ADOLESCENTS GROW IN GROUPS

Experiences in Adolescent Group Psychotherapy

Adolescents Grow in Groups

Experiences in Adolescent Group Psychotherapy

Edited by
IRVING H. BERKOVITZ, M.D.

BRUNNER/MAZEL • New York
BUTTERWORTHS • London

ADOLESCENTS GROW IN GROUPS
*Experiences in Adolescent
Group Psychotherapy*
Copyright © 1972 by IRVING H. BERKOVITZ, M.D.

Published by
BRUNNER/MAZEL, INC.
64 University Place, New York, N. Y. 10003

Library of Congress Catalog Card No. 72-190076
SBN 87630-055-7

DEDICATION

This book is dedicated to my family—the group in which I have grown—to Glenn, who helped put the book together, to Joel, who wanted to help, to Karen, who taught me much about teenagers, and to Anne, a writer, who waited patiently and helped by letting me write it myself.

MANUFACTURED IN THE UNITED STATES OF AMERICA

Preface

In the 60's and 70's the energies of teenagers have emerged explosively, creatively and/or chemically. Adults and adolescents often confront each other with mutual hostility, suspicion or lack of comprehension. It has fortunately also become well known in many settings that teenage peer groups containing one or two respected, knowledgeable adults often provide the kind of milieu where useful discussion, confrontation, mutual support and enlightenment can take place between teenager and teenager and teenager and adult.

In the present volume, 30 professionals of the three major disciplines—psychiatrist, psychologist and social worker—describe examples of experiences in such small groups. Many theoretical and technical principles are provided. Several vivid vignettes or brief glimpses into the group processes themselves are presented, from outpatient and inpatient settings. The mental health professional of any discipline and in any setting will find some suggestions or illustrative experience for working with teenagers. Of course, no book, however vivid, can substitute for experience and careful supervision. A thorough grounding in the individual treatment of teen-agers is an essential experience prior to attempting group therapy. However, it is hoped that those who hesitate to start groups and those who wonder where they are going with groups already underway will find some reassurance and guidance in these chapters.

IRVING H. BERKOVITZ, M.D.

Contents

Preface v

Contributors ix

Acknowledgements xiii

Prelude: Adolescent Group Therapy: Why, When, and a Caution .. 1
   Irene M. Josselyn, M.D.
On Growing a Group: Some Thoughts on Structure, Process,
   and Setting 6
   Irving H. Berkovitz, M.D.

PART I: EXPERIENCES IN CLINIC, OFFICE, AND
COMMUNITY GROUPS

1. The Importance of an Actively Involved Therapist 31
   Robert L. Anderson, M.A.
2. Younger Adolescents in Group Psychotherapy: A Reparative
   Superego Experience 37
   Walter E. Brackelmanns, M.D., and Irving H. Berkovitz, M.D.
3. Reflections on Selection 49
   Max Geller, M.D.
4. A Psychoanalytic Approach to Group Therapy with Older
   Teen-agers in Private Practice 63
   John R. M. Phelan, M.D., C.M.
5. Psychotherapy with the Adolescent in Self-Selected Peer Groups 80
   Max Sugar, M.D.
6. An Oedipal Revolt in a College Group 95
   Edwin M. Davidson, M.D.
7. Incest, Anger and Suicide 104
   Lorna M. Forbes, M.D.
8. "Turning On" the Turned Off: Active Techniques with
   Depressed Drug Users in a County Free Clinic 108
   Priscilla A. Slagle, M.D., and Dianne S. Silver, M.A.
9. Activating a Group of Passive Boys 122
   Harold B. Enns, M.D., and Irving H. Berkovitz, M.D.

10. "Playing It by Ear," in Answering the Needs of a Group of
    Black Teen-agers 126
    Dana B. Stebbins, M.S.W.

11. "Two Gray Cats Learn How It is" in a Group of Black
    Teen-agers 134
    Charles O'Shea, M.S.W.

12. A Drop-In Group for Teen-agers in a Poverty Area 149
    Martin Reiser, Ed.D., and Sylvia Kushner-Goodman, M.S.W.

13. Family Group Therapy for Adolescents 153
    Saul L. Brown, M.D.

14. Mediation within a Group of Multiple Families 162
    Lillian B. Vogel, Ph.D.

    Postlude: The Transference Dynamics of the Therapeutic
    Group Experience 173
    Martin Grotjahn, M.D.

PART II: EXPERIENCES IN HOSPITAL AND RESIDENTIAL GROUPS

    Editor's Note 180

15. Adolescent Group: A "Must" on a Psychiatric Unit—
    Problems and Results 181
    Florence Blaustein, M.S.W., and Helen B. Wolff, M.D.

16. The Value of a "Youth Group" to Hospitalized Adolescents 192
    L. James Grold, M.D.

17. "Bugging" of the Therapist in Group Therapy on an
    Adolescent Ward 197
    Robert L. Constas, M.D., and Irving H. Berkovitz, M.D.

18. "Should the Therapist Tell When He Hurts?":
    Countertransference in Adolescent Group Therapy 204
    James T. Barter, M.D., and Aurelio Buonanno, M.D.

19. Groups Promote Maturation of Sexual Attitudes in the
    Residential Setting 216
    *Irving H. Berkovitz, M.D., Paul Chikahisa, M.S.W., and
    Mary Lill Lee, M.S.W.*

20. The Peer Group as a Treatment Tool in a Probation
    Department Girls' Residential Treatment Center 225
    Karl E. Pottharst, Ph.D., and Marianne Gabriel, M.S.W.

    Postlude: Group Therapy Within the Wider Residential Context 233
    Donald B. Rinsley, M.D.

    Epilogue 243

    Index 245

Contributors

ROBERT L. ANDERSON, M.A.—Private Practice; Consultant to Zahm School for Individual Education; formerly Chief Psychiatric Social Worker, Department of Child Psychiatry, Cedars-Sinai Medical Center, Los Angeles.

JAMES T. BARTER, M.D.—Program Chief, Mental Health Services, Sacramento County, California; Associate Clinical Professor of Psychiatry, University of California, School of Medicine at Davis, California; formerly Director of Adolescent In-Patient Psychiatric Service, Colorado Psychiatric Hospital.

IRVING H. BERKOVITZ, M.D., F.A.P.A.—Private Practice; Assistant Clinical Professor in Child Psychiatry, University of California at Los Angeles; Senior Psychiatric Consultant for Schools, Los Angeles County Department of Mental Health; Southern California Psychoanalytic Institute and Society; Past President, Los Angeles Group Psychotherapy Society.

FLORENCE BLAUSTEIN, M.S.W.—In-Patient Psychiatric Social Worker, Cedars-Sinai Medical Center; Field Supervisor, University of Southern California School of Social Work.

WALTER E. BRACKELMANNS, M.D.—Private Practice; Assistant Clinical Professor, University of California at Los Angeles, Department of Psychiatry; Staff, Center for Training in Community Psychiatry, Los Angeles; Mental Health Consultant, Los Angeles County Department of Mental Health.

SAUL L. BROWN, M.D.—Chief, Department of Child Psychiatry, Cedars-Sinai Medical Center, Los Angeles; Associate Clinical Professor, University of Southern California, Department of Psychiatry; Faculty Advisor, Pacific Oaks College; Instructor, Southern California Psychoanalytic Society and Institute.

AURELIO BUONANNO, M.D.—Associate Professor in Psychiatry, Columbia University; Private Practice, exclusively with Treatment of Adolescents in a Residential Center; formerly Director, Child Guidance Clinic, Bergen Pines County Hospital, Paramus, New Jersey.

PAUL CHIKAHISA, M.S.W., A.C.S.W.—Unit Supervisor, Vista Del Mar Child Care Agency; Field Work Instructor, University of Southern California School of Social Work; Consultant, Casa Loreto Group Home.

ROBERT L. CONSTAS, M.D.—Private Practice; Staff Psychiatrist, Los Angeles County Department of Mental Health; Research Consultant, Experiential Physiology, Veteran's Hospital, Sepulveda, California.

EDWIN M. DAVIDSON, M.D.—Staff Psychiatrist, Brandeis University Mental Health Center, Waltham, Massachusetts; Clinical Instructor in Psychiatry, Harvard Medical School, and Tufts University Medical School; Assistant Attending Psychiatrist, McLean Hospital, Belmont, Mass.

HAROLD B. ENNS, M.D.—Private Practice; Senior Staff Psychiatrist, Kennedy Child Study Center, Santa Monica; Southern California Psychiatric Society.

LORNA M. FORBES, M.D.—Private Practice; Associate Clinical Professor, Child Psychiatry, University of Southern California; Consultant, Los Angeles County Department of Mental Health; Visiting Lecturer, Claremont School of Theology.

MARIANNE GABRIEL, M.S.W., A.C.S.W.—Caseworker at Los Angeles Family Service; Psychiatric Social Worker at Las Palmas School, Los Angeles County Probation Department; Consultant at Los Angeles Central Juvenile Hall.

MAX GELLER, M.D.—Clinical Instructor in Psychiatry, Harvard Medical School; Staff Psychiatrist, Beth Israel Hospital, Boston, Massachusetts; Consultant in Group Work, Arlington Schools, Arlington, Massachusetts; Private Practice.

L. JAMES GROLD, M.D.—Private Practice; Associate Instructor and Member, Southern California Psychoanalytic Institute and Society.

MARTIN GROTJAHN, M.D.—Clinical Professor of Psychiatry, University of Southern California; author: "Beyond Laughter," "Psychoanalysis and the Family Neurosis," "The Voice of the Symbol," and numerous papers; Private Practice.

IRENE M. JOSSELYN, M.D.—Training and Supervising Analyst, formerly of the Chicago Institute for Psychoanalysis and at present, in Southern California Psychoanalytic Institute; Past Editor, Journal of American Academy of Child Psychiatry; Author, "Adolescent and His World," "Psychosocial Development of Children," "The Happy Child," numerous papers.

SYLVIA KUSHNER-GOODMAN, M.S.W.—Caseworker, Special H.E.W. Project for Deaf; formerly Senior Psychiatric Social Worker, Pacoima Facility, San Fernando Valley Child Guidance Clinic.

MARY LILL LEE, M.S.W.—Consultant Social Worker for Somerset West Convalescent Hospital, West Sacramento; Board Member, Yolo County Mental Health Association; formerly Staff Psychiatric Social Worker, Vista Del Mar Child Care Agency, Los Angeles.

CHARLES O'SHEA, M.S.W.*—Associate Clinical Professor of the School of Social Welfare, University of California at Berkeley; Consultant to: Pediatrics Project and Mount Zion Psychiatric Clinic, California Youth Authority, Booth Memorial Hospital, Berkeley Unified School District; Private Practice.

JOHN R. M. PHELAN, M.D., C.M.—Private Practice; Assistant Clinical Professor of Psychiatry, University of Southern California; Clinical Associate, Southern California Psychoanalytic Institute; Consultant, North Hollywood Free Clinic.

KARL E. POTTHARST, Ph.D.—Co-Director, Western Psychological Center; Associate Clinical Professor, Psychiatry (Psychology), University of Southern California; Vice President, California School of Professional Psychology; Consultant, Las Palmas School for Girls.

MARTIN REISER, Ed.D.—Diplomate in Clinical Psychology, American Board of Professional Psychology; Department Psychologist, Los Angeles Police Department; Past President, Los Angeles County Psychological Association; Executive Secretary, Institute of Los Angeles Society for Psychoanalytic Psychology; Private Practice.

DONALD B. RINSLEY, M.D., F.A.P.A.—Director, Children's Section, and Chief, Adolescent Unit, Topeka State Hospital, Kansas; Psychiatric Faculty, Menninger School of Psychiatry, Topeka; Associate Clinical Professor of Psychiatry, University of Kansas School of Medicine; Associate Editor, Psychiatric Quarterly.

DIANNE S. SILVER, M.A.—Psychology Associate, Department of Psychiatry, Medical-Psychology, Child Out-Patient Dept., University of California at Los Angeles.

PRISCILLA A. SLAGLE, M.D.—Child Psychiatry Fellow, Department of Psychiatry, University of California at Los Angeles.

---

* Deceased 1971.

DANA B. STEBBINS, M.S.W.—Psychiatric Social Worker, South Central Mental Health Service, Los Angeles County Department of Mental Health; Consultant to: Department of Probation, Los Angeles County; Los Angeles City Unified Schools; Los Angeles Police Department; Member: Association of Black Social Workers.

MAX SUGAR, M.D.—Private Practice; Clinical Associate Professor, Psychiatry, and Former Director, Child Adolescent Psychiatry and Group Psychotherapy, Louisiana State University; Consultant, Family Service Society, Crippled Children's Hospital, Kingsley House (all in New Orleans) and Shreveport Mental Health Center; Vice-President, American Society for Adolescent Psychiatry.

LILLIAN B. VOGEL, Ph.D.—Private Practice; Consultant, Laurence School for Children with Learning and Behavior Disorders; Director, Research Project on Socialization; Volunteer, Leader of Multiple Family Groups, Valley Cities Jewish Community Center, Van Nuys, California.

HELEN B. WOLFF, M.D., M.P.H.—Private Practice; Associate Clinical Professor, Psychiatry, University of Southern California; Psychiatric Consultant, Council of Jewish Women; Clinical Associate, Southern California Psychoanalytic Institute.

ACKNOWLEDGMENTS

I wish to thank many others who helped: the social workers of Vista Del Mar Children's Home who shared their group experiences and started me in my interest in children's groups; my friend, the late Charles O'Shea, whose enthusiasm for his own special group experience sparked my enthusiasm to gather other such gems; the professionals of all disciplines who helped me to develop my concepts during the various courses I taught at the Los Angeles Group Psychotherapy Society, the Extension Division of the Southern California Psychoanalytic Institute, and the Los Angeles Center for Group Psychotherapy.

The twenty-eight other professionals whose work helps to fill these pages deserve special thanks. I hope that the months of letters, phone calls, and at times painful editorial surgery on very personal phrasings and thoughts have produced a contribution worthy of these efforts.

J am grateful for the time and talents of Mrs. 'Gene Stecyk, Mrs. Pat Hopgood, Miss Pamela Carr, and Mrs. Mary Koll, who were always willing and ready to type one more "final draft." Sonia L. Krasik provided useful editorial assistance on Part II. Fredric H. Jones, M.A., John A. Lindon, M.D., James E. Simmons, M.D., Alfred E. Coodley, M.D., and Bernard B. Nebenzahl, J.D., were generous with helpful suggestions.

Lastly—there are the hundreds of teenagers who participated in the many groups we are describing. Their problems, their defeats, their triumphs, helped provide the experiences and the lessons which hopefully can work for the benefit of future generations.

Thank you.

I. H. B.

PRELUDE

Adolescent Group Therapy:
Why, When and a Caution

Irene M. Josselyn, M.D.

MAN IS A SPECIES characterized by an inherent pattern of group formation. Lorenz, for example, has pointed out that in certain species there is a pattern of behavior closest to that of man. There is, "A type of social organization . . . in which it is the bond of love and friendship between individuals which prevents the members of the society from fighting and harming one another." It is in the group, the social structure, that man experiences an important aspect of the fulfillment of his internal wishes and needs. While the infant requires a relationship with others, particularly the nurturing person, as long as he is nutritionally dependent, his initial dependency extends with his maturation to an interrelationship with the family group and then to an expanding social world.

It is frequently pointed out, as stated in several of the articles in this collection, that peer group formation is characteristic of adolescence. This should not be interpreted, however, as either unique to the adolescent phase of development or originating at that time. Perhaps the earliest signs in the human species of a vague beginning manifestation of peer group seeking is observed in the difference in pleasurable responses of an infant, before he is able to walk, to the activity of adults and to the activities of other children. Children at this age may, with enjoyment, observe the activity of adults, but when watching the play of children older than themselves they have an eager response, as if they wished to join the others. This observation may be "adultamorphising" the infant. The most significant psychological strides toward socialization with peers, and the resultant formation of a peer group, occur during latency.

As the child finds some effective solution to the conflicts rooted in the infantile phases of psychological growth, he is free to widen his world through intellectual awareness and emotional response to the reality beyond the protective world of the family. Equally important, he is able to enrich his interpersonal relationships by gradually becoming a part of the nonparental social world of his peers. He melds into the peer group structure, influencing, and being influenced by, that society. The achievement of this maturational step, unless it is hindered by a lack of, or a faulty solution to, prelatency conflicts, or is inhibited by current reality-imposed limitations, is a gradual process, recognized in its effectiveness by the comment of adults that the child is making a "good social adjustment." Usually this implies a satisfactory participation in an acceptable peer group.

"Preventive group therapy," it could be said, is initiated by the child and his peer group during this age space. Sometimes by cruel methods, sometimes by more supportive ones, sometimes by offering "insight," (a child may say for example: "Don't treat me like you treat your brother, I'm not your brother."). Sometimes by behaviorist techniques, the latency group often without adult intervention aids its members in adaption to the social mores they have established on their own. The "rules of the game" are defined.

It is interesting to observe certain latency children who give no other evidence of being arrested in their maturation except that they do not appear to be a part of a peer group. They have a best friend, and neither partner seems interested in other friends. Yet their behavior is not alien to the peer group; their code of behavior is the same. They apparently learn the rules of the game by being an observer rather than a participant.

During latency the individual gradually structures a new self-image and a new ego ideal that are not as a child in his family, but as a participating member in a new social milieu composed of those living out the same phase of psychological development. This component of latency development provides an important supporting pillar for adolescence and begins to prepare the individual for an ultimate role in an adult social world.

To the extent that a child's latency phase has led to a comfortable and gratifying identity as a part of the peer group, the peer group during adolescence remains one of the major sources of support in attempting solutions to the typical adolescent pressure for self-recognition of himself as a child of his past and an adult of his future. It becomes a significant arena for the adolescent in which to struggle through the confused issues that adolescence typically creates. Within this milieu it provides support against common enemies, guidelines for acceptable behavior, a forum in which to discuss issues that can be safely explored only with those who are equally unsure, and tolerance for uncertainties and inconsistencies concerning ultimate goals. At the same time it provides a stage upon which, and actors with whom, can be acted roles experimentally, before a final choice of a role particular to each member is made.

There is another function of the group, however, that is not as often stressed. Each friend can, within the group structure, become a rival. Perhaps there is no clearer example than that which occurs in those groups of which both sexes are members or where a group of boys and one of girls tend to function in a complementary fashion. As an example that is hypothetical but applicable to many individual situations, John, a young adolescent, finds the courage to ask Mary for a "date" for a movie. John is attempting to break away from his child-like dependency upon his mother and finds in Mary a disguised substitute for his mother. Mary, likewise, is struggling with her conflict about her own mother, concerned about her awareness of her mother as a sexual person, uncomfortable with her own sexual feelings, and frightened by her sexually feminine identification with her mother. John's need for a mother is hidden under the mask implied in a "date." It also protects Mary from the more difficult problem of sexual stimulation; she is motherly to John. Soon John transfers to Mary his feeling of rebellion against his mother's solicitude and turns his attention to Jane, a girl freer in expression, at least in her manner of relating to boys, her growing potentiality of sexual femininity. John deserts Mary and seeks Jane. But Jane has been dating Fred, who is a very meaningful friend of John's. Fred sees Mary as "a good scout," but not like someone to date. Jane thinks John is immature. The loyalty of friendships is threatened by the needs and wishes of the individual. The arena has become an overt or covert scene of civil war in the group, and what had been a play upon the stage has become temporarily real life.

When crises arise, of whatever nature, the individual may find support from and clarification by the group and take a step forward toward integrating his multiple needs and wishes. On the other hand, he may be overwhelmed by the consciously recognized or more often unconscious implications of the struggle, and feel alienated from the group. While the overt response to this alienation is often anger, the more significant response is that of depression, a depression based upon the loss of a place in the chosen sub-culture, shame over the inability to live happily according to the peer level of maturation, or guilt because the peer code has been violated. If the experience leads to further growth, the group has provided spontaneous group "therapy." If instead the individual is unable to utilize the experience profitably, he may abandon the group and, responding with depression or a defensive denial of the value of peer group participation, become an isolate. He may instead seek another peer group that requires less adaptation and that has lower standards of conduct. His parents in the last instance may attribute this change to the bad influence of his new friends.

If the peer group provides "group therapy" for its members, it would be the therapy of choice for most adolescents. I would like to be arrogant enough to raise questions about certain aspects of group therapy with certain adolescents. I have perhaps little right to express an opinion. In the past when group therapy was less sophisticated than it is at present I did some therapy with adolescent groups and supervised others who were interested in it. At present, while I am not doing group therapy myself, I do see evidence of the positive values it has as practiced by several of my colleagues. Those whose work I know best know the patients on the basis of an individual evaluation before they recommend a group experience and carefully choose the group in which they place the individual. They have carefully formulated general goals for the particular patient.

In contrast to my observations of the effectiveness of the work of those colleagues, I have had some experience with adolescent patients who have participated in a group for which there had not been an initial screening and/or in which the leader of the group believed group therapy was the therapy of choice for all adolescents. From these experiences, granting that they are few in number compared to the large number of adolescents in group therapy, I have concluded that there are certain dangers in group therapy with the adolescent, perhaps more so than with any other age group. It is a *valuable therapeutic approach! It can also be a dangerous one!*

The turmoil of adolescence has two components. With the relatively normal adolescent the major component is that related to abandoning childhood patterns and finding a new identity as an adult. The latter identity is difficult for him to formulate, particularly in a culture such as ours that does not define it by rigid standards. His peer group is a significant aid in his explorations. But they too are confused, or may have taken steps boldly that a particular individual timidly avoids. A spontaneously formed group may frighten the timid individual, and it may encourage the overly bold to flaunt courage to destructive limits. A therapeutically planned group with wise leadership can lead to mutual support both for the timid and for the overly bold members in seeking a wise answer.

The other component of adolescent turmoil is that related to the recapitulation of childhood conflicts. It is in this area that I believe the indications for group therapy should be carefully appraised. Many adolescents can deal with those conflicts in a group situation if the therapist is aware of the correct meaning of the conflict and offers help both to the individual and to the group in understanding the significance of the conflict. When this is possible group therapy is effective and has many advantages. The solution of the latter component, however, requires ego strength both in the individual struggling with the conflict and in the other members of the group so that they can tolerate awareness of deep-seated anxiety over and/or poor defenses against a significant emotional problem.

While the ego of the average adolescent is surprisingly resilient, it can be overwhelmed by the resurgence of earlier conflicts. When this has occurred I question whether the most skilled leadership can handle the group situation constructively for the individual. This is particularly true with certain adolescents since a dependent transference to the therapist is difficult for some adolescents to handle, particularly if they thereby expose their need to the peer group. It can be kept a secret from others in individual therapy and thus is more tolerable.

The patients I have seen who have not only not been helped but have become acutely disturbed by the group experience either were frightened by the experience or were acting out a previously repressed conflict. All manifested seriously depleted ego strength; the last straw that brought on ego exhaustion was the group therapy sessions. In some cases I could place the onus on the limitations of the group leader. In others I do not believe the most skilled leader could have avoided the crisis as long as group therapy was the chosen form of therapy.

As indicated above, spontaneous groups are often therapeutic for the individual adolescent. They need and learn from group experiences. They also need wise adults who understand their individual as well as age-typical problems and provide some more sophisticated understanding than the adolescent himself has. Lastly, and from my viewpoint most importantly, if their difficulties require therapeutic intervention, the nature of that intervention should not be based upon conviction that one particular therapeutic tool is the tool of indiscriminate choice.

On Growing a Group: Some Thoughts on Structure, Process and Setting

Irving H. Berkovitz, M.D.

GROUPS GROW SPONTANEOUSLY or with cultivation. The types of groups described in this volume are those initiated deliberately by adults for teenagers. The hope in these groups is that structure will foster, and not inhibit, the emergence of intrinsic energy, understanding of interaction and verbalizing of fantasies. It is to be hoped that this energy and verbalizing will synthesize with useful adult feedback for mutually desired changes.

I would feel that some of these mutually desired changes are: (1) a greater enabling of interdependent autonomy. This would include emancipation from disabling attachments to parental demands and expectations but allow for a respectful appreciation of and reconciliation with positive qualities of parents and other adults; (2) reduction (but not crippling) of childhood narcissism, so that there is greater ability to respond to the worth of other individuals, beginning with peers; (3) enhancing appreciation for personal creative energies, so that a sustaining life goal and zest for what is available in living become more stable features in the personality; (4) a greater sense of sureness of self, in terms of familial, sexual and social identity, with a minimum of arrogance and rigidity.

MacLennan and Felsenfeld (1968) present several of these points in other language. They state, *"Group conditions are established for several purposes:***

---

* Editor's emphasis.

1. To provide constructive experience, which will assist the individual to feel differently about himself and others;
2. To give support or to add pressure to the individual's attempt to behave differently;
3. To provide opportunities for the individual to discuss and examine problems which he experiences in all areas of his life;
4. To give the individual a chance to examine and analyze his impact on others, as it is expressed in the group itself."

This chapter will touch briefly on many procedures which may need flexible structuring during the life of a particular group. On most of these structural details, there is no absolute right or wrong. I may state a point of view on certain issues, but this must be seen as purely personal.

Effective therapy depends on the *total spirit of acceptance and trust* developed in the group. The matter of structural guidelines is a large one and cannot be encompassed entirely here. Many additional principles and details will be suggested, implicitly and explicitly, in the more specific group experiences which are to be described in the chapters which follow.

"It has to be recognized that treatment groups, whether they are held in youth counseling centers, child guidance or psychiatric clinics, doctors' offices, schools or courts, all carry the implication that the teen-ager needs help. Teen-agers attend these groups for one of three reasons: (1) they recognize they need help, and they are willing to seek it out; (2) they obtain other kinds of gratification in the treatment; (3) they are forced to attend." (MacLennan and Felsenfeld, 1968.)

As the reader proceeds through these chapters, he may well be impressed with the important *influence of the setting* in which the particular group is formed, as well as with the personality or style of the particular therapist. Whether the setting is an office, outpatient clinic, residential institution, hospital, probation department school, etc., open or closed, will influence, and perhaps determine, many of the essential details and orientation of the group. Within the settings the groups may vary further in purposes and orientation. More specific comments about differences relating to setting will be stated later.

STRUCTURAL DETAILS TO BE DECIDED IN ADVANCE

Before beginning any group, certain mechanical, or housekeeping, items need decision, for example, the *number of members* to include in the group.

The setting may determine this, above and beyond the discretion or wishes of the therapist. For example, in an institutional cottage, a hospital ward or an outpatient drop-in group, it may not be feasible to exclude anyone, with the result that the group may range in number from eleven to thirty. If there is an option, most find six to eight comfortable, with five usually being the minimum. Very often, starting with two or three is possible, if absolutely necessary, for a short while, as long as other members are added soon. In the age group thirteen to fifteen, there may be a great amount of disruptiveness and horseplay, especially with boys (see Brackelmanns and Berkovitz, chapter 2, this volume). The therapist may prefer to keep the membership in such a group at five or six, in order to have the group more manageable and to allow maximum, direct attention to each member. A larger number insures sufficient attendance in the face of absences owing to illness or indisposition, factors to be expected with teen-agers.

Length and frequency of session vary. Outpatient groups are often scheduled once per week for one and a-half to two hours. Occasionally, in-patient groups last only for one hour. One may need to experiment with the time period appropriate for the setting. Longer sessions of two to three hours have been used to increase the degree of involvement, especially in office treatment. While many teen-agers complain that one and a-half hours are too short, increasing the session to two or three hours has still often left the feeling that there has not been enough time. Week-end sensitivity or marathon experiences have proved useful in outpatient settings (see Phelan, chapter 4). A frequency of twice per week, in outpatient or office groups, has helped to increase the amount of impact and involvement. In one residential setting, sessions five times per week were useful in this regard (see Pottharst and Gabriel, chapter 20).

The nature of the *meeting room* will influence interaction, initially. A small room will force proximity and increase tension. A larger room can allow avoidance of proximity and diffusion of interaction. Chairs around a table inhibit movement and block some directness of interaction initially, but not for long. The type of furniture and decoration in the room will influence feelings of relaxation, formality, etc, A rug on the floor may allow for more informal seating arrangements. A room that is poorly located, maintained or ventilated may imply an attitude of low value for the group program and should be used only if there is no other room available. One that is open to entry by nongroup members at any time will obviously inhibit and interrupt any freedom or flow of discussion. Some groups wish occasional outdoor meetings. Ultimately, the personality and style of the leader and degree of acceptance of the group by the institution will be most important.

Age spread may be dictated by the population of the agency, requiring, for example, mixing of ages thirteen to eighteen. If one has a choice, however, it may be wiser to limit the age range, as closely as possible, to one of the *three periods of adolescence*. In the *first period*, ages thirteen to fifteen, the principal conflict involves separation from parents, as well as lessening of homosexual and incestual anxieties (see Brackelmanns and Berkovitz, chapter 2; Berkovitz, et al., chapter 19). In the *second period*, ages fifteen to seventeen, there is further establishment of identity, the beginning of dating or exploration of relations to the opposite sex, experimentation with drugs, handling of money, responsibilities of driving and perhaps decisions about college or career. In the *third period*, eighteen to twenty (or older), the group can be very different from the previous two, depending on the setting. For example, a college group (see Davidson, chapter 6) will differ greatly from a group in a probation department camp. More usually, this age will be more talkative, less disorderly and closer to an adult type group. Some of the conflicts of earlier ages may, of course, be present, even in some of the older members.

Mixing these three age periods in the same group may run the risk of less interest on the part of older teen-agers in the concerns of younger members, or a tendency for younger members to seduce the older ones into regressive behavior. The younger members may be made anxious or identify prematurely with sexual or other behavior discussed by the older members. In an institution, there will usually be contact between the age groups in the dormitories and elsewhere, so that it may be beneficial for this exposure to take place in a group, where at least one adult is present to interpret and modify reactions. In outpatient groups, there is more chance to control the age spread. In walk-in groups, the number and ages may be more difficult to control, requiring a different kind of focus and process. Some therapists prefer not mixing high school and college youth.

Including both sexes in the group often has advantages. Where the institutional population is of one sex only, of course, this mixing cannot occur, unless members of the opposite sex are imported for the sole purpose of attending the group meeting. In a coed institution, a coed small group may encourage more intimacy than might occur in the otherwise usual social situations. In outpatient groups, mixed sexes is preferable, if enough of each sex is present from the clinic population. If nearly equal members of each sex are not available, it may be initially difficult to have one or two boys or girls with five or six members of the opposite sex. Homosexual anxiety and anxious disruptiveness are described as less prevalent in mixed sex groups. Having the opposite sex present brings into clearer focus the problems of heterosexual identity and concern (see Enns and Berkovitz, chapter 9).

What about a *male therapist* with an adolescent girls' group or a *female therapist* with a teen-age boys' group? Ideally, it is best, if possible, to have male and female co-therapists. When the solo therapist is not of the same sex as the group (if it is an unmixed group), anxiety may express itself in disruptiveness, overstimulation or flight. In one such instance a group of five girls, around age fifteen, decided, in concert, not to continue with the solo male therapist. They simply did not appear for further meetings, thus ending the group. One is left to speculate as to whether the incestual anxiety was so great, or if hostility at the "ungiving" father figure, or some other dynamic was responsible. In a residential setting, a boys' group, aged thirteen to fifteen, displayed such provocative sexual talk and action, directed to the female therapist, that dissolution of the group was required for the comfort of the therapist. With boys prior to puberty, the asexual mother role protects the female therapist, and the relation can be more manageably therapeutic.

Presence of a *cotherapist* helps to reduce anxiety, especially for beginning therapists. There is a greater opportunity to observe, while the other therapist may be interacting, at any particular moment. Feedback and comment between mutually respecting colleagues deepen understanding of the group interactions and of one's own behavior. Conflict between co-therapists can create "a broken home" atmosphere in the group, while honest and open discussion of differences can provide a corrective experience for the members. An example of two adults who can disagree without violent argument or divorce may be reassuring, and even novel, to many. If the therapists are of opposite sex, the parent analogy is all the more evident to group members. Participants will play out on the two therapists many of the feelings and maneuvers that they used with their own parents. Even if the two cotherapists are of the same sex, usually one is more active or less punitive or less aggressive, so that there may be a "good" and "bad" parent projection onto each. At times, even other group members may be used for these roles.

Diagnostically, a wide range of members is possible (see Geller, chapter 3). It is generally more feasible to include than to exclude. A teen-ager who appears psychotic, disorganized or too passive in initial individual evaluation may change for the better in the group more rapidly than one might have expected. If one's choice is not dictated by a particular agency population, the therapist might not wish to mix, for example, a mentally retarded, organically brain-damaged or extremely psychotic teen-ager with a majority of more intact adolescents. Some degree of intact ego function, despite these diagnoses, however, may justify inclusion (see Brackelmanns and Berkovitz, chapter 2).

Teen-agers with serious and conspicuous deforming *physical handicaps* may be anxiety provoking to the non-handicapped members. The therapist may be able to make use of the reactive anxiety in the non-handicapped members and deal with any secondary gains in the handicapped youngster.

If one does have the choice, it is desirable to have no more than one or two disorganized, *psychotic teen-agers,* with a majority of more neurotic members. One or two adolescents involved with bizarre or intense fantasies may help to reduce intellectualizing in others. Emotionally uncontrolled youngsters can trigger useful behavior in some members but also sorely tax the therapist, as well as the group itself. Members of the group will frequently come to the defense and protection of one or two psychotic, depressed or very anxious individuals who are not "too far out." Occasionally, decompensation of a more fragile member can occur, which may require the member's leaving the group. More often the group, with the therapist's help, can provide accessory ego strength to such a troubled member.

Severely antisocial individuals may be disruptive and manipulative, resisting effective therapy for themselves, as well as interfering with therapy for others. In outpatient groups, *delinquents,* latent or overt, may require extragroup contacts with probation officer, parents or auxiliary therapists, in order to help the teen-ager maintain control and avoid incarceration. Influence toward antisocial behavior on suggestible members may occur. At times it may help to prepare parents, of all group members, in advance for the possibility of some drug use, or other types of behavior, if these have not already been present in the life of the adolescent (see Brackelmanns and Berkovitz, chapter 2).

At times the proportion of similar type neurotic problems in any group will influence a group's progress. Five or six passive members can slow a group and exasperate the therapist (see Enns and Berkovitz, chapter 9). Although diagnoses may seem to be similar at the start of a group, individual variations will often show themselves fairly soon.

In current clinic practice, *walk-in or intake groups* for teen-agers are becoming more common. These preclude the possibility of selection or limitation of number in advance. From six to twenty members may be included, presenting a wide range of ages and diagnostic categories. Some of the members may get help from one or two sessions. Others may find themselves exasperated, confused and frustrated because of the changing population and inability to know the individual members for very long. Some walk-in groups can develop into "stay-in" groups and develop a more stable, on-going group life (see Reiser and Kushner-Goodman, chapter 12, this volume).

ISSUES ARISING AT THE START OF THE GROUP

Once the previous issues have been decided, one is now ready to begin contacting members for starting the on-going group. *Preparing the chosen members* for the coming group involvement may vary from plunging the individuals right into the group, as occurs in the walk-in groups, or allowing a certain number of individual sessions prior to the first group session. These prior individual sessions may help to assess the teen-ager's psychopathology and motivation, as well as to establish some one-to-one relationship, which may be useful later, especially if the relation with the group does not gel immediately. At times, contrary to practice with adults, it may be more valid to evaluate a teen-ager in the group situation. It is also important to assess one's own conflict and anxiety, especially if the therapist is starting his first group (see Davidson, chapter 6). Apprehension in the clinician can trigger apprehension and uncertainty in the prospective group member. A consultant can be useful in this regard (see Berkovitz, et al., chapter 19).

One type of introduction may be a variation of the statement, "Groups are useful in helping teen-agers to solve their own, as well as each other's, problems. Therefore, we have chosen you to be a member of a group." I try to explore anxieties or defenses used in previous group situations. The *withdrawn, depressed or schizoid teen-ager* may not initially welcome the invitation to join a group. These individuals may be difficult to involve in groups until an extended one-to-one relationship has taken place, in which they have been able to test the value and risk of communicated introspection. It is striking how often the initial resistance to group involvement gives way to a strong loyalty after only a few sessions. *Introducing new members* may not be a difficult matter in most outpatient groups. In institutional settings, some of the prospective new members are often known already to the members of the group. There may be strong antagonisms or alliances, which precipitate strongly positive or negative reactions to the entry of the new member (see Phelan, chapter 4).

A therapist may wish to enunciate certain *rules,* either individually prior to the member's entering the group, or in the early group sessions, to all the members. If all the members are new to the group, the first session undoubtedly will see anxiety expressed in cautiousness or disruptiveness. Younger adolescents, especially girls, may at times suggest their own rules to make the group feel like a club meeting. The therapist may wish to state rules, such as "no hitting, no interruption of others while they are speaking, stay in the room," etc. He may wish to explain the function of the group or to make a statement about common teen-age problems, or he may simply ask each member to introduce himself, discuss a problem, describe his life, family, etc. I try to minimize the number of initial prohibitions, since the proclivity to defiance and rebellion against any given rules is ever present with this age group.

One or two *members who have been in groups previously* can be especially useful. They will already have experienced certain rules of procedure and can be helpful in orienting new members to the group ethic, for example, introspection, examining interaction between members, etc. Of course, if one is starting a group for the first time, these convenient "aides" may not be available. On the other side, there can be a danger of depending excessively on one or more "aides," to the detriment of the therapy for these particular teen-agers.

More usually, unless one has a very passive, frightened group of adolescents, *interaction* will begin almost immediately. It may be difficult to enunciate any kind of rule about respecting each other's time to talk or allowing someone to speak his point before interrupting. A prime goal of the group experience, for some narcissistic, impulsive teen-agers, especially the younger ones (thirteen to fifteen), may be the experiential understanding of this need for mutual respect. Repeated confrontation, exhortation and firm control will be necessary in such a group (see Brackelmanns and Berkovitz, chapter 2).

Use of first names will probably seem natural by the therapist toward the members. The question of what the young people may, or will, call the adult therapist or cotherapist may not be as routine. It may seem awkward for the clinicians to address each other by first names and then expect the adolescents to call them "Doctor" or "Mrs." Some defiant or experimenting youngsters may hesitantly or counterphobically use first name to therapist or cotherapist. I usually state that first name usage is acceptable, but without specifically encouraging it. Most young people will avoid using first names to the therapists. The option to do so is useful in encouraging decreased fear and, at times, some open exposure of hostility or friendliness toward adults.

The matter of *smoking* may require a decision, especially if one is working in a particular institution where smoking is against the rules. It may require permission of parents in order to allow some teen-agers to smoke. In some outpatient groups, the therapists may allow thirteen- to fourteen-year-olds to smoke, if that had been their custom. Nowadays one may face the dilemma presented by a teen-ager trying to light up a marijuana cigarette in group. Besides the legal implications of such a maneuver, there may be other defiant, hostile or disruptive aspects involved, which deserve consideration.

What about *refreshments?* Some therapists provide doughnuts and coffee to older adolescents and candy or soft drinks to the younger ones. I prefer a large bowl of candy and gum. Teen-agers are often eating, and it is likely that the anxiety of interaction will stimulate a more intense wish to eat. This age group is still close to the child's use of orality. In addition, many may have emotional deprivations which express themselves in a greater or, at times, lesser need for food. Most will come to the session with some candy or other refreshment in their pockets, if none is provided at the session. In institutions, it does seem to increase the attractiveness of the meetings when soft drinks or similar special treats are provided.

The uses made of the food can become a useful part of the discussion and an aid to understanding relationships between the members, as well as some of the past or present acquisitive, deprived, greedy feelings. Bottled drinks may be used aggressively, or erotically, when squirted at each other. With groups of obese teen-agers, the use of food will have to receive special attention.

Many sessions will result in a *messing of the room.* One may or may not wish to include the cleaning of the room as part of the group session. Some members may voluntarily assist in cleaning up. If the room is an office where other patients are to come in immediately after, or if there is concern about the reaction of one's colleagues to entering a messed-up meeting room, there may be a wish to enlist group members in cleaning up. In some more active group sessions there may have been paper or refreshment throwing and chairs disordered.

The question of *individual sessions* supplementing group sessions will depend on the setting, the availability of private time or finances, as well as on the philosophy of the therapist. Individual sessions can be a way to avoid relating with peers in the group sessions, or they may represent seeking out necessary, more intimate relating with the adult therapist. In some cases this may be indicated, especially while a more immature member is attempting to adjust to peer group tensions.

Absences from sessions do require attention. In most institutional groups there will be some degree of control, positively or, at times, negatively, by house parents. The house parent can express feelings in reminding or not reminding the child to attend sessions, or even by scheduling other activities at the time of the group session. In outpatient groups there may be the question of how soon to contact the absent member, whether after one or two missed sessions. Will one be seen as nagging or oversolicitous? How many absences should one tolerate before dropping the teen-ager as a member? Does one charge for missed sessions? If a member is suicidal or a runaway, etc., there may be some urgency in contacting him after a missed session. A factor to be considered is the extent of family pressure or lack of support for the particular adolescent to attend the group. I prefer to bring up, in group, questions of motivation indicated by absences, unless a private discussion seems preferable. If the therapist delays or neglects contacting the teen-ager after one or two absences, it may suggest lack of interest on the part of the therapist, which in turn may lessen the feeling of involvement on the part of the young person.

It may seem premature to consider *duration of group life* at this point, but in some cases a decision may be necessary or desirable in early sessions. Many groups will continue only for the length of the school year, since summer plans will often interfere with consistent attendance. One may wish to allow a summer to pass without sessions, in order to permit new experiences or consolidation of the work done during the previous nine months. If a strong feeling of involvement has developed, the members may not wish to discontinue for the summer. The question of how long each member should continue in the group will, of course, be an individual one, especially in the outpatient settings. In the institution or residential setting, criteria for discharge may prevail over criteria more related to the individual's performance in the group.

THERAPIST ACTIVITIES

After the previously mentioned issues have been decided upon, the group has begun. So far, we have mainly confined our discussion to qualities of members and matters of procedure, with only brief mention of activities of leader or therapist. In the words of MacLennan and Felsenfeld (1968):

> "Some of the *functions of leadership** are: to bring membership together; to help the group identify its goals; to teach the group how to function; to help the group keep to the task; to serve as a model for the group; to present a value system to the group. Leadership activities may include: stimulating interaction; making suggestions; providing for the needs of the group; seeing that the ground rules are set; influencing goals of the group; keeping order; assigning tasks; planning for, or with, the group; deciding upon membership, initiating action; evaluating the group.
>
> "The *more active the leader is,** and the more he takes over responsibility for the group, the more dependent or defiant the group members are likely to become. In groups of immature members, when increased maturity is a goal, the leader must help the group set limits and structure which will allow the members to take maximum self-responsibility within those limits. The *group leader plays many roles;** he is a teacher, a reflector, an informant and resource man, an explorer, a model for identification, a clarifier, an interpreter, a transmitter of values, a supporter (someone who cares and respects the group members). In his work he can choose to emphasize one or more of these roles; what he chooses and what levels he works at will depend very much on the population and on the goals of the group. A leader must know his population, understand the significance of behavior and be able to communicate in their language."

Some of these same *leadership activities may be performed as well by the members themselves* for each other, whether in identification with the therapist or from their own knowledge of dealing with people. It is necessary to decide at each moment the importance of allowing continued interaction of group members, as compared to the therapist's making comments. Very often, the experience occurs in which the clinician's planned interpretation may be made by one of the group members a few minutes later, often more effectively (see Grotjahn, Postlude, Part I).

I feel that the therapist has to be active and responsive enough to show sincere involvement, prevent damage and introduce some ideas; otherwise, the young people should be helped and allowed to do the job for each other as much as possible (see Forbes, chapter 7). This is similar to what Ginott (1961) describes for group play therapy with younger children:

---

* Editor's emphasis.

"The therapeutic process is enhanced by the fact that every group member can be a giver and not only a receiver of help."

There are many specific *types of interventions* available to the therapist. He may choose, for example, to describe appearance, mood, posture, facial expression, dress, tone of voice or other outward indicators of feelings. The particular directness or timing of such *confrontation* may possibly be taken as criticism at times and impede, rather than facilitate, understanding or acceptance by the member. It is often striking, especially in the younger teen-agers, how surprised, startled, impressed, amazed or offended the individual may be when a very obvious indicator of mood is perceived by the therapist or peer members. This seems mystifying to the member, as if others have just read his mind. Such communication can often enhance ego self-awareness.

Reality clarification may be well accepted by a member, if not given in a humiliating way. A member may be telling a story which is obviously distorted, misinformed or full of contradiction. Other members may not be aware or choose to ignore this. The therapist, after judging the degree of humiliation or narcissistic injury that may result, may choose to supply the correct reality information. Important in all interventions by the adult therapist is, of course, the *kind of language used*. One cannot expect full acceptance of a polysyllabic, scientific, psychoanalytic or other "jargon" statement. On the other hand, very current, teen-age vernacular may be distrusted or rejected as "phony," unless the therapist feels comfortable with the vernacular and uses it with discretion. There are certain words that have been taken over into adult vocabulary that many adolescents accept easily, for example, "cool," "groovy," "uptight," "busted," "shine on," etc. Sometimes it may be necessary to make a statement in two or three different ways, in the hope that one formulation will be acceptable and more understandable to the teen-ager. The better one knows the particular youngsters and the longer one has been in the group with them, the more the therapist will be able to word his statements appropriately and effectively. Ethnic and cultural factors can have special importance (see Stebbins, chapter 10 and O'Shea, chapter 11).

A third type of intervention may be called the *transactional* or interpersonal. Here one may describe, either to the member involved or the observing members, a particular transaction including one or several of the members. It might have been loving, exploitative, defensive, etc. Nowadays, many persons talk about behavior in terms of "games" being played. This figure of speech often provides a special stimulus for considering ways that people use other people. At times there may be opportunities for combining the intrapsychic and the interpersonal in the same confrontation or interpretation. For example, one might say, "John must have interrupted Sue's talking about her parents because he was reminded unpleasantly of his trouble with his own parents."

The *educational* intervention has to be used with discretion. If well timed, not too lengthy, and clearly phrased, it can be an asset. Examples might include explanation of sexual facts, certain general concepts about relationships between parents, children or other persons. There is the danger of being moralizing, preachy or "school teacherish." When a therapist feels anxious, he may use this kind of intervention more frequently than is necessary or appropriate. It does stop any interaction going on between members and turns the attention of the group in the direction of the therapist, as the expert. Even though statements about morals, ethics or attitudes of "good" or "bad" may be considered "corny" these days, youngsters may be deprived if adults refrain excessively from making them. Such pronouncements, given in a flexible and unauthoritative way, may provide a confused youngster with an honest and valid expression of limits and standards.

Yet another kind of intervention might be termed *"empathy,"* e.g., "I know how you feel." At times this can be very close to *"self-revelation."* There are at least two types of self-revelation by the therapist which occur in group. One is that which is offered spontaneously in reaction to a piece of behavior described in the group. Another type is the providing of facts or other material from the therapist's personal or family life, in response to questions from group members. The first type can serve to show that the adult also had an adolescence, which presented various difficulties and examples of the kinds of alternative behavior that can be useful. This kind of self-revelation can come close to making the therapist seem, or feel, like a member of the group, but it may also dilute his authority position and possibly render him less effective. Done judiciously and sparingly, it can serve an important therapeutic purpose, often lessening the remote authority position into which many adolescents isolate the therapist (Barter and Buonanno, chapter 18, this volume).

Another volunteered type of self-revelation is the *admission of feelings*, especially frustration, anger, envy or affection, in response to some behavior in the group. It is understandable if a therapist feels envy of these younger, energetic persons, who, in many ways, may be having more freedom and license than was present in his/her generation. The experience of witnessing an adult's expression of anger with control, and without extended hostile recriminations, may foster a similar kind of honesty and openness in an adolescent's communication. Unfortunately, some therapists are indiscriminate and profuse in sharing their own feelings, to the confusion of the teen-age members.

The dilemma of *whether or not to answer any or all questions* from group members, no matter how intimate, is one which creates discomfort for many therapists. It is not always possible to practice anonymity. To reflect the question back to the youngster may make him feel rebuffed or give him the impression that the therapist is uncomfortable and "copping out." On the other hand, if the therapist does feel uncomfortable in answering certain personal questions, it may be more respected if he states as much. The meaning of the question to the teen-ager may be hard to elicit, whether one gives or withholds the requested information. Reassurance of trust and mutual openness may be more crucial at times than persistence in eliciting underlying fantasies. On the other hand, there is the danger that the group members will enjoy the experience of stripping an adult emotionally naked, rather than exposing themselves (see Phelan, chapter 4).

In many ways the dilemma described in the preceding pages may seem somewhat similar to those which will arise in any adult group. Important differences are the greater emotional lability and immaturity of the teen-age population, and the minor legal status. This brings up the question of *legal and moral responsibilities of the therapist.* Some therapists, especially in agencies, may feel compunction about giving advice or information, for example, about contraception or abortions or politics, etc., fearing repercussions from parents. If there is some parental reaction to material discussed in the group sessions, this may be a clue that some form of family interview may be necessary. A therapist's advocacy of special points of view, especially those which may seem to encourage violation of the law, such as draft evasion or use of marijuana, might be construed at times as contributing to the delinquency of a minor. The susceptibility to influence of some teenagers and their readiness to want to please a loved authority figure justify caution and judgment in disclosure of some personal, controversial attitudes. Well-intended, honest self-disclosure, at times, may subvert the desired fostering of autonomy and self-determination. Attempts to persuade adolescents to one's special point of view in some areas can be a misuse of group therapy and a seduction of the innocent.

With regard to revelation of *use of dangerous drugs,* or narcotics, etc., by the group members, there often may be a dilemma for the therapist about whether to inform the parents or to respect the teen-ager's confidence.

When there is a possibility of danger involved in the usage being described, this dilemma is similar to the one which would exist in the case of an adolescent being treated individually. Protection of the health of the youngster should take precedence over any feared violation of confidentiality. Objective judgment of danger to health requires monitoring of one's own attitudes about drug use. Premature panic can damage a teen-ager's trust in the therapist and drive the young person further into dangerous drug use.

Use of *drugs* and *marijuana* provides a variety of predicaments to the therapist and deserves more attention than is possible in this brief discussion. Several articles in this volume will discuss some pertinent facets (see Brackelmanns and Berkovitz, chapter 2). Occasionally, members will come to the session "stoned." The clinician will have to decide whether to make an issue of this himself, to encourage the group to confront the member or to wait until group concern arises spontaneously. Extensive discussion of drug experiences by members can be frequent, either as avoidance of more anxious topics, a flaunting of risk-taking, or as a need to catharse and share frightening experiences. Uncritical approval, or unsympathetic disapproval on the part of the therapist, may not assist the teen-ager in examining the meaning and consequences of this type of behavior (see Slagle and Silver, chapter 8). Some therapists curtail such discussion, rather than search for meaning in it.

THE GROUP PROCESS

The group has begun, and the leader has his functions in mind. The question now at hand is one of understanding the events in the sessions themselves. How does one organize the frequently rapid, seemingly disorganized discussion which occurs between the members? The answers to this question will depend on the concepts of the particular therapist and the particular school of psychology frame of reference which is used, whether psychoanalytic, Gestalt, transactional, etc. At times it may be difficult to pick out a coherent theme to each session, since learning and change may be going on at different speeds and timing for each member, in each session.

MacLennan and Felsenfeld (1968) state that *certain conditions are necessary for the establishment of relationships* which will advance the benefit of the group: "face-to-face interactions; willingness to take the risk of self-exposure; desire for closeness; a mutual demand for reciprocity; mutual attraction; trust, and some degree of predictability; willingness to listen to, and respond, to the needs of others." Scheidlinger (1955) has listed certain generic elements characteristic of all psychotherapy, including group.

"Among these elements are: (1) relationship, (2) emotional support, (3) catharsis, (4) reality testing, (5) insight and (6) reorganization of defensive patterns."

In the *early sessions* (perhaps the first four or five), the therapist's inner concern may be to consider which members are included in the discussion and which are excluded; which alliances are being formed and which antagonisms; how each member deals with being in the room with six to eight peers; which are monopolizing, isolated, fearful, aggressive, etc. In many ways this could be considered a diagnostic period for each member, as well as a determination of which group milieu is being formed (see Geller, chapter 3). The therapist may wish to be active in bringing in some of the less active members, as a means of testing their degree of alienation and their intensity of fear of involvement. Status roles may be in the process of formation. The therapist's function may be compared in many ways to a *radar system,* scanning the group at frequent intervals, picking up verbal and non-verbal cues of anxiety, anger, sorrow, etc. Yet, he cannot be a detached observer (see Anderson, chapter 1).

There are types of situations and individual behavior common to groups in all settings. Opposite ends of the spectrum might be reflected by two who might be called the "nonparticipating" and the "monopolizing" members. It is a matter of individual appropriateness as to how much pressure, attention or interpretation can be given to the *nonparticipating member.* It is often evident that a member, even though not participating fully, may be learning a great deal in listening and observing, so that constructive changes may be occurring in his life outside the group, even though his/her group interaction is less than ideal. One such boy, in an outpatient, mixed group, did not participate much of the five or six months that he was in the group. Finally, in one session he said that he was tired of the whole business and announced that he was quitting the group. This was more anger than he had displayed previously. It may have been that in working up to expression of this much anger his main problem of expressing anger and other feelings was partially lessened.

Monopolizing members, when not too competitive, may be consciously or unconsciously used by the therapist as a type of unofficial cotherapist. Such members may very often make insightful comments about other members and may derive an important leadership experience for themselves. Perhaps, just as often, this "leader" role may be defensive against feelings of helpless vulnerability. At times the monopolizer may be disruptive and suppressive of significant disclosure or interaction between the other members. Interpretation and/or confrontation in the group sessions, as well as in individual sessions, may be necessary to reduce the monopolizing. If the situation does not change and is thought to be inimical to the course of the group and the individual, it may be necessary to remove the monopolizer from that particular group. It may be that in another group the members would be more able to deal with his efforts at exclusive control.

Certain criteria can be kept in mind for use in describing the *movement in the sessions*. One dimension can be the amount of disruptive or integrative movement. Disorder or disruption might be related to the degree of anxiety in individual members, inherently, or the particular topic or emotion of that particular session. Integration may be seen in terms of cohesion or mutually involved discussion. It would be surprising if a large proportion of mutually respectful discussion would occur in early sessions, except possibly with older adolescents. Age level, maturity, degree of anxiety, previous group experience may all be factors determining the type of interaction in the first sessions. There will be less mutual dialogue in the younger groups, and more with the older age groups. One goal for a group may be increased interest in the comments of others and less intense self-interest (see Brackelmanns and Berkovitz, chapter 2). More often there will be alternation between orderly discussion sessions and disruptive meetings, especially during the consideration of anxious material. Mutually respectful discussion may arouse anxiety if it is based on premature inhibition of strong impulses. Disruption may be a defensive reaction against threatened engulfment by adult authority or by the group as an authority—a threat to autonomy, or fear of annihilation.

An important element is the *degree of trust, closeness or distance* tolerated with each other and/or the therapist. This may be a very fluctuating and anxiety-provoking part of relating in a group, especially since individual adolescents are oversensitive to the loss of individuality or ego autonomy involved in relationships. In boys with a male therapist, especially without a female cotherapist, there may well be a strong homosexual anxiety, mistrust or fear of seduction, reflected in hyperactive, anxious behavior (see Enns and Berkovitz, chapter 9; Berkovitz, et al., chapter 19). In groups of teen-age girls there are reports of as much as twenty-five minutes of giggling before any discussion could take place. Older adolescents may express their competitiveness and hostility to the therapist more openly (see Davidson, chapter 6; Constas and Berkovitz, chapter 17).

The telling of a dream by one member may arouse the narration of *dreams* by others. This can encourage revelation of fantasy in the group and deepen understanding of seemingly unclear daily behavior. Too detailed recounting of dreams can be defensive and obscure insight into feelings. Deeply instinctual and symbolic interpretation of dream material, I feel, is often confusing to the teen-ager. I prefer to focus on an ego level, relating the manifest content to attitudes about the group or other current events, unless I know the youngster very well. In a long-term group, more deeply psychoanalytic interpretations may be possible and useful (see Phelan, chapter 4).

In some groups, one member may become a focus for a large part of the session. This may be similar to the *"hot seat"* technique in some Gestalt groups. Occasionally, the process of "going around" may occur, either in soliciting attitudes from each member in sequence about a certain occurrence in the group, or attitudes toward one of the members or toward a certain subject.

Activity between members outside the group may occur at times, taxing the objectivity and judgment of the therapist. Unlike institutional groups, teen-agers in outpatient groups usually scatter after the meetings to various parts of the city or community in which they live. If such a group truly begins to be involved emotionally with each other, the wish for more sustained contact may give rise to extra-group association and the formation of a "network" (see Sugar, chapter 5). Some therapists interdict such extra-group association, but in some cases the socializing can be therapeutic. Comments and observations about parents or friends can bring new data into the group sessions. At times, self-damaging behavior will be confronted more effectively by a peer. Occasionally, some members may invite the entire group to a party, where various kinds of encounters occur, which may be referred to in the sessions for some weeks thereafter. Members will often exchange phone numbers. This can be used defensively against dependence on the therapist or as support for those who feel the need for contact with the therapeutic process between sessions. At times a therapist may have to trust the group relationships and allow members to get support from each other.

Sexual liaisons may cause special difficulties. In one such case, the boy involved soon left the group; his girl friend felt uncomfortable but stayed. As a result of the affair, she came to see the boy's personality in a way that differed from what she had known in the group sessions, but out of loyalty to her brief lover she did not feel free to bring the material into the meetings. Ultimately, this relationship did interfere with effective therapy for both. In another group, two older adolescents (19-21), who had previously not had easy or happy relationships with the opposite sex, became involved and married, after about nine months of group experience together. The marriage seems secure after one year. This marriage represented the greatest risk in consistent, intimate relating that either had previously dared. Ordinarily, such relationships developing during the course of a group therapy experience can reflect some avoidance of examination of feelings and poor toleration of frustration. The intensity of close feeling for each other that can develop in a group experience can, at times, be quite difficult to handle with restraint, especially in this age group. Each situation requires individual criteria as to whether growth or resistance is in process.

At times some members wish to *bring friends into the session* or unexpectedly attend with boy friend or girl griend. This may be similar to a "network" situation (see Sugar, chapter 5), in which a self-chosen, smaller, intimate group is being used within the larger, stranger group. Some therapists allow the visitor to stay and observe for one session. If he wishes to return he must become a member. More frequent attendance as a visitor would pose a problem of parental permission, as well as payment for the sessions. Such visitors often do not wish to return after the one visit. They may have come originally out of curiosity, or a member might have been using the presence of a friend to gain status, support or distraction, in the face of feelings aroused during the sessions. For example, some girls protect themselves against homosexual anxiety by bringing a boy friend. Occasionally, a visitor can be of special value. In one college student group, a member invited his parent for a single session. This turned out to be very productive for all concerned. In residential settings there may be curiosity on the part of nonmembers. Occasionally former members are welcomed for a session or even a series of sessions.

The problem of *confidentiality* is one that may best be dealt with as the group goes along, if required. Though it may not yet be meaningful, it should at least be mentioned in the initial ground rules. It takes some time before real trust of each other and therapist develops. In an institution there may be leakage of material, from other group members, from the therapist to other members of the staff or from the group records, if any are kept. If parent groups are meeting simultaneously with the adolescent groups, there is the possibility of leakage, from one parent to another, of material from their own youngsters and vice versa. Each teenager will have his own degree of mistrust as to how much adults side together against young people (see Phelan, chapter 4).

What kinds of *auxiliary therapy* should be going on in addition to the group therapy? Some teen-agers can be in group, family therapy and individual therapy simultaneously, while the parents are having occasional sessions, all with the same therapist (see Brackelmanns and Berkovitz, chapter 2; Brown, chapter 13). Should all these forms of therapy be with the same or a different clinician? If the same therapist is involved, vital information can be more readily available at crucial moments. However, there may be difficulties in the therapist's loyalties and alliances. The adolescent or other family members might be concerned about confidentiality. This may need periodic additional consideration. On the other hand, if more than one therapist is involved, communication may be incomplete or fragmentary. Some therapists see several entire families in one group (see Vogel, chapter 14).

There may be times when the therapist or members wish to introduce some *activity other than discussion* (see Stebbins, chapter 10). This activity might take the form of games, books, movies, guest speakers, trips, etc. In the very young teen-age group, crafts may be useful at times, much as in a latency-age activity group. Some individuals may bring a book into the session to quote a particular passage. Some may even wish to show movies of themselves or, if it is their hobby, movies they have made. Guitars may be used in some sessions. In one group, with a majority of passive boys, it became trying for the therapist to develop discussion. To stimulate discourse, popular adolescent themes were introduced, for example, records or from material read aloud, such as "Catcher in the Rye" (see Enns and Berkovitz, chapter 9).

In all settings, groups may be set up for more specific tasks. Some examples of *task-oriented groups* might be a discharge group, formed for the purpose of helping individuals to make a better transition from an institution to a foster home or some other form of living outside the institution. Other types of such groups might be those for unwed mothers, often in a home where expectant mothers are awaiting delivery of their babies. Sex education groups on a mental hospital ward or in an institution may begin as a time-limited, two- to three-session project, but frequently these can develop discussion which may very well become the basis for a more on-going group experience.

FURTHER CONSIDERATION OF DIFFERENCES RELATING TO SETTING

It has been apparent in the previous discussion that *differences in setting* influence the character and composition of any particular group. In office practice and outpatient clinics, especially in middle-class neighborhoods, a large number of adolescents referred may be similar: neurotic, passive, underachieving in school, depressed or, in recent days, freshly "busted" and on probation for the possession of marijuana or drugs. In lower socioeconomic neighborhood clinics there may be more of the antisocial behavior, psychotic disorder and more hard drug usage. The residential setting population will vary with the focus of the particular institution. *Degree of impulse control and introspective capacity* will be two of the variables which can differentiate individuals or groups in these various settings. For example, a mental hospital will probably include teen-agers with extremes of lack or control but with some capacity for introspection (see Blaustein and Wolff, chapter 15; Constas and Berkovitz, chapter 17). A probation department residential setting may have more young people with poor impulse control, as well as poor introspective capacity. The need for structuring and rule setting may be greater in such groups, even though a closed, institutional setting already provides greater structure and limits (see Pottharst and Gabriel, chapter 20; Grold, chapter 16). Some structuring in the outpatient groups may come from the members with greater ego strength and depend on the proportion of these members in the particular group. The residential center or institution which has a repressive authority structure may encourage a greater expression of hostile impulses during the group's sessions.

In one *residential center for delinquent girls,* a particular procedure evolved for increasing the degree of introspective ability and involvement in the group sessions (see Pottharst and Gabriel, chapter 20). The groups met five times a week, one hour per session, in the living units for girls. This frequency increased the time available for examining behavior and allowed less time for material to become repressed between sessions. In addition, if a girl did not become motivated toward introspection to the degree considered desirable by the therapist, that girl was moved to a locked cottage with decreased privileges, and more intense attempts were made to involve her in group. This was seen not only as a punishment, but also provided an opportunity for a greater intensity of care and attempt to induce change. This was, by far, the most vigorous program described in this volume.

In an *open residential center* there may be laxity in ascertaining the whereabouts of each youngster, so that attendance at sessions is often less than ideally consistent. Despite other group activities in the institution, however, a small therapy group may provide an intensity of interaction, which many of the youngsters value and find useful (see Berkovitz, et al., chapter 19). In one such setting there was a great amount of discussion of the house parents' being "at fault" or "defective." Some of this was seen as a displacement from complaint about the natural parents, as well as an attempt to divide the case work staff against the house parent staff.

One *important difference between an institutional or residential group and the outpatient group* is that ongoing relationships already exist between members in the institutional or residential setting, a "network," so to speak (see Sugar, chapter 5). In the outpatient setting one object of the group situation would be to establish a meaningful interaction between members. The avoidance of such close relating is likely one of the problems of many of the members, which led to their referral for group therapy. In an outpatient group, where members come together only for the one session per week, various supplements to intensified contact may be sought, as previously described, such as extra contacts between members between sessions, phone calls, longer sessions, etc. The institutional group, on the other hand, may already involve so much closeness between the members in dormitories, dining rooms, etc., that the more intense interaction of a small group arouses anxiety and defensiveness, so that disruptiveness and horseplay may occur more readily. The role of the small group in the total milieu needs careful assessment (see Rinsley, Postlude, Part II).

In a residential center the *power structure prevailing* in the cottage or living unit will often be carried into the group sessions. It may be hard to dislodge a strong, bullying leader, since reprisal may take place in the cottage between group sessions. This may require action on the part of institutional administration, as well as in the group therapy.

There are undoubtedly many more possible events in the life of a teenage group which deserve comment. Some additional issues may be touched upon in the chapters which follow. Others may have to be experienced, learned from, and perhaps be described in some future volume. Many of the foregoing paragraphs highlight the difficult dilemmas and vicissitudes of small group experience with adolescents. This is but one aspect. There is also the thrilling joy and excitement of being witness and partner to young minds discovering, inventing and communicating new knowledge of self and others. We hope that some of this joy and excitement will be conveyed in the experiences to be described on the following pages.

REFERENCES

GINOTT, H. G. (1961), Group Psychotherapy with Children, The Theory and Practice of Play-Therapy, McGraw-Hill Book Co., N. Y.

MACLENNAN, B. W., & FELSENFELD, N. (1968), Group Counseling and Psychotherapy with Adolescents, Columbia Univ. Press, N. Y.

SCHEIDLINGER, S. (1955), The Relationship of Group Therapy to Other Group Influence Attempts, *Mental Hygiene*, Vol. 39, No. 3: pp. 367-90.

Part I

EXPERIENCES
IN
CLINIC,
OFFICE,
AND
COMMUNITY
GROUPS

CHAPTER 1

The Importance of an Actively
Involved Therapist

Robert L. Anderson, M.A.

THE SEEDS OF SUCCESS of a group are sown in the first session, by the therapist. Certainly, there will be some groupings of adolescents that are just not going to click, in spite of the therapist's genius. What must be accomplished early is very much related to the reason teen-agers come to group therapy in the first place. The majority bring a great sense of estrangement —from themselves, from their parents, from their peers, from the school situation, etc. They are isolated and looking for connection. They want to be related. They want someone to force them into a sense of relatedness once again. (I am not referring to schizophrenic youngsters.) Very often these are kids who are functioning rather well, but there is an awareness within them that there is a great deal that they are missing. Satisfaction is just not there. They cannot discuss this with anyone. The therapist must help the group as quickly as possible to develop a sense of unity within the group, some sense of beginning intimacy or the promise that it can happen. The group will begin to fall apart very quickly if some of this is not *demanded* by the therapist.

I look back with horror at some of my early experiences with adolescent groups. In accordance with the group therapy approach of that period, we professionals used to sit around and say, "We'll begin at a very slow pace. We'll start where they are. Let's see who's going to speak first, and let's be very interested in who's going to speak second, and who are the silent ones, and begin looking immediately for a scapegoat." Our role would be a very passive one. I think there is never a time to be passive with an adolescent group. Even if one is not saying anything, the therapist must be "alive." If he is not showing it, he is setting a poor example.

I don't know if they are much concerned even about whether the therapist will like them. Mostly they want to be liked by their peers, but they want to see what kind of tone the therapist will set. What will be permitted? What will be encouraged? Will he understand their reason for being there, their needs and their wants? One of the first demands upon the therapist, therefore, is that he be active and even free in his own emotions to touch the emotions of every other member of the group. He must begin questioning why they are not free and help them learn what they really want to be. This is a lot of pressure that has to come quickly in the early sessions.

Techniques for doing this are highly individual. Each therapist has his own way of pressing for accomplishing a sense of intimacy with a group of people. There may be inhibition that must be consciously worked on in the therapist, to overcome any inhibitions in relating to teen-agers. If they sense a readiness and openness in the therapist to face his own feelings, they will complete the job for him. They will let him know when he sounds phony; they will call him on just about everything, for all sorts of reasons. Some will be hostile, but some who want intimacy can tell when the curtain is drawn.

It is important to put a group on its own as quickly as possible, to avoid the pitfall of allowing oneself to be set up in some stereotyped role, such as teacher, father or mother. If that begins to develop, it has to be talked about immediately. I have noticed a change over the past four or five years, in terms of what teen-agers expect of therapy. They are afraid they will find someone who will hold in his feelings. He will take a phone call, which makes him irritated and angry, and then come back and sit in the group with a denying smile. They may say, "What's this? Can he be angry one minute, then turn it off the next? What does he do with it? Where does the anger go? Is he going to be coming at me now?" A certain openness must prevail. Whether he wants to or not, *the therapist becomes a model*, by his own behavior and his own way of reacting. The ideal model, I believe, is close to what is described by leaders in the family therapy field: someone who is an initiator, an activist, a provocateur, someone who will pick a fight, maybe just to get some feelings out.

The frequency and duration of sessions is an important issue, when considering intimacy. Would a group meeting daily for an hour or two for a two- or three-week period get people into a deeper level of therapeutic working and personal connection with each other? Then one can experiment with tapering down to less frequent meetings. I feel we lose a lot of groups because the feeling of intimacy does not happen quickly enough and individuals begin pulling away. The infrequency of the meetings reinforces the very distancing that members do. Our own schedules force this on kids.

Another consideration would be selection of members. If there is a variety of personality types, chances are good of getting the group under-way. It is good if there is someone in the group who lives fairly close to his primary process. These are the ones who will cut through the phoniness more quickly than other members of the group, or even the therapist. They keep getting at others and keep the therapist on his toes.

Use of one's own feelings is a tricky issue. The following is an example. A group was being rather lively and focused on a youngster who had been on a drug weekend. He was very upset about the group's reaction, not knowing what to do with the concern being expressed and the feeling of caring that was coming from the group. Both my cotherapist and I were commenting on the way he was handling the group reaction, which ranged from "The Hell with him. I've given up on him," a very disappointed note, to anger, "Why do you keep doing this to yourself?" to hurt, "We were counting on you." His tendency was to fend off these reactions and be very philosophical and flip. The transaction here was for both of us therapists to move in quickly on him and comment, "This is a pretty hideous thing you're doing. Everybody is giving you their reactions. They're telling you they care about you, and your reaction is shitty. You're not coming back. You're just sort of saying, 'Not me,' and it's a lie. You're being very phony. You're not telling. We couldn't help being upset about what the reactions are. Anybody would."

While all this was going on, Eileen was dozing in her chair. Her head was dropping. I looked over and recognized that my first reaction was one of anger. I thought of saying: "Look. All this was going on. This is great. This is intimacy. We're getting at Bruce, almost, and everybody else is being very honest about their feelings, and Eileen is dropping her head over there." I thought for a minute, instead, and said what I thought might be going on inside her, "Eileen, what are you so angry about?" Perhaps there was projection in my statement. Twenty minutes of lively discussion ensued, in which members wondered if they were getting their money's worth, whether Eileen really was angry. I replied, "Yes, you're mad because you thought I'd stomped on her out of a clear blue sky, because you were all absorbed in this other discussion."

Eileen happens to be an unattractive girl, who neglects herself physically. We had talked about this the week before, or at least I had. Since then, she's come in with make-up on and looks different. We didn't let her get away with being isolated, but insisted that she join us. I *was* mad at her, not just because she was dozing in MY precious group, but because of my knowledge of her background. She and her family considered this group their last chance. She is very bright and artistic but keeps herself totally uninvolved with people, wanting such interaction but not being able to reach it. She had gone through two previous groups and a long course of individual therapy, relatively untouched. She came to this group expecting that involvement might be here, because a friend of hers had gone through a change in this group. When the group confronted me with the question as to my anger, I told them. I addressed it to Eileen. I said, "You and I know what this group means to you. You consider it your last chance, and here you are—you're just dozing off. You're going to go through the old business of feeling angry and withdrawn, and it makes me very angry, because I know you have a chance. You're not using it; you're blowing it." I think I told her, "The next time you do that, I'm going to throw a pillow at you!"

Other factors which might influence the *degree of caring interaction* in a group may be involved in procedures I use to get my groups organized. First of all, I have a rather large office with a deep, thick carpet. Most of our group sessions take place with participants sitting right on the floor. There are chairs, but the carpet is very inviting and lends a certain openness, relaxation and informality to the group. My clientele comes mainly from what we call "West Side middle class." I have different groups for the different age ranges between 12 to 22. The youngest is from 12 to 14; the middle group is from 14 to 16; other groups are 16 to 22. All groups are coed. The average number in each group is eight, four boys and four girls, with occasional variation in ratio.

In a new group, there is some turnover initially. Some people drop out after the first session and some after the second or third, when we begin to develop some feeling of intimacy. Some are just not ready for this feeling. I press hard for it. With all of these groups, my work is to arrive as quickly as possible at the working group that's going to stay together.

I have been seeing some of the youngsters individually in family therapy. Individual sessions may be once a week, every other week, or even two or three times a week. Some teen-agers are referred by other therapists, who continue to see the youngster and family members in therapy concurrently. Half of my groups are closed groups, in that I get a working group organized and we settle down to what I hope will be six months or a year together. One such group is just beginning its second year. Some of the groups are openended, i.e., members are coming in and going out at different times. The most effective therapy occurs in the closed groups, where we have been able to achieve a strong sense of relatedness. I feel very connected with each member, they with me and with each other. This is the prime condition for developing an intimacy of working together, an increase in openness and a freedom of revealing oneself.

Most of the youngsters in the groups are well motivated. *I always start out with a family meeting,* seeing the entire family, to get acquainted with the dynamics and also to give an opportunity for all of the family members to see "who this guy is" who is going to be working with this particular member of the family. It does take care of later sabotaging that might occur. I do it even when the family may be in therapy with another therapist. I want to show them what this office looks like, to answer questions and to make a friend of the family if I can. With clinic groups that I have had, there is frequently somewhat less motivation. Kids can be dragged to a clinic by parents. Clinics sometimes will tend to go along a little more with seeing youngsters who are resistant. The clinic structure, the institutional atmosphere, lends itself to a little more coercion in getting a youngster to come for therapy. Over 50 percent of the teen-agers that I see in the office are self-referred or are referred by another youngster that I see. This has evolved over a period of time, after private practice of about 12 years. Somehow they feel there is something magical or something very human or honest when they are referred by their peers. Usually the person is a close friend.

In private practice there is a realistic concern that after getting just enough people to start a group, one or two may be lost along the way, and that there may not be a group very soon. To get referrals, one has to spread the word. It is amazing how many people are looking around for groups for teen-agers. To put one together, I combined efforts with a colleague who had three teen-age girls in individual therapy. I had four adolescent boys and one girl. Together they made a group. We worked as cotherapists, billing our own patients. We then began getting referrals from other people. This group continued for about two years.

Many therapists in private practice are edgy about taking on referrals just for group therapy. There is a feeling that one eventually will get involved with the family and midnight phone calls, or that he will need much time for collaboration with colleagues. I make it very clear to the people referring that I am not going to collaborate very much. The experience that I am offering my adolescent group is a transactional one, directed to the "here and now," interactions within the group, and relating to each other. This is really a separate and unique experience. If it is valuable enough it will appear in the individual's private therapy. This, therefore, relieves me of guilt. I may get together with the other therapist for lunch once or twice a year. There are occasional crises which require communication, but there has not been the burdensome problem that many people anticipate.

In most instances, group has provided me with an exhilarating feeling of involvement. This feeling very often was in direct proportion to the amount of energy needed from me to increase the amount and degree of involvement between the group members at that particular moment. Many of the group experiences in this volume will provide vivid examples of how each therapist, in his or her own way, had to work out the needed degree and intensity of involvement, deemed necessary for the young people concerned. There are many roads to involvement.

CHAPTER 2

Younger Adolescents in Group Psychotherapy: A Reparative Superego Experience

Walter E. Brackelmanns, M.D., and
Irving H. Berkovitz, M.D.

A NUMBER OF PROBLEMS repeatedly arise in work with younger adolescents in individual psychotherapy. Youngsters in this age group (twelve to sixteen) often present themselves negativistically and resist engaging in treatment. There is a conscious, as well as an unconscious, rebellion which frequently results in termination or stalemate. These young people are action-oriented and are actively involved in dealing with dependency and aggressive feelings. There is less emphasis on sexual feelings and conflicts concerning identity at this age. They are invariably brought to treatment by their parents who are the very persons with whom they are having a significant conflict. In the treatment situation, younger adolescents are placed in a restrictive setting conducive to the generation of intense positive and negative transference feelings. They are most often closed in terms of discussing themselves, their concerns, and their problems, and they are not ready to use introspective searching nor are they willing to discuss feelings.

Resistance to forming an alliance with the therapist is often manifested in at least two forms of behavior. The first of these is represented by the youngster who passively accepts his fate and allows himself to be carried back and forth to the office, but refuses any involvement. There was an example of a thirteen-year-old boy who offered no overt resistance to coming to treatment but, upon arrival, sat silently for the entire time. More often than not, he appeared drowsy or fell asleep. The second form of response, more common in girls than in boys, is a more open hostile rebellion to treatment. This type of young adolescent is full of promises of failure, feeling of distrust, threats of termination, and raw insults, both personal and professional, which are directed at the therapist. The frustration involved in these experiences led the senior author to form a younger adolescent group.

In many ways, the two types of younger adolescent responses described above are ones for which group is specifically indicated. These types of young people frequently will not accept or work in either of the other two principal modalities, namely individual psychotherapy or family therapy. Both types frequently state an unwillingness to be helped, and stress the therapist's inability and incompetence to help. Other types for whom group may be specifically indicated are the silent adolescent and the adolescent with poor peer relationships, particularly if there is denial and reluctance to accept the reality of the problem. In terms of increasing the potential for early group mutuality, it is helpful if the members have problems which are not so dissimilar which will enable them to more quickly relate to and identify with each other.

Two *relative contraindications* to group psychotherapy are overt psychosis and severe narcissism or non-empathy. The latter is an interesting problem which the group and therapist find difficult to deal with. This patient tends to be very verbal and preoccupied with himself and his own problems and has little genuine concern for other people. He angers the group, but they find it hard to control him because of their own narcissism, their concerns about being critical and being criticized, and the way in which this patient transmits an aura of being fragile and helpless. An attack on him (or her) results in the attacker's feeling guilty. It has been very helpful to have this type of patient also in individual psychotherapy, and to educate him in group conduct with emphasis on developing his skills toward greater empathy and more effective interpersonal interaction.

A *patient with physical handicaps* was not found to be a contraindication. There was a very immature fifteen-year-old, mildly mentally retarded, cerebral palsied boy who was introduced into the group. He was brought by his parents because of difficulties in peer relationships and hostility toward his family. Aside from his disabilities, he differed from the other group members in his conspicuous lack of acting-out behavior. This patient turned out to be an extremely valuable group member by expressing personal things about himself which other members were unable to do. Initially, he presented himself as fragile. The group treated him gently, but at the same time confronted him with his isolating behavior. Despite his relative silence in the sessions, reports from home indicated that his behavior was very much improved. As time went by, it was clear that he was identifying with other group members, and he began to look more like a typical adolescent.

Group psychotherapy with younger adolescents is an effective *ancillary therapy* to individual and/or family therapy. The group provides an arena to help the scapegoated child separate himself from the parental marital conflict, as well as a place in which he can test out effective, constructive, independent movement into the world. He can be confronted with his behavioral problems and feelings. Responsibility for self is heavily reinforced by the powerful influence of other adolescents. The preferred treatment with any younger adolescent must be determined on an individual basis, after consideration of practical, as well as psychodynamic issues. The most common treatment modalities, individual psychotherapy, group psychotherapy, and family therapy, can be used concurrently or in any combination indicated, by the same or different therapists. It is our judgment that it works best for the group psychotherapist to undertake also the individual and family therapy. This allows for maximum input of data in the treatment process. There can be the problem of a subtle kind of sibling rivalry which arises between family members, or it may be difficult to achieve a relationship which will allow effective intensive individual psychotherapy, if this route is elected.

The focus in group psychotherapy with younger adolescents is on *peer group interaction,* with emphasis on self or identity, in the context of a group situation apart from the family. This is the treatment situation which is safest in terms of dealing with the dependency-independency conflicts. The influencing forces are the patient-therapist transference and the peer group with its feelings, attitudes and behavior. Determination of the more crucial of these depends upon the skill of the therapist in integrating individuals into a group that can deal with feelings toward each other and the therapist. Too little activity on the part of the group therapist allows the group to avoid dealing with him by escaping into the group, and identifying with the group's dysfunctional behavior.

The *focus in family therapy* is on the family system and the forces which are perpetuating the symptomatic behavior of the child. There is an effort on the part of the therapist to help all family members to become aware of the family dynamics and allow the child to move out of his role of being responsible for the family integrity. When the conflict focus moves away from the child to the marital conflict, the young adolescent is free to attempt to deal with and to attempt to resolve his intrapsychic conflicts.

The Question of Acting Out

The therapist must consider the danger of *mixing non-acting out adolescents with acting out adolescents*. It is possible that the young person, as he makes separation from his family and engages with the peer group, will identify with acting out adolescent behavior in order to gain acceptance. In addition to this process, the group often provides a sanctioning body with the tendency to encourage certain kinds of acting out behavior in order to deal with feelings. Initially, the therapist must project himself very actively in order to encourage a group value system which will operate constructively with rapidly changing and malleable young people.

Later when the group has formed and is more stable, this may be less of a problem. An unfortunate example in the early months of the group to be described below was Daniel, a fourteen-year-old boy with essentially no history of deviant behavior. He had been immature and resistant to entering into adolescence. He finally began to identify with certain group members, following which he grew his hair long, dressed in typically adolescent fashion, began smoking marijuana, developed problems at school and dropped out of the group. Attempts by the therapist and group members to retain him in the group were unsuccessful. In retrospect, family psychopathology interfered with his continued attendance.

Susan, fourteen, was an example of one who also was not acting out and who was doing well at school. She had poor peer relationships and a passive helpless mother. She had been in individual psychotherapy for one year where she had used a passive resistant defense. It seemed she had not been able to deal with her feelings toward the therapist. In group, there had been frequent absences, always with good excuses, and always supported by her mother. After five months of group psychotherapy, she terminated, stating that she felt alienated and different from the other group members. She refused to reenter individual psychotherapy. The relationship individually had been tenuous, but the attention to her specific problems had provided some dependency gratification which had allowed the therapy to continue. Her resistance to group involvement, her repressive superego, and her wish to escape the intensity of a one to one situation were factors which led to termination. It is probable that she was at the point where commitment to the group meant commitment to looser instinctual coping mechanisms and a less rigid super ego. Prior to termination, she had moved significantly from looking and behaving like a preadolescent to looking and behaving like a young adolescent. This patient had a strong super ego and a mother who had little or no capacity to provide external control. She felt unprotected and frightened by her feelings which prevented experimentation with a different type of control.

It is our feeling that young people who have not been using acting out behavior as a coping mechanism and whose parents do not provide adequate external controls need special attention. In some cases, it might be advisable not to include them in a younger adolescent group where most members are acting out.

Description of the Group

This particular group has been in existence for three years. It met once a week for one and a half hours. The number of group members has ranged from as low as three to as many as nine. Group members terminated for a variety of reasons. These were (1) inability to tolerate emerging feelings; (2) inability to tolerate group reaction; (3) inappropriate treatment; (4) satisfactory resolution of intrapsychic or interpersonal conflict. New adolescents were introduced into the group as members left. In each case, the group was prepared for this change. In the majority of cases there was great resistance to joining the group. The therapist would often make a deal that the adolescent would only have to commit himself to three to six sessions, and then would be free to discontinue. This grew out of the experience that once exposed, the young person would want to continue.

Some of the problems in bringing new people into the group were related to age and sex. As time passed, the adolescents grew, and over the three years several group members went from age fourteen to age seventeen. Experience showed that adolescent girls were usually more experienced and mature than adolescent boys. As the girls grew older, it was possible to bring in younger girls and boys, but also necessary to bring in older boys. The mean age of the group increased from fourteen years to sixteen years. In three years, the age range changed from a twelve-sixteen year old group to a fourteen-eighteen year old group. This aging process significantly influenced the behavior of the group and issues considered. The direction became away from family problems and peer interpersonal conflict to intrapsychic conflict, with emphasis on sexual and identity problems.

In general, the group members attended regularly with few absences. The majority had declared explicitly that the group was very important, and that they came not only willingly but eagerly. An example of this was a fourteen-year-old boy who ran away from home. In the group session following his return home, he stated that he had timed his runaway so that it was only long enough to scare and intimidate his parents, but not long enough to make him miss the following group session. This was a young person who had been seen individually for three months, and who had been unable to get involved in the individual treatment process.

One of the important dimensions of this group was the change in *limit setting* which occurred as the group developed a more stable internal structure, and the therapist's relationship with the group became more solid. Initially, the limits set were location, time, no physical contact and no throwing things. Another limit which was more relative than absolute was that social relationships between group members outside of the group were discouraged. However, this was not rigidly prohibited. On several occasions, superficial social contact outside of the group had been constructive for those members involved. Two examples were (1) group members sharing rides to the office and (2) a group member introducing a newer member, a recent arrival to Los Angeles, to the peer group in the high school they both attended. An inability to find friends was central to the problem of the newcomer.

Another relative limit, initially, which instead of becoming less rigid became more rigid, was the discouraging of members coming to the group under the influence of drugs. It was stated that the emphasis was on verbal interaction, and the goal was to talk about problems and feelings. As time went on, limits were tested in various ways. On one occasion, the group attempted to meet in the hallway. They often encouraged the therapist to convene the group in a wooded area many miles from the office. Hitting and throwing things occurred frequently, and had to be stopped. On one occasion, a member asked what the therapist would do if he persisted in disruptive action. He was told firmly that he would be expelled from the group. After nine to twelve months, coming to the group under the influence of drugs became more firmly prohibited. The important part of this shift was that the group members rallied around the therapist. The enforcement of this limit was as much or more related to group pressure as to the therapist's disapproval.

In the process, it became clear that the therapist was *repairing the vacuum left by a powerless parent*. The therapist was powerless in that he could and would do nothing directly about behavior outside the group.

However, he was a concerned surrogate parent in that he did set some limits in the interest of the process, and voiced disapproval of certain pieces of destructive behavior. The therapist's power derived from the young person's regard and wish for his and the group's approval, rather than the fear of punitive potential. This can be seen as a corrective experience allowing a maturational shift, from the externally enforced to the internalized super ego. As described in a later section, (Relationships with Parents), the majority of parents of these group members were of the passive-helpless type. As a result, these young people probably did not experience stable effective superego models. The therapist's and group's limit setting helped to repair this deficiency.

There were other significant changes, both in terms of process and content. Initially, the members operated as a stranger group, composed of individual fragments, loosely tied together by mutual adolescent interests. They moved to the point of becoming a unified group, committed to, interested in and involved with each other. The content changed from joking, laughing, disruptive comments and talk of adolescent issues, such as trips or parties, records and mutual friends, to discussion of problems more specifically related to parents, peers, and school. It was *never* possible for them to talk spontaneously about feelings. This was the task of the therapist, and his comments in this direction were accepted as often as they were rejected.

STAGES OF YOUNGER ADOLESCENT GROUP PSYCHOTHERAPY

(1) The Fragmented Stage:

Prior to entering the group and during the early sessions, each of the members had feelings that they would not be accepted. They felt that they would be attacked, that nothing they had to say would be considered important, and that nobody would be interested in what they had to say. Each person felt very protective of himself and his feelings and very sensitive to the reactions of others. As a result of these concerns, the group operated, in the beginning, in a very chaotic, disjointed and disruptive fashion. There was a tendency for several discussions to be going on at the same time. No group member was allowed to finish any thought without interruption, usually by introduction of something irrelevant to the matter being discussed and of little value to the group process. It was during this stage that they showed two things, which illustrated the growing commitment to each other, and their capacity for orderliness and organization.

One group member designated herself as the purchasing agent, and collected money from each member in order to buy candy for the next meeting. There was a couch in the office which was favored by the adolescents. Within thirty seconds after entering the office, they had worked out a somewhat complicated time plan, allowing group members to rotate in their use of the couch.

Almost from the beginning, each member was open about his activities, but the group, as a whole, was very protective in terms of any in depth discussion. Much emphasis, by the therapist, was on helping these young people to do less projecting and externalizing of feelings, and to develop greater skills in dealing with their parents, toward the end of achieving greater independence and autonomy. During this stage, the *therapist often felt like a "traffic cop."* Most of the time was spent turning off certain kinds of behavior, redirecting discussion and content, and encouraging the members to operate as a unit. This period lasted approximately three months.

(2) Pre-working Stage:

During this time the group was very committed to each other, and operated as a unit. They still tended to be protective of each other, and all actively worked toward changing the subject, and diverting from stressful problem areas. The therapist's efforts during this time were in the direction of filtering out relevant from irrelevant content. The therapist felt free to eliminate subject matter introduced, and to bring in for discussion important general comments, group process observations or interpretations, and material related to specific group members which may have been obtained via a telephone call or from a meeting with the parents. This stage lasted about six months.

(3) The Working Stage:

By this time, the scope of verbal activity allowed by the therapist had narrowed very significantly to discussion of problems and feelings. The focus was mainly on problems related to parents, peers, and school. It was as if a corrective superego experience had occurred which allowed the young person to move more independently toward adulthood.

In the working stage of the process, the *open conflicts with the parents generally had subsided.* Most of the issues that ordinarily helped to fan this fire of conflict had been channeled into the group sessions for discussion and resolution. To illustrate, in this stage the therapist often traded drugs with the young person, generally the therapist's Valium for the adolescent's drugs. The contract was that the young person would use no other drugs, and take the Valium as prescribed (usually 10 mgm, four times per day). The parents knew about the prescription, but were not involved in any other way. If the teenager violated the contract, the therapist discontinued writing prescriptions. He did not indicate anger or disappointment, but utilized this violation of trust as a point of discussion and understanding. The hope was that the trade would work. In practice, it failed one hundred percent of the time. The real value of this interaction was to focus parent-child feelings into the group sessions, more specifically between the adolescent and the therapist.

One of the major defenses in this phase was the "secret," namely, things not stated were labeled "personal," and not relevant to the group. It was interesting that there were rarely any sibling difficulties discussed. This may have been because feelings in this area were intensified by virtue of the group situation, and the varying relationships each member had with the therapist. During this time, there was much more focus on the therapist, with expression of negative and positive feelings related to his efforts. The working stage never stopped, but blended into the termination stage.

(4) The Termination Stage:

As suggested above, a termination stage can only be artificially described. The termination stage of an open ended younger adolescent group of this nature is only relevant in that these young people are continually growing older with members leaving and new members joining. In four years, this group aged from a younger adolescent group to an older adolescent group. It was no longer a group which could accommodate youngsters between the ages of twelve and fifteen. In a sense, it is more relevant to think of the termination stage in terms of individuals within the group rather than the group as a whole.

Different group members terminated at different times, depending upon their completion of the psychological work necessary for each one of them. These areas of resolution varied from dealing with parent conflicts to feeling more comfortable with the peer group, to feeling a greater sense of personal achievement and success, to more effectively being able openly to experience and express feelings and thoughts. The younger adolescent group served as an effective forum for the young person to be able to work through his dependency-independency conflict, and to begin to move more effectively away from his parents and their conflicts into a satisfying relationship with acceptable growth facilitating peers, both in the individual close friend relationship and in the more casual peer group relationships. The younger adolescent group cannot solve all problems related to entering later adolescence, but when successful can equip the growing teenager with better reality testing and more constructive super ego.

RELATIONSHIPS WITH PARENTS

Therapeutic involvement with the family, more specifically the parents, varied widely from patient to patient, and covered the range from ongoing family therapy or marital therapy to occasional family or parent meetings. The purpose of this concurrent therapy was to deal with psychological issues relatively unrelated to the patient, or to deal with problems or a crisis centered around the child. The degree to which the therapist was involved with the family was determined by two factors: (1) the needs of the family to involve themselves in the treatment process in order to deal with their own personal problems; and (2) the therapist's evaluation of the extent to which the identified patient was actively caught in the total family psychopathology or the marital conflict.

With this therapeutic approach, there was a greater understanding and acceptance of the behavior of the young people by their parents. There was quieting of the conflict and hostility at home. There was a shift in attitude on the part of the parents away from viewing the therapist as a parent surrogate who would immediately stop all unacceptable behavior, to viewing him as a professional who would help their child to understand his/her actions, assume responsibility for behavior and find better ways of dealing with feelings. There was a tendency, on the part of the parents, to feel less guilty in their role, and more secure, through their pursuit of help. They were able to view the problems of their children more realistically, in terms of type and severity, and were able to allow time for the process.

The parents varied in regard to degree of intrapsychic problems and overt versus covert marital problems. They also varied significantly in the power they had over their children, from passive-helpless parents to dominant-authoritarian parents.

Of the patients involved in the group experience described, the majority of the parent units were in the passive-helpless category. Initially, all of these couples brought their children with the hope that the necessary missing power element would be provided. During treatment, they struggled with their responsibility to control unacceptable behavior of their children, and felt frustrated, lost and powerless. Occasionally, behavior of the young adolescent exceeded their limits of tolerance, and there would be an emotional crisis in the family. The parent would explode in anger, over-react to the behavior, and threaten to expel the child from the family or give up parental responsibility. Invariably, the therapist would receive a phone call from the parents at such times, and these events would become a central issue of discussion in the group sessions.

One example was that of a fifteen-year-old girl, living with her mother, stepfather and stepbrother. There was overt, unresolved marital conflict and a hostile relationship between the patient and her stepfather, which caused chronic friction in the family. The patient began to take the family car at three A.M. for joy riding. After a couple of weeks, this activity was discovered by her mother, who read a letter which had been left in open view. The immediate reaction by the mother and stepfather was to have the adolescent declared incorrigible, and sent to a locked residential probation facility. They decided to give up trying to help her. The therapist insisted that the parents give themselves a moratorium before making a final decision. There was a family meeting, and the crisis passed.

There were many phone calls from the parents relating problem events at home, and these matters were brought into the group for discussion. Telephone calls or meetings with the parents concerning complaints or difficulties with the youngsters were not held confidential, but meetings regarding intrapsychic problems or marital conflicts were. Absolute confidentiality about material discussed with the teenagers, either individually or in group, was maintained. The net result of this was that the young people in the group were open and honest about all of their activities, and there was easy access to the problems going on at home from both sides. Strict *confidentiality* was requested of all group members. This was violated frequently by almost all. There was a greater tendency, on the part of the young people, to tell their parents about the activities of other group members which almost invariably resulted in generating concern about the "bad influence of the group." At first glance, this action seems paradoxical. On the one hand, there was the great commitment to coming to the group, and on the other hand, there were these activities which seem designed to provoke the parents into removing them from the group. It was the reverse of the open hostility at home and the covert dependency relationship. This discovery resulted in a change in procedure. Prior to bringing a new member into the group, the therapist met with the parents, and discussed, in general terms, some of the problems of the other group members; for example, that "there are young people who act out sexually, take drugs, are disinterested in school or refuse to go to school." This allowed the parents an early opportunity to deal with some of their feelings around these issues.

CONCLUSION

The therapist must be flexible in his role, and willing to move from transference object to real person, from the position of powerless parent to powerful adult friend. Most adolescents referred for treatment feel powerless, inadequate, and incompetent, and deal with these feelings by exerting themselves against their parents in self-destructive ways. The parents' over reaction and feelings of helplessness allow the child to deny his own feelings, and to get dependency gratification without overtly acknowledging these needs.

The therapist must be increasingly firm in his limit setting, and, at the same time, accepting, but willing to express judgment about the constructiveness of behavior for the young person. He must be careful not to support the group members' hostility toward parents, and their active efforts to project and indict them as "unjust dictators." Much work is done in helping the adolescent to assume responsibility for his behavior, and to recognize his parents as people with faults and feelings.

The therapist, in dealing with this age group, has to be somewhat directive, help the group verbalize problems, and focus on the major areas of conflict, namely, parent-child, peer relationships and school. Open, spontaneous discussion of felings can be too great an expectation at this age. The most useful directiveness or limit setting is not rigidly or mechanically supplied, but respects group and individual readiness and timing. This need for directiveness is appropriate to this developmental stage, age thirteen to fifteen. In this stage, loosening from parental superego (if this is tolerated intrapsychically) creates a period of vacuum, varying according to previous parental rigidity or helplessness. The therapist and group superego support can modify previous malformation, and facilitate progression to consideration of older adolescent age-appropriate intrapsychic issues and life goals.

CHAPTER 3

Reflections on Selection

Max Geller, M.D.

ANYONE WHO HAS CONCERNED himself with the group treatment of adolescents and young adults has found it to be a rather broad, difficult, and complex area beset by much diversity of opinion. Using the focus of selection for treatment may highlight some of the distinctive issues involved.

The criteria of selection to be presented are based on work with about forty young people aged sixteen through the early twenties. They were seen in about equal numbers in two outpatient groups. One is a clinic group now in its seventh year of continuous operation, the other is a private group currently in its fourth year (1970).

The groups involved eight or fewer members of both sexes who had a variety of symptoms and diagnoses. They met once weekly for an hour and a half and were essentially closed, i.e., members were not added to fill vacancies except when new members could be usefully added without major disruptions to group continuity. Additions of one or more members usually occurred on a once a year basis, and never more than twice a year. Group vacancies were filled by those with ages close to the average in the group.

Ground rules were rather simple. Topics for discussion were open and wide ranging. Spontaneous comments about thoughts, feeling, etc. were encouraged; assaultiveness and damage to property were explicitly prohibited. Payment of fees was structured as the patient's responsibility, even in the rare situation where a parent or other third party had been permitted to assume the financial sponsorship of the therapy. Both groups were observed, the clinic group through a one-way mirror for training purposes, the private group by a non-participant observer in the group room. Group events and content were considered confidential both for the members and professionals involved. No information was divulged without the usual clearance of the members beforehand (e.g. to school authorities, draft boards, etc.), except in emergencies (e.g. suicide attempts, etc.). Parental overtures and contacts with the therapist were always reported, kept to a minimum, and actively discouraged, barring urgent developments. Outside contacts between group members beyond the barest minimum were not encouraged.

Basically, group sessions were unstructured. The therapist's commitment was to share his thoughts or impressions when he felt he had something to contribute. A primary focus of the group work was determining the issues which concerned the group as a whole and understanding how it dealt with such issues, collectively and individually. Such group issues became discernible when the individual associations of various members linked together in a pattern. When sufficient material emerged to support the existence of a particular theme, such thoughts were shared with the group.

The progression of material in the first session of a newly formed clinic group vividly demonstrated the emergence of such a group issue. After the introduction and comments about the ground rules, members initially talked about selfish preoccupations and the wish "to get all one can get." This discussion soon shifted to the topic of society and its taboos, couched in anthropological terms. The issues of nakedness, moral structure in primitive cultures, the fear of sex, etc. were introduced. One member tried to dispel the mounting tension by joking about nudist colonies, displacing it as far away as Africa, then gradually bringing it closer to home with an acknowledgment that they exist even in Massachusetts. The major preoccupation of what does and what doesn't "go" in the group emerged in this way and was pointed out. The group members went on to elaborate a variety of concerns about what safeguards would be available against being "bopped," "killed," "labeled" (idiot, crazy, etc.) and how their "deformities" would be handled.

As familiarity with individual styles, defensive maneuvers, personal conflicts, etc. increased, additional remarks were made about each individual's manner of dealing with the key issues. Such comments were not added in a rigidly formalistic manner, but in relation to a continuing assessment and reassessment of each person's potential readiness to receive such observations and cope with them.

Such a technical approach, characterized by a minimum of structure and relative lack of direction in the exploration of personal and mutual issues, inevitably had consequences. Anxieties were evoked by the uncertainties of the situation. Concerns about trust became manifest. The ambiguity of the situation led to mounting tensions which mobilized characteristic ways of handling discomfort and highlighted specific defensive maneuvers. Leading conflicts emerged. Expectations aroused by the therapeutic situation were frustrated and resulted in affective reactions of various kinds. Difficulties relating to closeness, intimacy and communication arose. Regressions were experienced directly or threatened by observing others becoming more dependent. Transference reactions became apparent. Other issues such as exposure, observing and being observed, sharing, competition, etc. confronted the individual members of the group with a number of stresses.

The aim of this technique was to marshal these reactions and resonating issues in an appropriately orchestrated manner for the group's benefit. The therapeutic goal was to change to some degree those painful and repetitive qualities of behavior which made for social isolation and inadequate functioning in various sectors—i.e., at school, work, play, etc. In maturational terms, emphasis was on a more successful disengagement from dependence on family of origin, the achievement of a better sense of personal identity, the development of a greater capacity for intimacy and increased comfort with sexuality. In the groups described above it was considered desirable for the therapist to have a minimum of outside contacts with either patients or parents. Decompensation, crises, extreme acting out in the transference, etc. were handled outside of group sessions as circumstances required. Such interventions were regarded as parameters in Eissler's sense: to be used sparingly, and for as short a time as required to meet the necessities of the occasion.*

Selection for treatment in groups must take into account the potential reactions likely to be induced by the group processes described earlier, as well as consideration of the extent and nature of the adolescent turmoil in a given individual. Some of the guiding principles in choosing candidates will be examined and relevant clinical examples presented.

NEED, MOTIVATION AND CAPACITY FOR ENGAGEMENT

It is desirable that the prospective group member be able to convey in some way or other, that he or she is suffering and wants to change. Peter,

---

* Eissler, K. R. The Effect of the Structure of the Ego on Psychoanalytic Technique. *Journal of the American Psychoanalytic Association*, 1:140-143, 1953.

a nineteen-year-old boy distressed by homosexual preoccupations, applied to the clinic. His worries had made him feel apart from others, and this in turn had led to much social isolation. Because of his loneliness, his wish for help, and the absence of any specific contraindications, he was asked to join a group then in progress.

Participation in a group is often of significant benefit to those suffering from self-imposed social isolation. The opportunity to experiment with new modes of behavior, test out old premises of human interaction and witness alternative approaches to similar dilemmas in fellow group members provides unique possibilities for corrective emotional experiences.

Referral of adolescents for psychotherapy usually occurs as the result of a second party's discomfort or concern—i.e. parent, teacher, court, etc. This is so frequent that at one time in our child psychiatric unit there was the unwritten rule: "Respond immediately to any teen-ager who seeks evaluation or treatment on his own initiative, whatever the length of the waiting list!" Despite the external initiation, one can usually distinguish the distress felt solely by an outsider from the distress experienced by the person involved. When this is apparent, a reformulation of the problems in personally meaningful terms will often engage the patient sufficiently to make some efforts at further exploration possible.

The following illustrates the matter of *engagement*. Barbara, a 16-year-old high school student, was referred by her mother, who felt her daughter to be in a "mad rush" to finish high school in intense competition with her older brother. The girl had become involved in a series of manipulations with the school authorities to allow her to manage this. Her behavior and pre-varications indicated that she was becoming involved in situations she was not quite ready to handle. She was a bright, articulate, appealing teen-ager, who came to see me grudgingly. However, she was cordial enough, and was soon engaged in a detailed listing of mother's faults.

A prolonged evaluation seemed indicated, but her reluctance seemed to be a considerable barrier. I finally commented that her mother did not seem to be her idea of what a woman should be. She agreed, giving another catalogue of deficiencies. When I added that she seemed to be on the way to becoming much like her mother, I supported this impression with pointing to a few of her activities. She was rather surprised and dismayed. After a few more exchanges, I told her of her mother's reaction to my comment that I could see her only at 7:00 a.m. for future regular appointments. Mother's reply had been, "She'll never come!" The girl rose to the challenge, asked which morning was available and said that she would think about it. Two weeks later she took the 7:00 a.m. appointment time and did keep it.

At times, other factors have to be reconsidered with the patient in order to promote an opportunity for involvement. Laura, 22, was referred for group therapy in spite of past failures of sustained involvement in treatment. She had been subject to longstanding instability in academic and work situations, as well as in relations with family and friends. She had frequent episodes of depression, was readily stimulated to extremes of anxiety, and had tried to deal with these painful feelings by a variety of impulsive acts, including homosexual experiences, heterosexual promiscuity, blatantly seductive behavior with father, suicidal attempts and prodigious lying. She had consulted a succession of therapists over the preceding four years.

Each treatment period was characterized by a stormy course. While there had been some diminution of impulsivity and crisis these changes were not sustained. Hospitalization was used in an effort to interrupt her self-destructive behavior—first, in a private mental hospital for about six months, and later in a public teaching facility. In both places, she was active, non-cooperative, constantly testing out the extent of the limits, escaping when frustrated, etc. In the second hospital, the staff's patience with her behavior, e.g., sleeping with a borderline patient on an open ward, was short-lived. They discharged her after one month with the recommendation for hospitalization on the closed ward of a state hospital. About a year after the above events she was referred for group therapy.

When I first saw her in individual evaluation, she had just been dismissed from her job, and had broken up with a boyfriend. She was obviously bright, articulate, appealing and miserable. The range of her behavior was acknowledged and amplified upon. While she recognized these facts as constituting her problems, external considerations were too readily used as rationalizations for her behavior. Without getting into a hassle with her about the issue of responsibility in an abstract sense, I confronted her with this issue on a practical level. At the time she was having her rent paid by her parents. All other expenses were covered by her earnings. I agreed to accept her for inclusion into an on-going private group, on the condition that she came regularly, and would be personally responsible for the payment of her fee, which was a flat rate for each member. She agreed to these conditions, joined the group and found another job to meet this commitment. For the two years or so of her treatment, she has been a regular and involved participant in the group.

In this case the conditions for my participation were quite clearly spelled out. I would accept certain responsibilities if she would do likewise. This approach has shown itself to be an extremely important overture to these young people. When I first began using this procedure with clinic patients, I discussed financial matters with each prospective member. I indicated that the bill was something they could handle by themselves. This money was to come out of allowances, savings, or summer or part-time job earnings. When told of the clinic's sliding scale policy, a rather frequent response was, "What is the *average* fee in the adult clinic?" The majority set fees for themselves which clustered around this average amount.

One of the crucial struggles at this period of life is the attempt to emancipate oneself from dependence on one's family. Through the use of a tangibly recurring agency, the fee, the tug-of-war is joined at the outset. It is experienced as an entering wedge by both patient and parents and emphasizes for whom the treatment is being undertaken. As a challenge accepted, it begins the development of an alliance directed toward personal growth. The fee's usefulness continues during the course of treatment when focus on it highlights the vicissitudes of the person's efforts for progressive development.

STATE OF COMPENSATION OR PSYCHIC EQUILIBRIUM

The stability of the young person's state of compensation (or ego strength) is an important variable in determining selection for group. Walter, a young man in his mid-twenties, was referred by his individual therapist for concurrent group psychotherapy. The aim was to offset his chronic and reclusive loneliness, to offer him an opportunity to learn about his manner of communicating to others, as well as, to test his feelings about others, in their presence. His parents were divorced when he was quite young and he was shuttled between his mother and his grandparents for years. What remained of these events was a strong conviction of his mother repeatedly trying to "room him out." There were few acquaintances in his past, and fewer close friends.

Walter had entered individual treatment some months earlier, in what was described as an "obsessional crisis." This had led to a major disorganization in his functioning. He had responded to an active, supportive therapeutic approach combined with the use of Stelazine. He had been able to reintegrate sufficiently to deal with his affairs. His therapist's vacation led to a reversal in equilibrium, necessitating interim hospitalizaton. Upon his therapist's return, Walter became preoccupied with suicide while becoming overtly angry with his doctor for having taken a vacation. The doctor's absence was clearly experienced as a repetition of earlier rejections by mother.

He had reservations about joining a group, due to anxiety about a "nasty streak" which had emerged in his dealings with others at school. However, he felt desperate and was willing to try anything which might help. It was clear that he was in tenuous equilibrium, staving off a more intense psychotic episode. With the support of an individual therapist the effort to get him into contact with more adequately functioning people seemed worth a try.

What impact the particular events in the group may have had on his gradually worsening condition is hard to say. Whether the actual referral to group was experienced as yet another "rooming out" episode, can be only conjecture in the absence of supporting data. What is evident is that he was in a rather shaky state to begin with and the addition of group therapy on an outpatient basis did not help to stem the tide.

Several other attempts at including people who were in similar unstable equilibrium have been uniformly unsuccessful. Established members who decompensated for short periods were quite manageable and were tolerated well by the group, which often responded with necessary support. For example, upon the termination of two members, the size of one group was reduced to three. The matter of adding new members was broached about six to eight weeks before the therapist's vacation, with their entry set for several weeks after his return. On that occasion, Jerry, a 25-year-old established member, came late, midway into the session. Initially neutral, he gradually began to bristle when one of the new members raised the issue of changing the day and time of the session. The matter of lack of control emerged in a derivative way with another member in relation to his mother. Jerry became more direct, gradually expressing his mounting anger because he felt the additions were beyond his control and veto. Suddenly, he pulled out a plastic water pistol in one hand, a mini-Mace cartridge in the other, and began threatening the group. Angrily he shot the water, primarily at the observer. When several of the group rose to overpower him, he became quite frightened and more verbally threatening. The therapist waved them back to their seats, indicating that he was not the "Texas Tower killer," to whom he had alluded earlier, but had only sprayed them with water. As they sat, Jerry "accidentally" released the cartridge directly into his own face, defusing the intensity of the situation.

These occasions were rare and reasonable reconstitution occurred before the meeting ended. Basically, such persons were severely disturbed personali-

ties who occasionally experienced transient breakthroughs of primitive impulses. They worked quite beneficially when they did not encounter aggressive provocateurs in the group. Their slowly emerging self-control and
progressive social adaptability were most heartening to them, and provided
remarkable impetus for attempts at change in the less disturbed, but chronically anxious and inhibited members.

The capacity to tolerate the stimulation of one's own impulses by exposure to the fantasies, acts, behavior, and feelings of others in the group
is a factor which must be considered in evaluating the suitability for group
therapy. For example, Lucy, a chronically depressed 16-year-old girl, with
a history of suicide attempts at ages 10 and 15, was referred for group
therapy. She had been involved in long standing battles with her parents
from early childhood. Initially there had been feeding difficulties which
finally required strict medical orders that she not be forced to eat. Vomiting
and stomach cramps were recurrent problems from the first year of life
and at times were consciously used to manipulate people.

Her tendencies to somatize were intense. When mother was "on her
back" she developed back pains. When she saw a player hurt at a baseball
game, she developed similar symptoms in identification with him. In more
recent years, her fury was directed more towards her father who was
exerting pressure for academic accomplishment and who was also quite
sexually stimulating. Father had a modest clerical position but had serious
and pretentious ambitions to be a writer. He had written several books, all
rejected, and would turn to Lucy for editorial advice. The content was a
transparent use of family history, interwoven with illicit sexual themes
which fascinated and disgusted her.

After this interview, I received a letter from her father which read:

> Dear Sir:
>
> I am Lucy's father the girl you interviewed Saturday—. After
> questioning my daughter about her talk with you, I found out
> that she didn't reveal an important fact about herself. She wears
> a wig. She's very self-conscious about her thin hair. This is a big
> problem with her, I think. My best,
>
> Sincerely,
>
> P.S. . . . Please keep this letter confidential.

Despite Lucy's eagerness to have group treatment due to the referring
physician's persuasiveness, she was not accepted. To have added her to the

on-going group at this time would have been too stimulating for her. Incestuous wishes were then being alluded to in the dreams of one member and also in the waking fantasies of another member. Such discussions would undoubtedly have served as stimuli exciting her to further disequilibrium. Her voyeuristic tendencies and primitive hysterical identification potentialities, as reflected in the sketchy history above, would have been activated by the climate in the group at that time. The intense bind between father and Lucy, and father's early intervention by letter gave indications that significant extra group involvement would occur. As Lucy progressed, her father would probably try to undercut any therapeutic improvements. The reference to Lucy's wig indicated in capsule form how intrusive he could be and suggested the potential of his assaultiveness on Lucy's emotional integrity. Further, the history of suicide attempts as early as age 10, as well as Lucy's acknowledged manipulative use of symptoms earlier in life, presaged a stormy course in treatment which would probably require a number of therapeutic parameters. In view of these considerations, despite her obvious motivation for some help, she was not considered a good candidate for group therapy. It was felt that individual therapy, with the concurrent treatment of father, would be more appropriate.

POTENTIAL FOR INTENSE RESPONSES

Reviewing the nature of referrals received, from a practical standpoint, a group of patients emerge who, on the basis of their life experiences, neurotic conflicts, or transference possibilities, are likely to have rather intense responses in a therapeutic context. To dilute or minimize such reactions, a number of therapists have considered group therapy as an alternative approach.

Sandy, a 20-year-old college student, applied to the clinic because of a severe depression and frantic hyperactivity in seeking personal attachments. Her past history revealed much emotional deprivation. Her parents divorced when she was 3 years old. She attended boarding school ages 7-16. When Sandy was 18, her mother died suddenly and unexpectedly. Sandy made several suicidal gestures in her teens. Her summer roommate sent the clinic a lengthy and eloquent description of Sandy's overdependence on her and others: "She went to bed leaving John and me in the livingroom discussing her, with the words, 'Well, you two can discuss it and decide what I should do and let me know in the morning.' " At the intake conference she was repeatedly described as a "desperate lost soul" who would require treatment of a "nutritive" kind in order to finish college work and try to find a place for herself in life.

Patients in this age range can tolerate a great deal—from bizarre and "crazy" behavior to confrontation with the feared wishes and tendencies—under appropriate conditions of dosage and timing. What they have poor tolerance for, is the severely dependent and self-centered regression some members are likely to experience in group sessions. They tend to set rather clear and firm limits to extreme, repetitive attempts at infantile behavior—limits which are more readily responded to when coming from peers. For Sandy the expected search for a gratifying dependent position in therapy was soon in evidence. Her maneuvers in the group were contested by the even more expert manipulations of two other members. This led her to take the rather mature role of intelligent adviser and supporter. With the dependent avenue closed in group, her attempts at contacting the therapist outside of group sessions began, mainly limited to phone calls which were always presented in "crisis" terms. As the therapist's responses grew briefer and he directed her to bring such material to the group sessions, such requests declined. The lengthy difficult treatment which followed was sustained by her developing a sense of family within the group. This in turn led to attempts at reintegration into her own family, i.e., with her estranged father, distant aunts, uncles, and cousins.

Certain patients have a greater susceptibility to excessive transference developments which are not really contained when stimulated. The following example demonstrates the strong reaction in one young man and the subsequent management of this tendency in a group. Sy, a 20-year-old, chronically anxious, tense, depressed college student with learning problems, entered individual treatment. With therapy, he began to disengage himself from his parents who were overbearing, restrictive and unable to permit him to develop in any self-assertive direction. Despite an abundance of material relating to homosexual concerns and tendencies, this issue was not significantly touched until 1½ years into the treatment. He led the way and set the pace in the context of his then current sexual wishes and preoccupations. Despite this, he became intensely anxious and interrupted treatment.

Two years later, he contacted the therapist with a request for further help. He had become involved with a girl and there had been talk of possible engagement. The courtship had advanced gradually, sustained in large measure by her prudishness. However, the prudishness diminished after a time, making him so anxious that he wounded her to the point where she broke off the relationship. When he found he could not undo the damage, he realized the need for further treatment.

Despite Sy's recognized readiness to develop intense transference reactions, the therapist suggested group therapy. Sy joined an on-going mixed group, and has done quite well. The sexual issues were engaged through the concurrent exploration of other members' difficulties with sex, e.g., multi-determined promiscuous behavior, belated sexual awakenings, homosexual fantasies, etc. Sy came to grips with some of these matters. With gentle group encouragement, he began to make bolder overtures towards females, although with temporary lapses into homosexual behavior. Finally, he felt a more sustained capability of being with a woman and succeeded in having intercourse without his usual panic reaction. He became more self-assertive and sublimated his former "mom"-like behavior by training for one of the helping professions.

Both Sandy and Sy suffered from conditions presenting technical problems which would make for a difficult course of treatment in either individual or group therapy. Both were chosen for group therapy on an experimental basis. Their examples do illustrate that strong distress and tendency to intense responses, when channeled and mobilized in group therapy, can lead to significant gains.

RESISTANCE TO GROUP THERAPY

Patients who have been referred to group therapy for such reasons of expediency as unavailability of an individual therapist or financial considerations, and who feel ambivalent about group therapy, rarely become involved in a committed or sustained investigation of their problems.

Mary, an 18-year-old college coed was directed to the clinic because of her concerns about masturbation, inability to study, chronic unhappiness and confusion. Despite marked reservations about group therapy, she agreed to join a group then in progress because of her positive transference to her evaluating doctors. They supported the recommendation to enter group therapy because she was upset, wanted treatment urgently and was not going to receive it soon on an individual basis. The initial agreement was that if she didn't like group therapy after a reasonable trial she could withdraw and be placed at the end of the waiting list.

She appeared to be a bright, generally sensible girl, caught up in a severe struggle with her parents. Her initial responses in the group reflected intense distrust. The structural arrangement in the room, namely the observation window and microphone, became the focus of much sarcastic anger. The therapist's comments, whether fostering further discussion, or used for clarifying or interpretive purposes, became the targets of biting disparagement. This was almost invariably true when such comments referred to the contributions of various members to a particular theme or group issue.

When an attempt was made to draw her into group discussion she redoubled her criticisms. For the most part, she remained a silent observer, but was very alert, sometimes asking strikingly cogent questions and at times making some appropriately timed clarifications herself. Though she indicated her misgivings about the usefulness of group therapy and repeated her wish to leave on several occasions, she remained in the group on the strength of the above noted recommendations and her curiosity regarding the problems of other members.

During the few months that she was in the group her relations with her parents became more tolerable, and she changed her plans for the immediate future. She decided to stay in the area, work during the day, go to school at night, and get her own apartment. Her gripes about elders and authorities became directed more towards housemothers and college dormitory regulations. She participated in civil rights picketing at City Hall (at a time when such activities were not commonplace) which almost led to her being jailed with an entire group.

She finally decided to leave the group, feeling she could not talk about such things as masturbation, which still bothered her intensely. The timing of her departure from the group did not seem correlated with any specific issues then under discussion in the group. The striking and surprising aspect of her group tenure was that she remained as long as she did, having started with such intense ambivalence. Subsequently, she spent two years in individual therapy with another therapist. A review of that treatment indicated that she tended to be constantly depressed, felt poorly about herself, and considered herself "bad and dirty." Whenever sexual feelings were explored she experienced dizzy spells and confusion, primarily as defensive reactions.

Masturbation, sexual problems of various sorts as well as a range of sexual practices were available for discussion in group with far greater freedom than was anticipated. The oft noted lessening of rigid morals and strict attitudes of conscience in groups has been useful in relieving tensions about sex and has permitted a filling in of rather enormous gaps in sexual knowledge, even in most sophisticated young people. However, this period is one in which sensitivity to lowering of self-esteem can be extraordinarily acute. For those persons whose narcissistic vulnerability is so high, that protective measures are required against revelations of sexual failings, guilt-inducing behavior, etc., self-exposure in a group is too threatening. When such disturbances are the prominent focus in seeking help, exploration is usually severely blocked, as in the preceding example, or abruptly terminated as in the following circumstances.

Les, a recent high school graduate, apprehensive about the transition to college, became depressed after several sexual experiences in which he was impotent. This occurred in a relationship with a girl who provoked his jealousy quite readily. As a result of her flirtations with other boys at a party, he became furious and beat her. Subsequently he was shocked by his behavior and felt extremely guilty. Group referral, made on the basis of expediency, was pursued quite reluctantly. He was unable to state his objections or concerns in any specific way, but conveyed a vague, but intense uneasiness. He was an active participant in the first session themes referred to earlier. However, a few minutes before the end of the session, he left, giving some lame excuse. Despite his "see you next week" parting, he did not return to the group again.

In this instance, the extent of his guilt and shame about his unbridled anger, as well as his sense of sexual inadequacy, was too severe to unveil before a group of peers. The particular discussion during that one session involved considerations of taboos in primitive cultures which could only have reinforced his intolerable apprehensions.

Several such experiences have led me to honor such ambiguous or definite reservations about treatment in groups. If preliminary efforts in the one or more sessions used for diagnostic assessment do not demonstrate a softening in such attitudes, I respect such signals and no longer recommend group therapy.

The foregoing discussion has been based on experiences encountered with young people with a wide variety of diagnoses and a wide range of severity of illness. The broad scope of problems suggests that anyone whose need for psychiatric help is clearly demonstrable and for whom there is no contraindication can find group psychotherapy of some significant value, either alone or in conjunction with individual treatment. Diagnosis in the formal sense, when used for screening purposes, without consideration of the factors elaborated earlier, can be an unnecessarily restrictive screening instrument or alternatively an unfortunately inclusive one, e.g., psychotics "out," neurotics "in" for outpatient treatment. The nature of problems, in conjunction with the above factors, which may cut across the diagnostic spectrum, seems to be the more salient focus. Social isolation as the compelling concern is a case in point.

Participation in a group has been of significant benefit to those suffering the self-imposed exile from the world around them, whether it is based on inhibitions and overcontrolled behavior on a characterologic basis, the chronic anxieties of the phobically included, the provocativeness of the paranoid, the concerns of the self-deprecating, the insecurity of the repeated failure, or the uncommunicativeness of the severely disturbed. To repeat, the opportunity to experiment with new modes of behavior, test out old premises of human interaction, witness alternative approaches to similar dilemmas in fellow group members, provides unique possibilities for corrective emotional experiences. The built in safeguards of this protected environment—confidentiality, proscription of physical assault, some degree of titration of emotional assault to the limits of tolerance, restriction of the consequences of failure to the session without their spilling over into other sectors of one's life—encourage the utilization of one's potential and promote the initiation of change.

CHAPTER 4

A Psychoanalytic Approach to Group Therapy with Older Teen-Agers in Private Practice

John R. M. Phelan, M.D., C.M.

I BELIEVE THAT GROUP THERAPY is by far the treatment of choice for adolescents. In my experience, the few contraindications could include: (1) psychosis of a nature that would arouse intolerable anxiety in the patient or the group; (2) absence of superego controls, such that a grave danger would exist that group members would be exploited or injured, in or outside of the sessions.

My beliefs are based on experience with several different types of teen-age groups in private practice and in a metropolitan free clinic. The group I will use as an illustration is an open-ended group, which had been meeting for three years. Membership had generally been limited to adolescents between 16 and 20 years of age. We began meeting once a week for 1½ hours, but soon, in response to the group's enthusiasm, we changed to a 2-hour session. Attendance was quite regular, despite the early Saturday morning meeting time. That Friday night late hours did not interfere attested to the responsiveness and responsibility. The group consisted exclusively of private outpatients, referred by their family doctors or by other psychiatrists.

First, I will describe the group members and some of the group's therapeutic highlights. Then, using this information as a point of reference, I shall focus on (1) the special dynamics of adolescence; (2) techniques of treatment especially pertinent to adolescent groups; and (3) special problems of adolescent group therapy. I will describe only six of the 17 who have been members. These six play a greater part in the events to be described later. Let me introduce you to some of the group members in their own words. More clinical descriptions of each can be found at the end of the chapter.

Ruthie (17 years old): "Hi, gang! My name is Ruthie, and I had a sister that was raped and murdered. I've got a nervous stomach that's making me miss an awful lot of school, but I make it up at home. I've never "barfed," but I'm always afraid I'm going to. . . . I want to get married some day, but I'm gonna stay virgin till I do. Not that I have anything against sex, it's just that I think it should be something special. . . . The one thing I'm most worried about is that I might end up a little old lady with a 'condition.' "

Lynn (16 years old): "I got caught shoplifting, so my mother broke open my diary to see what else I was doing. When she read that I was sleeping with the boy next door, she and my father said, 'We're taking you to a doctor to put a stop to this.' They don't like my boy friend because he's a year and a-half younger than me and he's Italian. I came to see Dr. Phelan by myself a few times, but he never answered any questions for me, so I thought maybe this group would help me more."

Tom (16 years old): "This is all bull shit! Every week I feel like walking out of here, slamming the door and never coming back. . . . If anybody throws it up to me that I said the same thing six months ago, I'd just as soon punch 'em as look at 'em. You know, I don't get the dizzy spells I came here for anymore, but the thing that I'm really worried about: Is it normal to have weird thoughts go through your head a lot? Like about girls, and strange kinds of sex, and funny feelings that probably nobody else has? I live with my mom, and I wouldn't dare talk to her about this kind of stuff. And my dad, well, he's busy with his new family."

Hal (15½ years old): "The only reason I'm here in this group is because my dad's a shrink and I'm kind of interested in this stuff. I think it's really neat to find out about yourself and to help other people. I probably will become a shrink myself. I haven't got any problems. I'm just curious, so I thought I'd try it for a while."

Alice (16 years old): "It's all my own fault I had to come here. I got sick and tired of everything and took a whole bunch of pills to kill myself.

They say I came pretty close, but at the last minute I chickened out and called my mom at work just before I passed out. I'm really a burden on her. She can't really afford this. My parents are divorced, and every Saturday night my dad comes to our house drunk and throws the alimony at my mom and screams, 'There's your blood money.' If she's not there, he screams at me, instead. I guess he can't help being the way he is. Last year my sister had a baby without being married, so she's moved away, because my mom said she couldn't support them. I have to take care of the baby most of the time, so my sister can work, but I don't mind very much. But when I think about it, life is really shitty."

Henry (19 years old): "Every time my parents go anywhere without me, I get this funny feeling in my stomach, like I might throw up. Or if I've got to drive far from home on the freeways, sometimes I just can't do it. I get all dizzy and shaky and have to turn around and go back. I know it's a weakness, and I tell myself, 'Just do it—*force yourself,*' but I can't. I'm gonna try to get into the Army. Even though I got a draft deferment on account of all this stuff, I think maybe it'll cure me if I get on my own and have to follow the rules. Besides, I had a friend killed in Vietnam, and I don't think it's fair for me to stay home just because of this."

Not all the patients portrayed in the above clinical vignettes were in the group simultaneously. My aim was to have eight members, divided equally between the sexes, when possible. During the group's first two years, there was a total of 17 patients, 7 boys and 10 girls. The average duration of treatment for the boys was 14 months, ranging from 4 through 21 months. For the girls, the average was 9 months, skewed by two girls who were in the group only one month each. There were seven members still continuing treatment, including one "charter member."

THERAPEUTIC HIGHLIGHTS

An essential element in the success of any group is the development of an intangible something called *group spirit.* It is this something which changes a number of individual people, meeting in the same room at the same time, into a unit, a psychological whole, far greater than the sum of its parts. Although none of the members had had more than a few months of individual therapy and only one or two had any degree of psychological sophistication, an esprit de corps developed which transformed this particular gathering of adolescents into an effective working group, with its own sense of identity, purpose and continuity. The original members happened to be above average in intelligence and articulateness, with a wish to learn and to progress. There was no formal lecturing in psychological mechanisms or the analytic school of thought, but they enthusiastically soaked up techniques of personality exploration. The fact that there were others in the group with whom they could apply their knowledge and share their insights softened the frequent pains of self-scrutiny.

Lynn, for example, came to therapy because her mother broke open her diary, that is, assaulted her privacy, her dignity and her "adolescent rights," though she could not have defined it so clearly at the outset. Since she regarded the therapist as a representative of the parental establishment, she understandably looked at him as a natural enemy. In the few interviews she had before beginning group treatment, she hesitantly answered questions with questions, denied there was anything on her mind, etc. When it was pointed out to her, with an attitude of interested curiosity, that these reactions of hers might be ways of testing and judging the therapist, she reacted with something like elation at unexpectedly learning something about herself which she could apply to her habitual ways of relating to parents, teachers and others. Once in the group, she lost little time enthusiastically pointing out "passive-aggressive personality manipulations" to other members whenever the occasion afforded. That she did this with an air of excited, friendly "know-how" and very little of a "put-down" attitude led to an interested acceptance by the group and the beginnings of group introspection.

An event that crystallized the *emergence of the group as an entity* and contributed to an understanding of their unity as being similar to that of a family came with unforgettable clarity a few months after the group began. As the group was talking, a sudden, explosive shout came through the wall from the next office. The shout was followed immediately by a muffled curse and the rapidly diminishing sounds of angry voices. The group was electrified: "What was that—a shot?" "Somebody is being hurt!" "It must have been in the street." . . . "I didn't hear anything. What are you talking about?" . . . "It sounded like my mother and father fighting at night." There was a long moment of dramatic silence, then a flurry of free and jumbled associations: "Mother and Dad fighting." "Somebody being killed." "I used to pull the covers over my head. God, it was scary." "I wonder why *I* didn't hear anything?" As the tension lessened, we were able to explore in some detail the vivid imagery and the powerful emotions evoked in almost every member of the group. Even those who minimized or denied the evidence of their senses were unable to deny the emotional impact of this episode. It was a powerful demonstration that a chance event could trigger off outpourings of both feelings and ideas, dating back to early childhood and shared among the group, in reality or in fantasy. The group had an exultant air of discovery and mutual achievement that day.

The next week I learned that, in contrast to their usual compliance with my recommendation that group interaction should be confined to group therapy as much as possible, the group had left the session together, got on an elevator and toured the building en masse. A chance meeting with a stranger in the hall led to a friendly bantering which informed the outsider, "We're the group from the padded cell." They explored further in the building and came upon a candy and soft drink machine on another floor. This led to a pooling of their cash for a shared snack, which, in the retelling, sounded like a fraternal banquet. More good-natured raillery with the building occupants continued to foster a cohesive, unified spirit.

Prior to this nodal session several of the initial members had left treatment precipitously. Up to this time I had asked each member before beginning in the group to give it a two-month trial, but I had made no strictures regarding the manner of stopping treatment. Their exits and the advent of new members were received by the group with little overt expression or feeling. The group seemed to endure these events, rather than to explore them, but from this time forward, members' leaving or joining the group assumed new significance. There were no further precipitous withdrawals for more than a year. New members joining the group provided opportunities for serious exploration of the feelings aroused.

The group reacted consciously to newcomers in a dual way: one, as real persons with feelings of their own and provoking reality responses from group members; secondly, as symbolic "baby brothers" or "baby sisters" joining a family, replacing ambivalently held "lost siblings," and thereby evoking feelings and reactions in the group preconditioned by past psychological events. This was an extremely important development, because it provided new members with an introduction to the purpose and meaning of the exploration of process, rather than merely of content. Perhaps even more importantly, it conveyed to the new member that he or she had joined a group which had its own existence, method and purpose, which continued to function without depending on the presence or absence of any particular individual.

Not every development was so happy. As mentioned, Alice had attempted suicide and was expert at denying her feelings. Slowly and painfully, she shared with the group the problems of living in a family full of psychopathology, except for a "perfect" mother. Alice's desperately suppressed rage was expressed more openly for her by the group. Other members tried to show her that she was offering herself as an expiatory sacrifice to her mother's need to be the "good person, wronged by all around her, in spite of her best efforts." As Alice began to tolerate the idea that mother was less than an injured innocent and that she herself had a right to be aggravated or even angry and to prepare for an independent life, the mother began to react. In essence, her response was, "Darling, I certainly want you to get the help you need, but it is an expense; you're getting awfully sassy lately, but I do want you to keep on with your little group." With an air of sad resignation, Alice left. She assured us that as soon as she was old enough she would make her own life, free from what she had begun to recognize as the baleful influence of her "long-suffering" mother. Although more than two years have passed since Alice quit treatment and only one member is left who knew her personally, "Alice's Mother's Syndrome" is still a part of the group's lexicon.

Current popular belief holds that today's young people are the beneficiaries or the victims of a permissive upbringing, which has lowered the age limit for and expanded the boundaries of sexual experimentation. It is surprising, then, that this group, intelligent, verbal and apparently accepting of the idea that there need be no taboo topics in the therapy situation, *took nearly a year to allow conflicts about sexuality to emerge.* The group offered a fair cross section of an adolescent suburban population, ranging from hip to square, from agnostic to religiously orthodox. There was mutual acceptance and tolerance and considerable intragroup supportiveness. Two members had even been referred specifically for sexual symptomatology. Yet for many months the topic of sex lay in the midst of the group like the proverbial iceberg, mostly beneath the surface. The overt sexual problems that were mentioned were discussed, to the group's apparent satisfaction, in a rather compartmentalized way.

As we neared the end of the first year of treatment, enthusiasm and group spirit were mounting. There was *pressure to have a marathon.* "After all," it was pointed out, "we only meet for two hours a week. It always seems like it really warms up in the last 15 or 20 minutes, when bang! We run out of time." I was a little reluctant to try such an experiment. Practical reasons, such as time and expense, interfered. We worked out a compromise. We would have a "mini-marathon" the night before a holiday.

We would begin at 6:00 p.m. and end when we all felt like it, sometime after midnight.

The mini-marathon produced two incidents that excited the group's attention and wonder, and they have remained etched in memory, though most of the participants are no longer with the group. The long session proceeded smoothly, with many interesting discussions, some attention to feelings and much conviviality, along with coffee and sandwiches at the midpoint. About 1:00 a.m. we decided we would stop at 2:00. About 10 minutes before 2:00, one of the members pointed out, with an air of dawning recognition and ruefulness, "Things have really warmed up in the last 15 or 20 minutes, and bang! We're running out of time!" Those who had inveighed against the weekly restriction of two hours and thought of the mini-marathon as the perfect solution took to heart the astonishing workings of the human psyche!

The second memorable event also occurred late in the mini-marathon. Hal, the psychiatrist's son, who professed great interest in psychological matters and had some acquaintance with Freudian theory, took a remark about an attractive girl in the group and turned it into a subtle double entendre, having to do with her breasts. When other members elaborated on it, Hal, seemingly nonchalant, remained silent. He was absent for the next two sessions consecutively, which, by this time, was a rare occurrence for anyone in the group. At the third meeting he amazed us by offering the explanation that he had obtained his father's permission to miss therapy, "because I had an exam coming up." The second week he "just forgot." "Forgetting" had long before been established by the group as a psychological mechanism with identifiable meaning. Hal had always presented himself as never asking permission for anything, if he could avoid it. Hal was open enough to be capable of participating in a psychological scrutiny of his absences, which showed them to be directly related to shame and guilt aroused by his making a sexual remark about a girl's breasts. Through the group process he was able to bring into the open dependent fantasies about women which had hitherto been unconscious. He recognized his wish to deny them.

The connection between Hal's absences and his "Oedipal sex hang-up" remained vividly in everyone's mind. The episode was often brought up as an example of the power of unconscious defenses, particularly where sex was concerned. The group related it to newcomers as incontrovertible evidence that frightening emotions, even in an intelligent person, can motivate his behavior without his knowing it.

The *end of the taboo on discussion of sexuality* and the expression of sexual feelings occurred in the eighteenth month. A new girl of near-genius intelligence, with a blandly intellectual approach to everything, matter-of-factly narrated a homosexual interlude with a school chum which had occurred shortly before her beginning therapy. Over the next few weeks it was as if a dynamite charge had exploded in the center of the iceberg. Tom, who, up to then, had studiously affected a "cool" manner, was the first to react, with an attitude of reciprocity. He talked about his inner fears and fantasies that he might be homosexual. With growing seriousness, he recounted his attempts to prove his manhood by casual, almost brutally direct sexual conquests of girls, his willingness to fight at the drop of a hat, should anyone question his virility, and his gnawing fear that there was an incurable cancer of homosexuality within him.

This provided a touchstone for the entire group to begin examining what it means to be a man or a woman, and to be growing from childhood toward the adult state. Tentatively at first, but with increasing freedom, the group settled down to hard-working exploration. With a disarming naivete, they reassured themselves they would not let curiosity, titillation or even that frequently encountered bugaboo, denial, interfere with their work. They soon became aware of—and fascinated by—the pervasive roots of sexuality in personality characteristics: self-confidence, aggressivity, coldness and, most of all, the complex relationships between sexuality and intimacy. The topic of masturbation was given serious attention for the first time. The values, meanings and feelings about male-male companionship and (less traumatically) female-female companionship were explored with steadily lessening tension on the part of those members with the greatest uncertainty about their sexual identity.

Typical of this new-found freedom was an occurrence a few months after the lifting of the sexual taboo. Henry, who was coming to realize that his hang-up with his overprotective mother was responsible in great part for both his wishes and fears about becoming a man, had *a dream* in which the central point was his leaving home on a train, which then crashed. Someone offered the observation, "That could kill you." Hal, with his customary Freudian bent, laughingly announced that a train always reminded him of a penis. Tom, who had apparently ignored Hal's association, focused on the crash. Excitedly, he told the group that very thing had almost happened to him the previous night. He had been riding around with a friend, looking for some Friday night excitement, when they approached an unmarked railroad crossing. They drove across the tracks just seconds ahead of a passing freight train. It was a milestone in Tom's psychotherapy that he was able to accept the suggestion from another member that he really had heard the equation, "train equals penis," coupled it with "that could kill you" and unconsciously recounted his feelings of excitement and danger at being alone with a male companion, seeking excitement at night. He volubly assured us that several months previously he would not only have denied any meaning to the stream of associations but would have been ready to take a poke at "anyone" ("outside the group, that is") who would suggest that he might have had erotic feelings, conscious or unconscious, toward another young man.

THE SPECIAL DYNAMICS OF ADOLESCENCE

Adolescents generally tend to be volatile, to prefer action to thought or speech and to be exquisitely sensitive to the values and judgments of their peers. Emotional distress exaggerates these characteristics. Activity, intellectual or physical, social or antisocial, helps the adolescent avoid painful affect and disturbing personal relations. When activity is not available as a defense, retreat by personal withdrawal and isolation, or by the use of drugs, is a frequent maneuver. Toward the later years of adolescence, increasing knowledge and verbal skill often help the emerging young adult to organize and rationalize his rebellion against authority, both the individual authority of parent or teacher and the personification of authority, described as "the Establishment." At the same time, a large number of young people possess a truly remarkable degree of self-sacrificing idealism, often accompanied by a wish for a strong teacher, leader or guru. This quest for a "good parent" often underlies even the rebelliousness of the action-oriented patient whose strong belief in a "generation gap" may make him approach treatment with resentment or suspicion.

It seems clear that the expectations of the adult population frequently either are not clearly conveyed or are not acceptable to a sizable number of today's youth. It remains to be seen whether this is a unique "generation gap" or whether it is merely our own variant of the *age-old conflict between the settled adult way of life and the quest for identity of "upstart youth."* The reader may recall quotations as recent as Mark Twain, as far back as Gregory the Great, Bishop of Sixth Century Rome, wherein the youth of the day are described as the most unruly, disrespectful, destructive, etc., of all time. A major reason for these jeremiads on the part of aging authority is the very heart of adolescence itself: the need to develop independence, the need to become an individual of one's own and, eventually, on one's own. This frequently leads to an iconoclasm that is more apparent than real, to bold assertions of absolutes, which are replaced by their opposites—or forgotten—on the morrow. Such rapid shifts are a testing, a trying on for size, of both new and old ways of life. To the rigid authority, parent or other, who has forgotten his own adolescence and its purpose, these things may be threatening, unsettling or ridiculous, but taken as a part of an over-all, healthy struggle for growth, they can be understood and, if not enjoyed, tolerated.

Erik Erikson has elaborated on the adolescent's need for shifting values with his concept of "role diffusion." Classical Freudian theory is sometimes thought to hold that the basis of the adult personality is permanently cast, like the rigid mold of a statue, by the end of early childhood. Clinical experience with adolescents makes more plausible the view that the roots of personality are, indeed, laid down in early childhood—crucially so—but *adolescence offers each individual the chance to revise or to consolidate his foundations.* The results of earlier development and training, both strengths and mistakes, may be intensified, modified or drastically changed over the period of years we call "adolescence."

TECHNIQUES OF TREATMENT PERTINENT TO ADOLESCENT GROUPS

At the beginning, the *criteria for admission* to the group I have described were simple: being in an age range of about 16 to 20 years, a willingness to give group therapy a two-month trial and a reasonable hope on the part of the therapist that this kind of treatment would be helpful. As time passed, the criteria became more exacting: a reasonable degree of articulateness, the clinical appearance of being able to form transference reactions to the therapist and to the group as parent-family surrogates, and the therapist's clinical hunch that the capability existed to develop a psychological set, which could lead to the use of insight as a means of resolving conflicts. Placement in a separate group was made for those who were relatively inarticulate, strongly disposed toward action or drugs to avoid conflict and had little ability to tolerate close relationships in the group setting.

The most obvious, aggravating and productive technique was the *therapist's regular and predictable*—within limits—*refusal to answer questions.* Queries were reflected back to the group, with steady insistence that the feelings behind them be identified, explored and evaluated. Very quickly "What are you *feeling?*" became a shibboleth, often chanted in unison.

"We're avoiding feelings!" became a kind of "in" joke, an almost always correct answer to the therapist's question, "What do you think is going on?" This attitude, analytic rather than supportive, often provoked anger and even hurt. Nevertheless, the group was impressed with the remarkable frequency with which intelligent, alert young people could continue to use all manner of means to avoid feelings, the unconscious repetition of the very process about which they joked.

The discovery of *body language* in the early days of the group established another beachhead for psychological exploration. When asked the nature of her "problem" on the first day of the group, one of the girls quietly pulled her coat more tightly around her and folded her arms before giving an evasive answer. Several weeks later, when she confided to the group that her difficulties had to do with sex and attendant feelings of shame and guilt, someone remembered her evasion and the gestures accompanying it. This led to a field day of examining such things as pushing chairs closer to or away from the center of the group, strategic coughs, blushing and the like.

Important in any analytic group, and especially so with adolescents, is *precision of communication*. To facilitate the free and clear expression of emotion in a teen-age group takes time and patience. Gradually, the members recognize that they may say whatever they want. It is important to be able to identify and deal with psychological mechanisms, but where a good clear vocabulary is necessary, jargon is not. The open expression of genuine feeling and mixtures of feelings is desirable; saying "Fuck you" for its own sweet sake is usually not. Nonverbal emotional communication needs, also, to be respected and even encouraged, provided that eventually, at appropriate times, the group will try to analyze what it means and what are its effects. This may be done by free association, by the expression of empathic emotional response or sometimes simply by "rapping," that is, a free-flowing discussion of ideas and responses. Gradually, language becomes a workable tool for the expression of things that many adolescents may not be aware of or only feel.

The more analytic capability a group develops, the more useful *dreams* will become. In an atmosphere of trust, it has been my experience that a timid or blustering adolescent will often use dream imagery, his own or others', to relate inner feelings or uncertainties which otherwise would remain buried. The technique of free association in response to dreams is often stimulating, revealing and worthwhile. It frequently leads to a playful kind of group creativeness which can be turned to productive use.

Individuals, groups and therapists differ considerably. One's technique is probably a composite of personality, instruction and trial-and-error experience. Even group therapy based firmly on psychoanalytic principles will vary within wide limits, but I think it is safe to generalize that with any adolescent group, *flexibility is invariably essential.* There are times to adhere staunchly to technical rules, and there are times to respond specifically to the unique situation. Such things cannot be learned from a book, but they can be pondered, then clinically tested, so that the therapist's intuitive responses usually become helpful ones.

SPECIAL PROBLEMS OF ANALYTIC ADOLESCENT GROUP THERAPY

Problems with *authority* make for one of the prime pitfalls of adolescent treatment; successful therapy demands the avoidance of any semblance of authoritarianism in the therapist. It has been pointed out that adolescents tend to seek a "good parent" and to rebel against the "bad." This makes it imperative to foster in the analytic group the ability to recognize transference reactions toward authority, so that they can be dealt with, when appropriate, as irrational or neurotic. At such times it is useful to point out the wish for a powerful authority or law giver, who might diminish the pain of developing personal responsibility. Meanwhile, the therapist must be constantly vigilant, to control unhealthy *countertransference* needs and wishes of his own. These may fall under three headings: an authoritarian need to dominate, which is generally fatal to rapport with adolescent patients; a wish for gratification by being the beloved "good parent," which is more subtly inimical to treatment; and finally, a neurotic need to identify with the adolescent patient, attempting to win acceptance by becoming "one of the gang."

Another paramount problem of the adolescent patient is *confidentiality.* The older teen-ager, not yet an adult, certainly not a child, is in an anomalous position vis-a-vis treatment; he is the patient, his are the confidences, but usually the parents foot the bill. So, I routinely explain to my adolescent patients and then to their parents that since the parents have important responsibilities and concerns, I may have occasional contact with them. However, it will never be without the patient's consent, and he or she normally has the option of being present.

Furthermore, I inform both patient and parent that any communication from the patient to me is privileged but that the reverse is *not* true. When parents call me, I reserve in advance the right to discuss their conversations with the patient when it seems helpful. "Doctor, please don't tell him, but—" has prefaced many a conversation with parents. I interrupt as quickly and politely as possible to say that if I cannot be free to discuss it with the patient, I would rather not hear the information. Although adherence to the patient's right of confidentiality is of utmost importance, I have not yet had an adolescent patient who does not quickly grasp the idea that certain kinds of information ("I just stole $200, and tonight I'm gonna run away with the kid next door.") are barely disguised requests for my intervention and will be acted upon accordingly. Severe suicidal ideas also fall in this category.

Experience with several adolescent groups has convinced me that, for analytic groups at least, a mixture of boys and girls is preferable. The therapist, of course, needs to be alert to the fact that *sexual activity between group members can be used destructively as a defense,* for example, against depression and loneliness, or as a means of acting out rebellion against authority. A non-preachy discussion of how the use of sex to cure loneliness is like using aspirin to cure appendicitis, accompanied by the frank admission that the therapist cannot make a rule against this, cannot control members' behavior, that responsibility for their group rests with them, seems to suffice at the beginning. As time goes on, focusing on the dynamics and the transference aspects of sexual feelings, plus clarifying reality relationships, enables the group to become its own watchdog against destructive intragroup behavior.

Because of the intensity of the emotional involvement possible in this age group, *dependency problems* repeatedly arise and must be patiently handled, preferably by the group and, often, over and over by the therapist. The warmth of group camaraderie can stir up uncomfortable dependency feelings and their vigorous denial, "This therapy isn't the only thing in my life!" Gentle reassurance may be needed to point out that such things as punctuality and regularity are not signs of dependency, but of normal courtesy, and that the willingness to take oneself and the group work seriously is not a weakness. "Sure, this therapy is not the only important thing in your life, but in every session it should be helping with the most important things in your life!"

The *completion of treatment* for an individual in an adolescent group requires special handling. Classic analytic desiderata for a successful termination are often impossible to achieve. However, just as I request each prospective member to give the group a trial for at least six or eight sessions, as the group develops I point out repeatedly the worth of taking a reasonable period of time, as many sessions as for the trial, to conclude treatment. The example of members in the early days of the group who quit precipitously or who were abruptly removed by their parents served as valuable object lessons in what I meant, and the group rapidly realized the psychological mechanisms—and the wastefulness—in such behavior. After only a few such incidents, the members learned to rally around and dissuade the anxious, angry or frightened member who wanted to use impulsive flight as a defense.

Surprisingly enough, considering the narcissism of adolescence, the sorts of problems which come under the rubric *"sibling rivalry"* played only a minor role in this group. Claims for the therapist's attention, subtle and not-so-subtle attempts to win his approval by espousing his real or imagined values occur often but are readily recognized by the group and worked with quite effectively. A much more insidious problem is *intellectualization.* Particularly when there are group members in college, with a smattering of academic psychology, intellectual discussions about psychological topics ostensibly related to group behavior are most seductive defenses. A less sophisticated version of a similar thing is a diary accounting of recent activities or friendly inquiries into what others have been doing outside the group. Usually someone recognizes the evasion and handles it by asking a question that conveys boredom and implies, "This is chit-chat. Let's take a look at what's going on."

Requests for advice, medication and moral judgment are common but seldom provide serious problems, once the group is established. Dealing with such things analytically does not preclude occasions when the dispensation of the first two, and rarely the third, may be necessary. It is remarkable that even in a sophisticated adolescent group of considerable experience, outrageous behavior on the part of parents can unite everyone in an ingenuous and touching plea to the therapist to "Do something! You've just gotta do something *this* time!"

It goes without saying, but does not come without effort, that the group therapist must avoid the ever-present opportunities for pedantry, but even this is a minor peccadillo with an adolescent group, compared to the cold, aloof attitude of uninvolvement, with which a therapist may attempt to mask his own problem, by thinking he is following that hoary cliche, "the mirror-like psychoanalytic attitude." Of course, it is essential to demonstrate control over one's emotions under the stresses of group therapy, but it is equally essential to be able to *express emotions appropriately and with spontaneity*. For the therapist in this kind of a group to be warm, to care and to allow himself to be involved is crucial.

Other tests of the therapist's *countertransference* may include seductive young girls, more or less willing to act out an Oedipal conflict, and impressionable young men, quite susceptible to the reverse Oedipal complex. The manipulative, sometimes even cruel, actions of a parent in response to growth on the part of the adolescent patient, which threatens parental neurosis, provides an especially difficult trial of therapeutic skill.

I have also found that a considerable difficulty in working intensively with a bright, articulate group of adolescents is that their warmth, exuberance and sincerity can tend to sweep the therapist into a state of benign and affectionate acceptance, overlooking the problems of an isolated member of the group at a particular time, or group problems which the aura of good feeling may let shrink into the background. Again, vigilance to underlying process and communication—the use of the analyst's "third ear"— provides the answer.

To be able to express warmth and affection, to avoid seduction or cold impersonality, and to do it all in words, these are goals for which the therapist of adolescents must constantly strive. Given in turn the adaptability, the vibrancy and the potential for growth in youth, adolescent group therapy can be one of the most genuinely worthwhile professional experiences of a psychotherapist.

Countertransference notwithstanding, I feel a mixture of pride and delight and a sense of privilege at being able to work with these young people in what is a process of mutual growth and learning. The irrepressible Ruthie summed it up and warmed the cockles of my heart by saying with earnest conviction, in her final session, "All the eyeball-to-eyeball stuff, the hold hands and love each other stuff, the role-playing and sensitivity games I've had in my psych courses at school don't come close to the feelings we've got here. I'm not afraid to call it love, *and we do it all by talking!*"

CLINICAL DESCRIPTION OF MEMBERS

Ruthie, a winsome, bright and lovable chatterbox, called herself the group's "Jewish mother." She regularly dispensed peppermint Lifesavers for nervous stomachs—or anything else. Her store of advice seemed inexhaustible. However, she came to realize that the blight on her family from a tragic sexual crime prior to her birth affected her upbringing drastically. She was terrified at the prospect of growing up to be an adult woman and facing male sexuality. Aided and abetted by an oversolicitous mother and a passive father, she reached late adolescence intellectually a precocious young adult and emotionally an "innocent" child. Her family believed she knew nothing about the existence of her sister, much less the brutal circumstances of her death. Ruthie discovered in therapy that she had known all about it since preschool years. Keeping it out of her awareness helped her live up to her parents' tacit command that she never mature emotionally. Diagnosis: Hysterical neurosis, with conversion symptoms (psychophysiological GI disturbance).

Lynn could have been the model of the California teen-age girl: pretty features, clear skin and long hair, carefully ironed. Her parents, however, refused to accept her emerging young womanhood. Puritanical and controlling, they treated her as if she were still a pre-pubertal little girl. Sexuality was taboo, conformity a virtue and intellectual achievement a major measure of worth. In response, Lynn developed a strong passive-aggressive character. She struggled to please by academic excellence, in which she had little personal interest. Meanwhile, she rebelled, furtively, against many of her parents' middle class values, always with guilt and shame. "And why," she asked the group plaintively, "do I always get caught?" She began to perceive the depth of her feelings for her father and her wish to please him. As she and the group painfully began to connect these feelings with her choice of an opposite kind of person for her sexual object, she found rationalizations for a precipitate withdrawal from treatment. Follow-up a year and a half later revealed that Lynn had lived out the problem again with another "opposite" kind of lover, this time leading to a rather hasty marriage. Diagnosis: passive-aggressive personality.

Tom came to the group in the midst of a full-blown adolescent identity crisis, particularly about sexuality. He was referred for frequent dizzy spells, which had no apparent physical cause. Living with an ineffectual and rather seductive mother, Tom had tried since early childhood to be the "good boy" and make up for his (envied) rowdy, disrespectful older brother. In the process he fled from his feelings about his mother to a more comfortable world of male buddies. The onset of normal sexual feelings under these circumstances roused in him the specter of homosexuality, to the point where he found it necessary to prove his "virility" by punching anyone who offered real or imaginary challenges to him—all the while much afraid that he really was "a pansy" and that nothing could be done about it. Once these ideas came out in the open for group discussion, Tom's fears evaporated rapidly and he was free to resolve his ambivalent feelings about women, intimacy and sexual relationships. Diagnosis: Adjustment reaction of adolescence, with psychophysiological components.

Hal's considerable intelligence made it easy for him to rationalize his powerful fear of emotions, especially his own. The middle child in a family of high achievers, he felt lost in the shadow of a brilliant, erratic older brother, who monopolized most of his parents' attention. His insecurity drove him into isolation, which he hid behind a blasé facade. His father, an analyst, highly regarded in the professional community, probably fostered the idea of group therapy as "an interesting experience," rather than treatment for moderately severe emotional inhibition. Diagnosis: Adjustment reaction of adolescence.

Except for a brooding, haunted look in her eyes, *Alice* was an attractive young girl. She was above average in intelligence and thoughtful of people around her. She came to the group in a severely depressed state and was extremely reticent, afraid of "hurting someone's feelings." After a few months, with a great deal of group support and encouragement, the depression began to lift and its underpinnings of resentment toward her parents became evident. Alice could not tolerate this and fled to the status quo ante. Diagnosis: Neurotic depression, severe.

Henry was the group's "square." He disliked hippies and eggheads and despised himself for what he viewed as his weaknesses. He loved both his parents and thought his relationship with them was a good one. But he couldn't understand why his father let his mother push him around all the time and run the household. Henry did his best to be the man his mother wanted. At one point he was attending college full time, holding down a demanding part-time job and preparing to take a trade school course at night. His severe anxiety shortly put an end to all these activities. Over a year in group therapy taught Henry a great deal: that people with ideas and hair styles different from his could be worthwhile friends; that the problems and the solutions were within himself; and that having his mother's smothering love protect him from grown-up problems was not worth the price of his independence. Diagnosis: Anxiety state, with phobic reactions.

CHAPTER 5

Psychotherapy with the Adolescent in Self-Selected Peer Groups

Max Sugar, M.D.

PATIENTS WHO BRING a friend or relative to the psychiatrist's office are bringing along part of their social network. This frequent occurrence arouses as much uneasiness on their part as on the therapist's in regard to having them come into the session. At best, the intrusion is tolerated, rather than accepted as a communication or an additional therapeutic asset.

Speck (1965b) has coined the phrase "Network Therapy" to describe his use of the social network for therapy. Until he described his original and deliberate method of involving family and friends, little, if any, use was made of the patient's social network for therapy. His aim is to tighten the bonds between people and loosen the binds by the use of network therapy in a crisis that might otherwise eventuate in suicide or hospitalization.

Further attention to the patient's interpersonal and intrapsychic adaptation has resulted in increased therapeutic use of group and family approaches. When the patient is seen in a therapy group, many otherwise concealed aspects of his interfering character traits and dynamics come to light in the interaction with other group members. By seeing family members or friends of the patient, the therapist often observes previously closeted data that enhance understanding of the dynamics and successful therapy. The family or peers may thus vitiate resistances of the designated patient.

80

Scapegoating is a common phenomenon which family therapy may help clarify, but fear of reprisal back home may cause avoidance of the matter, or abrupt termination if the issue is too threatening. Adolescents often feel that they are the family scapegoat and resent being "the patient," while parental or other sources of psychopathology of consequence are left untouched (Ackerman, 1968). They sometimes have a great sense of relief when the rest of the family is brought in. Home therapy has been attempted to deal with the psychopathology of the puppeteer in the background who never appears in the consultation room (Speck, 1965a).

Langsley and Kaplan (1968) have contributed some valuable research and impressive clinical data on managing a crisis in a family member. They avoid hospitalization by dealing with that person and his whole family, at home as well as in the emergency room.

Speck's networks, vertical (multigeneration) or horizontal (adolescent peers), can become groups as large as one hundred people, who are relatives, friends, or even strangers interested in helping the patient. His usual arrangements involve a huge room, optimally multiple therapists, and one evening a week for the six to ten sessions that may be needed to deal with the crisis effectively.

In this chapter, I wish to focus on the flexible use of the network, or self-selected peer, psychotherapy group to deal with an adolescent's actual or impending crisis. Because my modification of the network for therapy with adolescents involves no additional office space or unusual time arrangements, it is readily applicable for work with adolescents in private or clinic practice.

THE ADOLESCENT IN A SELF-SELECTED PEER PSYCHOTHERAPY GROUP

I have found the application of the network useful in therapy with adolescents who appear to be suicidal or in need of institutionalizing without this intervention (Speck, 1965b; Sugar, 1971). Although what follows may be viewed as an open, still developing approach with further possible modifications, it may serve as uncongealed guidelines for others.

Arrangements

Network therapy is considered for an adolescent with a crisis (or one brewing) who has been seen for a sufficient time to assess his major dynamics and who appears to require hospitalization for disorganization or to avert an imminent suicide attempt. The risks of not hospitalizing him need to be carefully assessed. If he is felt to have sufficient organization and controls within, and from his environment, the alternative of using the self-selected peer group is broached to him and his family. He is asked if he would like to have a *group or therapeutic club of his own,* and told that he can bring in whomever he wishes to his sessions, having as many friends as often as he wants, to try to help him. If the reply is affirmative, it is pointed out to the family that his friends may have helpful data and experiences to share with us in the sessions and the family's permission is requested.

After explanatory sessions have clarified the approach to the patient and his family, the peer group sessions are initiated at a time that will not disrupt the friends' school schedules. The patient's other sessions may be continued at the same frequency, or increased if necessary. The fee remains as before, at the usual amount for an individual session. The friends are not charged, but are free to ask for help and speak of their personal problems in the session, since they and the patient are invited to discuss anything they wish. The therapist observes the usual confidentiality with patient and his friends, but no restriction is placed on the patient and his peers about discussing identities or content of sessions. They may socialize and continue their outside contacts as before, unlike the usual group therapy requirements. These arrangements are the responsibility of the patient to disseminate to his friends.

After the peers are welcomed, they are asked to identify themselves and their relationship with the patient. The basis of procedure is then *group process, but focused mainly on the patient.* The number of peer group sessions required to deal with the crisis has varied from one to ten. Thereafter, therapy in other forms may continue or not, as the situation requires. Friends may be unavailable for one session but may arrive at the next, as the patient wishes, until they are no longer needed in the sessions.

Clinical Illustrations

Attributes of, and contributions from, the peer group for therapy are multiple and varied, being determined by the particulars of the case, and no prediction can be made about some of this heterogeneity. The following cases may illustrate some of the possibilities.

Case I

At 15, Sara was seen because her mother was concerned about her poor school work; skipping school; using "pot," LSD, and other drugs with overdose effects obvious to the mother; threats to run away; associating with psychotic and addicted peers, including a known addict, who was her boy friend. She admitted lying, "taking grass and obetrol," forging doctors' signatures on prescriptions to obtain drugs, playing hookey, and erasing her school report to disguise her absenteeism.

Until age 13, she "had been a good student and had had no difficulties." Then "she met a neighborhood girl who was a troublemaker," which led to the behavior mentioned. Six months before that, while she was driving the car with her father and paternal grandmother, she had an accident which killed the grandmother. She did not attend the funeral, cried once, but had not mentioned it since.

Sara seemed depressed, angry, suggestible, manipulative, impulsive, with poor self-concept and controls, and super-ego difficulties. The diagnosis was character disorder with depression. She had some remorse and defiance, along with fear of consequences of her actions, if caught. The mother was given guidance to help her manage Sara, with implementation of controls, and Sara moved in with the maternal grandparents. The only other possibilities were boarding school, reformatory, or a hospital, none of which was acceptable to either parent.

The mother cooperated, became somewhat more assertive, and arranged for controls of Sara so that the girl could have psychotherapy. Initially, Sara was cooperative and had some ventilation and abreactive sessions with relief. After about ten sessions, however, she became antagonistic, and mostly silent, but kept her appointments. Simultaneously, her situation at home seemed critical again. Because she had spoken of her twenty-two-year-old maternal aunt as a person who understood her and with whom she could talk, I suggested network psychotherapy, inviting her to bring in her aunt and any friends she wished. I hoped thus to help her with her resistance as well as to avoid institutionalization.

Of the seven scheduled peer group sessions, she missed two and attended five, with her aunt alone on the first two occasions, with her aunt and two girl friends on the next two occasions, and with one girl friend on the last visit. Initially the girl friends, and especially the aunt, were very supportive and empathetic, and attacked authority with Sara. Some extra-strenuous controls were complained of, and since they realistically needed to be changed, it was suggested they discuss these controls with the mother. At first the aunt's presence seemed to reflect a wish of Sara's to have a well-organized mother-substitute, idol and model in this young adult. In fact, at times, the aunt functioned almost like another demanding, hostile, and provocative teen-ager, who had many unresolved authority problems and excess sibling rivalry and hate toward her sister, Sara's mother. At times she behaved like an older version of Sara, while the girl friends sounded like more mature persons.

In the fifth scheduled network session, the aunt chastised Sara for her misbehavior and recalcitrance, for missing two appointments during the Christmas holidays, and for many demanding, unrealistic concepts and requests. Sara was shocked, flustered, and seemed disappointed with herself and her aunt.

In the last two sessions, she was slightly cooperative, seemed embarrassed and lost without her aunt siding with her. Her schoolmate had no trouble at home or school, or with herself, and seemed to be coping well. Having her present instead of the aunt for the last session may have indicated that the aunt was in disfavor, and may have reflected an effort at identification with her better-integrated peer, who had less hostility and guilt and a more suitable superego.

Sara seemed to be fearful that she would hurt someone, especially maternal figures, to whom she became close, while simultaneously having wishes to do so. The realities that mother was divorced, grandmother killed, and her girl friend hospitalized, added to these fantasies. With this, there were apparent fears of loss: being deserted by mother, aunt, girl friend, boy friend, and therapist, which she partly attempted to provoke. Her absences from school and therapy sessions, as well as her silences alternating with hostile verbalizations, seem to have related to these dynamics.

Her school behavior and grades had improved over the three months of therapy, and her mother was now able to cope with and control her. Although the situation was only tentatively stabilized, it seemed to be less explosive or critical. The mother was asserting herself more with the father, setting limits on his intrusions, and expecting him to fulfill his responsibilities. The father became openly antagonistic, refused to finance Sara's psychiatric therapy, which he now disparaged despite his previous active support. Sara now refused further cooperation and terminated therapy on the basis of finances.

The father's antisocial behavior with revengeful manipulation, and the mother's dependency with secondary gain made the environment less than optimal. The mother's symbiosis with the father and her own parents was a further limiting feature. Nevertheless, there were some therapeutic gains to Sara and her mother. This case indicates how a shift in equilibrium in a family has multiple effects and may lead to crises, in this case from improved management to abrupt termination. Although the father was never seen, he was the active puppeteer behind the scenes. When threatened by the therapeutic gains to the mother and alterations in the effects of his power and maneuvers on Sara as well, he made threats and derogated psychiatry. When this did not succeed, he withdrew his support and abruptly ended the therapy.

Case II

Mary was an 18-year-old out-of-town college freshman who had attempted suicide by wrist slashing (requiring no sutures). She was to be sent back home, but this was avoided by having psychotherapy for a few weeks. When referred for further treatment, she complained of having received no benefit from any of her previous therapists and derogated herself, all family members, and classmates.

She had made three other similar suicidal attempts. She felt there was nothing else that she could do and therefore she wanted to die. She had vague goals, but episodically she felt that she had nothing to look forward to when she became depressed, after which came suicidal ideas and acts.

During her later high school years, she had had a close attachment to a female high school teacher, of whom the family disapproved. When this teacher moved elsewhere, the patient wanted to go to college in that area, but the family disapproved. When she wanted dates she had plenty of them, but she liked only one boy in her home town and had a similar situation now in college.

She seemed to be directionless and functioned in a kind of vacuum. Although bright, she seemed to have no clear-cut notions of what to do with her intelligence. She had experimented with some drugs and occasionally had had some weird "bad trips" with LSD and "pot." The diagnosis was schizoid personality.

She was ambivalent about wanting friendships, since she was distrustful and considered others to be as worthless as she. After each suicidal attempt, she was showered with affection and concern from her family, which made her feel good temporarily. When she was offered affection at other times, she distrusted it and moved away from the source.

At her first visit, Mary brought along a home-town girl friend who remained in the waiting room. Now a college mate, this girl had satisfactorily terminated therapy with me about six months previously. She had previously been hospitalized numerous times for suicidal attempts and threats over a period of several years. A threat of suicide and refusal to enter hospital, in fact, led to her referral and office treatment with me. She had refused network therapy when this was offered, but she continued and progressed satisfactorily in individual therapy. Thus, Mary knew a good deal about me from this friend, before having been referred from another, unrelated source. Apparently Mary brought her friend along for support, or perhaps as a talisman. This action may have been an indicator of her intense involvement with friends, especially the emotionally ill, and a readiness for network therapy. Interestingly, she did not ask this friend to come into the peer group session later, perhaps because she wanted someone better integrated.

After several sessions, during which she seemed to overcome some of her early distrust of and antagonism to continuing in treatment, she made a suicidal attempt with another wrist-slashing, which she did not reveal until the following week during her session. She could not describe the impulses or the need for this behavior any more clearly than she had previously. She was afraid that she would be asked to leave the college and had bound her dormitory-mates in a pact of secrecy to protect herself and them.

The suicidal risk was too great for her to continue living in the dormitory without some additional help in the form of intensive outpatient treatment or hospitalization. With her family's agreement, therefore, her sessions were increased from one to three times a week. After several weeks, I still considered her situation to be too tenuous, so I suggested that she set aside one of these sessions for network psychotherapy. I explained that she could bring as many of her friends as she wanted to help us, that this would be her therapeutic club. She seemed pleased with the idea, but had a number of questions indicating some fears about it. When Mary's closest dormitory-friend and roommate, who had attempted suicide coevally with Mary's first attempt, was leaving school, Mary got a separate room, as she wanted no more roommates. Their mutual friends were the ones who protected Mary from disclosure of her second suicidal attempt in the dorm. Some of these friends seemed as unstable and unsettled as Mary.

For the peer group session, Mary brought in a dormitory-mate with whom she had been somewhat friendly, but who had not been involved in the secret pact about the suicidal attempt. This girl seemed to be well-integrated, had goals, dated, and was doing very well in her pre-medical studies. She was very sympathetic and throughout the session seemed to be most concerned about Mary. Halfway through the session, she turned to Mary and expressed concern, annoyance, chagrin, and disgust about her suicidal behavior. She challenged Mary's reality-testing and her judgment.

Mary became extremely upset at having to defend herself against her friend, who was now confronting and challenging her. The girls, however, settled this issue between them amicably, so that Mary felt some support from her friend, and the friend felt some increased comfort that Mary could manage her impulses better and might call for help the next time before acting rashly. Bringing this girl along may have represented a wish to emulate her as an ego-ideal, and a desire to organize at a different level than she had previously enjoyed, alone or contagiously with her less stable friends.

Following this session, Mary seemed to feel much more comfortable, had some grasp of her impulsivity, and decided she did not want to have any further peer group sessions. Subsequently, she managed to get through the semester fairly comfortably, continuing her therapy three times a week, individually. At the end of the semester she passed, but decided not to continue in school. Although still uncertain about her goals, she did not want to stay at home, and elected to travel until she settled on her own goal, at which time she planned to return and resume therapy.

DISCUSSION

Early in adolescence there is a natural tendency for gangs of the same sex to form, which give way in mid and late adolescence to heterosexual groups. There are often frequent shifts in the ties, as values, interests, narcissistic ties and ego ideals undergo changes, along with different rates and types of development in ego, superego, abstract thinking, identity, object choice, and vocational pursuits. The spontaneous group seems to be one of the functional foundations for the self-selected peer groups and has also been capitalized on for group therapy (Richmond and Schecter, 1964).

Another apparent indicator for the possible usefulness of network therapy from my experience with these networks is the level of object relations, which should have reached the ambivalent level although it may fluctuate between anaclitic and ambivalent. This was manifest in the present two patients, in their having some very involved, firm and continued attachments to some current peers and a symbiotic tie to parents. The tie to friends appears to be anaclitic rather than sharing, in some of the cases. Thus, although strongly and positively tied to peers, they were similarly involved with the parents in a negative way and had not managed to satisfactorily separate and individuate. In several of my cases there seemed to be an apparent separation on the surface, along with a precocious or pseudo-independence, covering an intense symbiosis to a parent.

The adolescent's psyche is ordinarily weighted with developmental tasks, sexual and aggressive drive accommodations, psychic structural changes, and physical adaptations in the attempt to achieve individual identity. Where there are added strains to the revival of the oedipal and preoedipal conflicts in an emotionally ill youngster, the usual therapeutic approaches may not be sufficient to manage the complications. Among these may be acting-out a psychosis or neurosis for a parent, excessive guilt and need for external punitors, or excessive separation anxiety with a need for cuddling care by a mother-substitute. Some such adolescents may then feel hopeless and attempt suicide, or such an act may seem imminent, or they become disorganized and behave in a way that indicates the need for hospital treatment. In such circumstances, where the environment can be made minimally cooperative, either of these alternatives may be avoided by use of the self-selected peer group.

The active help of parents, guardian, or college officials, along with their continued understanding and contact, is therefore vital to ensure the cooperation necessary to manage the crisis. Therapy may pose a threat to the symbiotic tie with the parent, and it is vital that patient and parent not be abruptly shaken apart, but instead that they cooperate with the therapist. Subsequently, some separation and individuation gradually supplant the symbiotic tie to the parent, in successful therapy.

Flexibility in therapy and perceptiveness to the dramatis personae met in the waiting room are important considerations in the approaches used, especially with an adolescent. Immediate cues, such as who accompanies the adolescent in the waiting room or who is the main subject of his material, may indicate the need for individual, family group, combined, or peer group therapy.

In adolescent group therapy there are frequent complaints leveled at the therapist: that the other group members can't help him "cause they're just a bunch of nuts too," or that the therapist is really not on their side as he is "a member of the Establishment," or that even "telling about pertinent matters won't alter anything because the group members and therapist are not involved" in his daily life, or that he "couldn't talk with a bunch of strangers about personal things." Of course, these have many aspects of wishes and fears as well as various defenses involved, and such resistances may often be dealt with successfully in group therapy. But for some adolescents, even though peer grouping is a natural phenomenon, there is too much anxiety about exposure for them to be in a therapy group. When a crisis is looming, it would also be unwise to increase their burdens by entering an ordinary outpatient adolescent therapy group as a new member (Strean, 1962).

Frequently, adolescents are as rigid, intolerant, and uncompromising about other youngsters' behavior and defenses as they are about adults, as evidenced by the arguments and divisions between "straights" and "freaks," or "hoods" and "frats," or "mods" and "rockers." There is often envy, fear, or disparagement of other adolescents with opposite kinds of defenses. For example, the altruistic youngster is frightened by the hedonistic, selfish, egocentric, or impulsive youngster; the impulsive one disparages the inhibited or aesthetic one; the promiscuous look down on the frightened, shy, hard-working, or student-council member, while the shy are frightened and envious of those who are sexually active. Numerous other such pairs of opposites could be enumerated, but it is clear that one is striving hard to control impulses and is envious of another's seeming pleasure from the deficiency of such controls. The coarse expression of impulses in a primitive, intense way is threatening to a youngster with a different type of defense which has only recently and uncertainly been acquired. Therefore, each will try to find refuge, enhancement of defense, and confirmation of unsettled, unstable, or fragile sense of self through conformity, by choosing friends with defenses that augment their own. This may partly be a narcissistic tie or partake of the ego-ideal as well. In a therapy group these various defenses may be useful as catalysts, but if they are too disparate or intense in type or degree, or if the youngster's ego is brittle, they may serve as barriers to becoming a functioning group member or forming a cohesive group. For some youngsters with a fragile ego, a therapy group is therefore not acceptable or advisable. For such youngsters, therapy in a self-selected peer group may be more suitable and beneficial, since they select friends of their own choosing whose defenses are acceptable and supportive to them.

The self-selected peer group uses the wishes and needs of the patient and his family to be rid of, or separate from, each other. This is in reaction to the binds imposed on each other, and is a natural developmental need. These efforts may previously have led to hospitalization, suicidal attempts, or increased clinging, with ambivalence and guilt about moves in either direction by either party. This type of group promotes, by gradual, controlled, therapeutic inoculation and immunization, a therapeutic togetherness and simultaneous separation. The togetherness occurs by virtue of a diluted symbiosis with the therapist and peers, in which the patient sheds and molts some feelings and attitudes about parents, authorities, his misbehavior, hates and guilts, brought up actively by him or passively by the peers. This process involves a diluted transference to the therapist and a bond with peers whereby some separation from the family occurs. Ultimately, the tie to the therapist decreases. The bond with peers may remain for as long as the patient needs it, since this tie leads to peer symbiosis, which helps increase barriers to the family binds, and assists in the separation-individuation process. This starts with the beginning of the self-selected peer group.

Many adolescents enjoy the achievement of abstract thinking in middle adolescence (Inhelder and Piaget, 1958) and express it by "rap sessions," weaving many plans and talking almost incessantly. Numerous aspects of this, such as enjoying mastery, practice, comparison, and confirmation with and by peers, dealing with mild anxieties, or using it for minor exhibitionism, may not stir up any therapeutic enthusiasm. This ego-achievement is another positive basis for the use of heterogeneous and self-selected peer groups with adolescents.

In suggesting a self-selected peer group, the therapist reflects some possibilities for the adolescent's increased autonomy and self-esteem with some responsibility for himself. Asking him to bring in his friends indicates their importance, and increases his self-esteem. The potency ascribed to the therapist is reflected onto the adolescent in this procedure, since it offers him some autonomy in a prescribed situation. This indicates respect for him as an individual, for his ability to choose and have his own friends, and for his right to use his own judgment, to try out and experiment. The youngster may be introjecting the therapist, incorporating him, and the omnipotence ascribed by him to the therapist.

The patient may have questions about why he should bring in any more friends, or talk with the therapist in their presence. These may reflect an indirect question about his relationship to the therapist and his feelings toward him.

When friends are brought in, how often, and when, may be significant diagnostic and therapeutic aids. Their degree of organization, type of defenses, autonomous ego-functioning, and superego are clues to the type of material the patient may be able to deal with and wishes to have brought up, as well as to what level of therapy the adolescent is capable of using that day. Thus the ability of the friends to aid the patient by pointing out reality or making interpretations of his behavior is, to some degree, involved in his choosing them to come in for that session. The choice of a provocative psychopathic peer may indicate resistance. The therapist's awareness of this test of trust or attempt to anger the therapist in the same way other adults have reacted to that friend may be a crucial matter in managing the resistance. The patient may also unconsciously use this friend to focus on his own antisocial behavior. The frequency with which certain peers are present may give a further clue to the direction of therapy, since their productions, memories, and interpretations to the patient will have a particular theme and relevance. The presence of a psychotic peer in one instance seemed related to a wish for the patient to see some of his abnormal behavior through the reflection of his friend as well as to display some of his healthy islands of ego function.

The parents of one youngster did not want him associating with certain people because they were undesirables. This attitude on the part of parents interferes with the adolescents' developing autonomy, self-esteem, assessment of their judgment, and respect; with their striving for separation; and with their developing their own identities. To some extent, it also refutes the parents' own sense of certainty about the values they have previously imbued in their offspring. If challenged on this, many parents will embarrassingly admit their ambivalence about the impending separation. When this sort of response does not occur, it is quite likely that there is a pathologic symbiotic tie between parent and teenager.

In the self-selected groups, the issue of the youngster associating with "the wrong kind" of peers does not come up except as a complaint by the youngster against the parents. The therapist's acceptance of whoever accompanies the patient is an important test of the therapist. It is also a crucial reflection of what the youngster is struggling with developmentally and may be in conflict about, with his inner self and his family.

For the most part, the patients mentioned brought in peers who were managing well, and were helpful to them. In other cases, severely disturbed youngsters were brought in only one time. Mary brought in a well-integrated youngster, and did not ask any of her disorganized, suicidal, or severely depressed friends to accompany her. Sara brought in a fairly well-integrated young adult, her ego ideal in some ways. Later she also brought in some age mates who were also functioning well, although one was her school-hookey-mate. The friends that her mother most objected to were never brought in: a girl friend who had been in and out of the state hospital, to whom the mother reacted with a panicky, impulsive move to another home in a suburb; the boyfriend who was a school dropout and narcotics addict with whom she smoked "pot," and against whom mother felt almost as violent.

After the initial support of and sympathy with the patient, a particular crucial turning-point in the need and use of the peer group seems to occur when the peers confront the patient about his unrealistic attitudes or destructive behavior. They also thus express their concern for him and his self-destructive behavior. When the patient first hears this, he responds as if in shocked disbelief and seems to turn to the therapist for support. This affective response to a peer's confrontation or interpretation has been effective. Hearing it from a peer cannot be dismissed as "Establishment noise." *The defensive barrier also seems to be lowered appreciably* as a result of comments from peers selected by the patient, and with suitable timing. This again is related to the patient's unconscious and conscious wish to bring that peer in on that day, indicating a readiness to get aid from that peer. If this crisis of improved integration is well-managed (and it usually is by the peers without the therapist intervening much), the patient may within a session or two feel less need for the peer group and be out of the crisis that led to forming the self-selected peer group.

Not all adolescents who have been offered such a group have accepted. Of those who did not, subsequently about half, to my knowledge, required hospitalization. The other half said they wanted to continue individual therapy only, and it was then possible to work through the crisis that way. Perhaps this was aided by the parameter of the suggestion of a peer group, which led to some increase in hopefulness, self-esteem, and autonomy by the implications of using a group of friends of their choosing. Of course, there may also have been a wish to conceal their difficulties from friends because of fear of exposure, guilt, or shame.

Network psychotherapy may most easily be accepted by adolescents who have a strong conforming need for their own subculture. But I have found it applicable also with youngsters with a great deal of separation-anxiety (wrist-cutting syndrome), severe paranoid ideation, or severe depression, with too much shame to speak of their needs openly to an adult or to the strangers in an ordinary therapeutic adolescent group. It may also find application with less disturbed youngsters who are not in a crisis.

The effect of a more integrated peer's personality on an unstable or disorganized one may be inferred from cogitation on Thoreau's words in another context (Erikson, 1969), indicating the effect of one person's actions on others:

"I know this well, that if one thousand, if one hundred, if ten men whom I could name—if ten honest men only—ay, if one honest man, in this State of Massachusetts, ceasing to hold slaves, were actually to withdraw from copartnership, and be locked up in the county jail therefor, it would be the abolition of slavery in America. For it matters not how small the beginning may seem to be: what is once well done is done forever."

This is indirectly reminiscent of the value of integrated people and their effect on others, referred to in Genesis, where Abraham attempted to intercede and not have Sodom and Gomorrah destroyed if ten righteous men were found therein.

SUMMARY

Psychotherapy with adolescents in self-selected peer groups, or networks, has been a useful adjunct to deal with a critical situation and avoid a suicidal attempt or hospitalization. One to ten sessions may be necessary, provided that support and cooperation of the environment are present. Individual, family therapy, and group psychotherapy may not be feasible for some youngsters in such crises. The peers chosen are usually better integrated than the patient. There is potential for a diluted tie with them, which may be apparent from an intense, positive bond with peers. The peers selected may be particular indicators diagnostically and therapeutically of the patient's readiness to focus on certain conflicted areas. The meaning of deliberately inviting peers who may be unwelcome to the parents has many possible positive effects related to enhanced self-esteem and respect for the patient's potential for improved judgment, behavior and autonomy. This is especially significant in connection with their symbiotic tie to the parents and their need for separation and individuation which has been conflicted. The effect of better integrated personalities, via the peers, is, of course, nonpareil in value.

REFERENCES

ACKERMAN, N. W., (1958), The Psychodynamics of Family Life, Basic Books, New York.

ERIKSON, E. H., (1969), Gandhi's Truth, W. W. Norton and Co., New York, p. 200.

Genesis, 18:32.

INHELDER, B., & PIAGET, J., (1958), The Growth of Logical Thinking from Childhood to Adolescence, London, Routledge and Kegan Paul, Ltd., Chapter 18, pp. 334-350.

LANGSLEY, D. G., & KAPLAN, D. M., (1968), The Treatment of Families in Crisis, Grune and Stratton, Inc., New York.

RICHMOND, A. H., & SCHECTER, S., (1964), A Spontaneous Request for Treatment by a Group of Adolescents, Int. J. Group Psychother., 14:97-106.

SPECK, R. V., (1965), (a) in, Friedman, A.S., Boszormenyi-Nagy, I., Jungreis, J. E., Lincoln, G., Mitchell, H. W., Sonne, J. C., Speck, R. V., Psychotherapy for the Whole Family, Springer Publishing Co., Inc., New York, Chapters 12, pp. 197-205, and 22, pp. 293-304.

SPECK, R. V., (1965), (b), Psychotherapy of the Social Network of a Schizophrenic Family, *Family Process*, 6:204-214.

STREAN, H. S., (1962), On Introducing the New Member, *Internat. J. Group Psychother.*, 12:362-368.

SUGAR, M., (1971), Network Psychotherapy of an Adolescent, *Annals Adol. Psychiatry*, Vol. 1, Basic Books, New York.

CHAPTER 6

An Oedipal Revolt in a College Group

Edwin M. Davidson, M.D.

"EVERY THERAPIST GETS the group he deserves," says Anthony (1968), reflecting on 25 years with groups. The implication is, indeed, that they are just desserts. This paper presents the evolution and denouement of an adolescent group revolt, heavy with Oedipal implications. Group dynamics, transference and countertransference became interwoven in a confrontation between leader and group, with echoes of confrontations between administration and students on the one hand, and older, more primitive conflicts on the other. As Freud (1955) stated, "The leader of the group is still the dreaded primal father; the group still wishes to be governed by unrestricted force; it has an extreme passion for authority. . . ."

Scene:

The setting is a small, residential university, close to a large city but still rather isolated. The community is highly verbal and intellectual, with everyone much involved in everyone else's emotional business. Because of the closeness of the community, group therapy had not been attempted for a number of years. There was much doubt about whether it could ever be successful. Specifically, some senior staff members expected the problem of confidentiality to be insoluble. The group described here, therefore, was instituted with considerable doubt and anxiety. The leader himself had not been involved in group work since residency, 12 years previously.

Meetings began in the spring of 1967 and continued on through the fall and winter of 1967-68. The period of turmoil and revolution had begun in the universities. Confrontations with administration and the social structure had already developed at Berkeley, and increasingly throughout the college community.

The Group:

We started with eight members in April 1967, meeting weekly for 1½ hours. There were five male and three female students.

1. Joan, a freshman, was mildly depressed, feeling lonely and unable to get close to people. She felt alienated from both her parents, whom she described in derogatory terms. Her older brother was described as having gone to psychiatrists "since he was nine."
2. David, a junior, had presented himself originally as an observer, interested in group therapy. He saw himself as a potential therapist but was unsure whether to become a psychiatrist or psychologist. This rickety throne collapsed at the last meeting of the spring term.
3. Bill, a freshman, complained of anxiety about making decisions and working out relationships with girls. Both of these issues were associated with anxiety related to his directive and controlling father, who would periodically threaten to cut off Bill's funds. This boy was the oldest of four in a close family.
4. Sharon, a sophomore, was an older daughter in a small-town Jewish family. She was chronically depressed and alienated, with questions about whether to continue in school or drop out. She was having serious academic problems.
5. Sylvia, a sophomore, was the older of two children from a Jewish family living in the West Indies. She was a transfer student who had been dissatisfied with her first college, as well as with two previous therapists. In the group she complained of feeling alone and alienated. This pattern of dissatisfaction was habitual, having occurred in high school and continued into college.
6. Roy, a junior, had been a judge in student government and had resigned shortly before coming to the Mental Health Center. He was depressed, unsure of any direction for himself and unable to be in touch with his feelings. He felt quite distant from his father, who was a judge. Mother was described as infantile and hypochondriacal. His older brother had just entered law school. Roy had just been jilted by a girl friend. He became the central protagonist in the group, and his Oedipal conflict is crucial to the theme of this paper.
7. Paul, a sophomore, was depressed but articulate at first. He had considerable anxiety about coming to the first meeting. His father

had died when Paul was 13, and the boy felt he should be filling father's role at home, to rescue his sister. He dropped out of the group the following autumn and entered individual therapy.

8. John, a freshman, had major conflicts with his father over whether he deserved to be in school; he had serious scholastic problems. He was a constant talker and group scapegoat during the spring of 1967, went into individual therapy in the summer and dropped out of the group after one meeting in the fall.

The Engagement:

The group met four times during the spring of 1967. During this time a female member of the staff acted as recorder. I felt my role as leader was to promote and interpret group process, rather than "doing individual therapy in the group." This position, theoretically, was to enhance group development and interaction, but it also suited my initial anxiety. I introduced the members to each other, told them of the plans for our meetings, emphasized confidentiality, talked a little about group therapy in general—and threw the ball to them.

John began to talk compulsively, filling the silences with what the observer called "little maxims of optimism." Roy made several attempts to bring up anxieties. He wondered why people were glad to be alive. David asked if one would be attacked in the group. John swamped both these beginnings with his stream of talk. Questions about the motives of the therapist came up: "What are you doing this for?" "Is this a research project?" Finally, John made a slip about talking his parents down the previous summer, and the group tension was released into laughter.

During the next two meetings David suggested that the members present their opinions of each other. The group considered this and rejected it. John became silent, recognizing the scapegoat role toward which he was moving. Anxieties about being attacked and hurt became more insistent. Sharon complained about her family, "how little they understand."

At the last meeting before vacation, dissatisfaction with the group became more insistent. The observer could stand it no longer and emerged from silence for the first time. She told the group that they kept expecting everything of the leader and were letting slip by the opportunity to do something for each other.

After a moment of shocked silence, David opened up. He had gone to high school with Joan, and she had been his first date. She had been cold to him then. He had never understood why and wondered if she could tell him now. Joan tried to pass it off, "It was just one of those things; let's try to forget the past." The group turned on David: he is uninvolved, he always acts *like the psychiatrist*. At this point the observer spoke again— David was hurt and they were attacking him. Bill began to talk about his father and himself, and the observer spoke for the third time, "Do you realize that you always begin to talk just before the end of the hour?"

In the few remaining minutes there was general agreement among the group that they would return next fall, although Roy required some persuading by Sylvia. In the fall, Paul did not return. John came back for only one session, during which he offered to share some new insights from his individual therapy that summer and antagonized everyone. The observer was unable to continue. The group resumed, but it had now experienced three losses.

Insurrection:

As the group continued into the fall there was a sharpening of both the closeness and the rivalry between David and Roy. Both had been in the same group dynamics seminar during the summer, and both alluded to new knowledge and insight. I dealt with the loss of the observer by suggesting that the role be alternated among the members. This suggestion was at first accepted but quickly became a center of covert and overt resistance. Increasing anger became focused on me.

In the third meeting, when Joan read the notes of the previous week, she was immediately challenged by Roy. He attacked her for being aloof and not participating and then added that she must have noticed him staring at her the last session. He felt she was nice to stare at. Joan chose to hear only the attack. She protested that she did feel committed and involved and that things were much better for her this year. David quickly supported her position, which left Roy isolated in his challenge and advance. Then the group briefly got into the question of Sharon's decision to leave school. They discussed the fact that this option was open to a girl but not to a boy, because of the draft.

At this point David turned to me and wondered if I could help him get a psychiatric deferment from service. Roy promptly sustained David in his suggestion and further proposed: The administration of the Center should take some stand to help everyone get out of the service, because it's important to fight this immoral war with every possible means. I brought the challenge back to me. I asked if anyone would be able to write some notes, since Sylvia, whose turn it was, was absent. Roy spoke for himself and the group, saying he could but he didn't see why he should; if I wanted some notes, why didn't I make them myself? The battle was out in the open.

The following meeting David and Joan were absent. Roy was restless and anxious. He said Joan was usually ten minutes late and recalled how sensitive her comments had been the previous week. Sharon wondered aloud where David was.

Roy returned to the attack. He reviewed the question of the draft and predicted that the doctor would not take a position because of the legal system. He would risk getting a bad name as a psychiatrist if he did so. Roy did not think the doctor would give his opinion, in general. Anyway, he, Roy, was more interested in the group's opinion. I reminded them of the question about who would take notes and wondered if the real issue were not my commitment to the group.

Roy suddenly asked Sylvia how she liked taking notes. She said she hated it. Roy said he felt awkward meeting members of the group outside. Yet, bringing into the group what is known of each other from outside can be helpful—as it was with David and Joan—and with David and himself. Roy suggested, perhaps there should be more meetings, or a marathon all-night meeting, to show people in different moods. "Is the doctor willing to come to a marathon meeting?" asked Sharon. Roy suggested a united front, a "revolt against the leader."

The marathon session idea was picked up by Bill at the following meeting. Both Joan and David were present, and each endorsed it. David wondered if the doctor wanted to give up an evening. "It might interfere with his personal life and that's unfair." Sharon and Joan were uncomfortable. They wanted me at the all-night session because of my commitment to the group as a psychiatrist. David mockingly said that he was afraid to be alone all night. With the alignment of the boys on one side and the girls nervously on the other, the boys started kidding the girls. I found myself getting increasingly anxious and stressing the group issue of how much the leader is willing to give, while turning away entirely from the sexual rivalry with me and the challenge to me as leader.

At just this point David mentioned that he had decided to go into VISTA for a year and then go to medical school. He had recently turned 21 and he asked Roy to congratulate him. The questions of growing up and of relationships between men and women dominated the rest of the meeting. At the end I again raised the question of what the group expected of a marathon session. The issue was talked about again the next week, with

Roy finally saying, "We need to decide *now!* And we need an all-night session to achieve closeness."

At the next meeting Roy announced that he was leaving the group. He had talked with Bill and Joan about the group and its direction. Then, from prepared notes, he discussed each member of the group in turn, with the exception of himself and me. He characterized David as defensive, preventing group interaction and afraid to commit himself. He criticized the others in turn until he came to Joan. She was "beautiful." She was the only reason he had stayed in the group so long. He had wanted to get to know her better.

David defended the group. He attacked Roy as cruel, unfeeling and afraid of closeness. Joan and Bill came to Roy's defense, with Joan agreeing that little had been accomplished, that we were afraid to attack each other and afraid of a marathon session. I pointed out the agreement to have sessions regularly. The proposal for an all-night session was a change in the agreement. "Why can't we accomplish things in here at this time?" I also pointed out that Roy was saying that either things will run his way or he would destroy the group. David and Sylvia agreed. I recalled a couple of slips in which Roy had confused David and me, which suggested that some of his anger was really at me.

Roy finally turned to me, I had been "too passive, allowing people to work things out." I had not been giving enough, and I was using an analytic model which, he felt, was not the most helpful or appropriate for the group. The group wanted to get very close, but I wouldn't let them.

David asked what he meant by closeness and brought up the question of Joan, which had never before been out in the open. Roy said David had a dirty mind. I also asked Roy what he meant by closeness, if he had not felt before that someone in authority was not committed or helpful enough. He agreed. I said I thought he was on the verge of dealing with some things that were quite important and that he ought not to leave the group at that point. He sent me a note before the next meeting, indicating that he had decided not to return and none of my subsequent efforts could change his mind.

Mourning and Dissolution:

Three people came to the next meeting: Sylvia, Joan and David. Bill was sick. The first half hour was a depressed silence. David hoped I would speak to Roy. I said I planned to do so. David felt we were mourning. Sylvia wondered if we could accomplish anything without Roy. David thought we could.

Two meetings later Sylvia found she now had a conflicting class, which she would not change. David, after some discussion, felt he had achieved the things he needed in the group, the ability to get close and to talk about his feelings. He felt that he could now leave. I accepted this plan. Sharon and Bill decided to remain and did so for several more sessions. They each achieved some insight and strength. But the original group, as a unit, had really ceased to exist following the revolt.

Discussion:

What happened within this group of college students, I think, can be understood in terms of a delayed adolescent revolt, played out within the group, with Roy as the protagonist and me as the reluctant father. This was a revolt determined by Roy's own needs but, at the same time, an expression of the group's dynamic position. Roy spoke for himself but also for all of them. They resonated with his challenge until he, like Daedalus, scorched his wings and fell, destroying the group, as well.

An observation by Anna Freud (1969) illuminates these events: "What serves the preadolescent as some protection against the quantitative pressure of the drives proves wholly inadequate against . . . adult sexuality proper. Nothing helps here except a complete discarding of . . . the parents. This battle . . . is fought out in a variety of ways: by openly displayed indifference to them—by denying that they are important—by disparagement of them since it is easier to do without if they are denounced as stupid, useless, ineffective; by open insolence and revolt against their persons and the beliefs and conventions for which they stand. . . . That these reactions alternate also with returns to helplessness and dependence . . . does not make it any easier for the parents."

Roy's father is a judge. Roy had resigned from a position as justice in student government shortly after his older brother entered law school. Perhaps Roy felt his rivalry with father was surpassed by his brother's more actualized rivalry. Depressed and unsure of where to go and what to become, he entered the group. Here he found another rivalrous brother, David, one year older.

David had announced in the first meeting that he planned to become a therapist like the leader, and soon after he tried to reactivate a prior claim on Joan, the belle of the group. Roy's first response was to ally himself with me and with David. This soon gave way to the re-enactment of the Oedipal battle in the transference to revolt against the father-leader, to triumph over the brother, and to win Joan. The final break came after Joan and David were away from a meeting at the same time. In Roy's fantasy were they perhaps together—representing an Oedipal defeat?

"The group appears to us as a revival of the primal horde. Just as the primitive man survives potentially in every individual, so the primal horde may arise once more out of any random collection " (Freud, A., 1969). Experience with therapy groups repeatedly demonstrates the revival of these fantasies. What is it that makes it possible for them to be enacted, rather than only felt? Why was it not possible for interpretation to stop the acting out?

First, I think, the formality and relative inactivity of the leader led, as in individual therapy, to an increase in the anxiety of the group, to reinforcement of fantasies and an intensification of the transference. The rapid development of anxiety and anger was clear in the responses of the observer. Secondly, and uniquely for this group, the observer's activity during the fourth meeting demonstrated the vulnerability of both the leader and the group structure. It set a model for the later revolt, which began after another four meetings. The disappearance of the observer may have been felt as abandonment and fragmentation within the family.

I saw the idea of a marathon session, on one hand, as a challenge to me and, on the other hand, as a covert invitation to the members for sexual activity in the group. Both the girls, by their anxiety, and then David directly confirmed this. All of this made me anxious. I feared both the challenge and the exposure of my own fantasies.

Anthony (1969) points out the erotic countertransference feelings of older therapists with adolescent patients. He describes that "the therapist may find himself reacting as indignantly as the parents to reports of sexual misdemeanors and even adopting a strategy of moral expediency . . . in the name of reality principle." Kanter (1964) describes a similar phenomenon with a number of groups concerned with genital issues and contrasts this with orally focused groups: "The genital groups related to the group leader (of the same sex) more as a peer in the reality and as the same-sex parental figure in the transference . . . therapists were at times too anxious and then refrained from valid interpretations."

All of these considerations interfered with attempts to intervene and interpret what was happening. My early interpretations were addressed to the group as if it were primarily dealing with oral problems specifically, as if the only issue were how much I was willing to give. I glossed over the challenge to my leadership. After the revolt was over, during the mourning period, I was able to talk more freely about the revolt itself, my feelings about the group and the role of group leader.

A follow-up note further reflected Roy's dealing with his Oedipal conflict. After an initial decision to go to law school, I have heard that he changed his direction and entered medical school, with the plan of going into psychiatry. Possibly this change reflected a decision to renounce rivalry and identification with his real father, leaving that contest to his brother and replacing it with a new Oedipal rivalry with the therapist-father.

REFERENCES

ANTHONY, E. JAMES, (1968), "Reflections on Twenty-five Years of Group Psychotherapy," *International Journal of Group Psychotherapy*, Vol. XVIII, No. 3.
————, (1969), "The Reactions of Adults to Adolescents and Their Behavior," Caplan, G., and Lebovici, S., *Adolescence: Psychological Perspectives*, New York; Basic Books.
FREUD, S., (1955), "Group Psychology and the Analysis of the Ego," in *Standard Edition of the Complete Psychological Works*, Vol. 38, London: Hogarth.
FREUD, ANNA, (1969), "Adolescence as a Developmental Disturbance," in Caplan, Gerald, and Lebovici, Serge (ed.), *Adolescence: Psychological Perspectives*, New York: Basic Books.
KANTER, STANLEY, S., et al., (1964), "A Comparison of Oral and Genital Aspects in Group Psychotherapy," *International Journal of Group Psychotherapy*, Vol. XIV, No. 1.

CHAPTER 7

Incest, Anger and Suicide

Lorna M. Forbes, M.D.

TO THE AVERAGE ADOLESCENT the acceptance of the concept of the hostility inherent in a suicide attempt is relatively slight. The following is an example of the use of one adolescent's guilt over her father's death to confront three others who had made a suicide attempt in the past.

In this interaction, the key figures of the group are two 17-year-old girls, both of whom had had extensive sexual play with their fathers between ages 8 and 12. For Kay, this ended with father's suicide. For Lou, it ended with exposure of the problem to mother. Kay's father had often said to her that she would replace her dead mother, at the same time threatening suicide if she did not comply with his wishes.

Three other members of the group had made suicide attempts. Bea, 16, had grown up with constant criticism from father. Overt masochism on the part of her mother made her feel guilty of her very existence. She became an intense perfectionist, isolated with her books. When first seen she had spells of depression, crying and suicidal ideation. In a recent attempt she took an overdose of medication.

Carol was 16 and had grown up with a sister who required intensive care for a congenital malformation of the larynx. There were numerous episodes of surgical intervention, in which the sibling's death was anticipated. Carol was the "well one" who received little attention and resented her sick, overprotected sister. Finally, in a rage at her mother, she took an overdose of medication. She had also been angry at a former group member who, unfortunately, died by accident three days after the session in which Carol expressed her feelings. She felt responsible for his death for some time after this and had recurrent dreams of seeing his face.

Sue was 16 and had become involved sexually with a Mormon boy friend. He later rejected her and became more religious. Sue felt the church condemned her, while he was held blameless. From that time she became promiscuous sexually and used amphetamines and LSD. Each LSD flashback made her suicidal. On one occasion when she feared pregnancy, she made a suicide attempt.

Also in the group was Rick, a 16-year-old boy on amphetamines, acid, speed, etc. When he first came he was depressed. Wes was a 17-year-old boy with marked dependency on his mother. He was basically schizophrenic and in the past had fantasied conquering the world, being famous, etc. He had an obsessional interest in comics, in which he would be Superman or his equivalent. Fears of competition were strong. The last member, Tom, 17 years of age, had a sister with congenital heart disease. She had been preferred and overprotected. He experienced such open rejection that it was noticeable even to neighbors. The older sister had lured him into an incestouous relationship, about which he had much guilt. When she wished to control him, she would threaten to tell about it, saying the parents would blame him, since he was the male.

In one particular group session they discussed their self-hatred. Rick brought out the feelings that he had never pleased his father. Bea described a similar feeling and her positive anticipation of the group meetings. This led to Sue's expressing dissatisfaction with the group and denial of her own problems. Finally, after confrontation by others, she recited her guilt over intimacy with her present boy friend. There were minor diversionary topics. They also discussed the importance of eating in the group session, to lessen anxiety.

Then Bea began to talk about her need to draw attention to herself: "But I want to draw attention to myself. Today in class I was supposed to give a demonstration of something. Everyone picked something fancy. I wanted to be different, so I just picked a stick." She cried. "They didn't know—they didn't know it was a stick."

Therapist: "No, Bea, maybe you felt so insecure they didn't understand you and couldn't get your message that it was a stick. You feel unimportant like the stick. You were describing yourself."

Bea: "I know. When I write my boy friend a letter I get all wound up.

I think he should say how nice it was. Then I know how silly it is. I just wrote a few lines, but I want to be noticed. I want someone to say it's good. It's silly, isn't it?"

Wes: "No. I feel the same way. I have to do things to be noticed, too. In fact, I finally was. We gave a concert at school. I sang a solo, "Jill," that song I composed. It was a smash hit. My father came up and praised me—the first time in my life! Can you imagine?"

The entire group expressed pleasure at his success.

Wes: "But he has never given me praise."

Bea: "But I just plain want attention. My father always told me it was wrong. I don't have a right to it. He made fun of me if I tried to get it."

Kay: "I want to tell you all something I've never said before. Why did my father kill himself when I did try to satisfy him (sexually)? I didn't give him enough. He killed himself because of me!" She cried. Her entire body quivered. The room was hushed.

Therapist: "Kay, your father didn't kill himself because of your not satisfying him. I think you can see, though, how angry it is when one takes his life. You felt that if he really loved you he would not have done it. He would not have done it if he had not been thinking so much of himself. But he did, and you feel that to be his anger and rejection of you. I can imagine he must have felt very guilty over his seduction of you." Kay broke down hysterically. She was given a drink of water and a mild tranquilizer.

At once and in different ways, those who had attempted suicide asked, "Did my folks feel that way when I tried to kill myself? Did my parents think I blamed them? Is that why my parents were so upset?"

Carol: "I never realized before that my mother could think I was mad at her. All I felt was that I wanted to get away. How terrible."

Bea: "I knew I felt mad, but I just didn't want to live. I felt I couldn't do anything right. I'm just not important to anyone."

Therapist: "Bea, you're demonstrating how angry you were at yourself because you couldn't feel anger toward them. As you say, you were unimportant. It's yourself you feel hatred for, but you've been angry at them. You have often told me how guilty you are that you cannot do anything to please your father, yet you are angry at his demands."

Kay: "But how can you know he didn't do it because I couldn't satisfy him? He kept telling me he'd kill himself if I didn't."

Carol: "I took the pills to get away, but I know I've wished my sister was dead. I was angry at my mother for favoring her."

Therapist: "Kay, your father may have been very angry at your mother or felt rejected by her, in that he became involved with you. Remember how unimportant you felt, and his attention to you made you feel better."

Carol: "But Kay, you have to understand that when we tried to commit suicide we didn't feel we wanted to hurt anyone."

Kay: "But I feel I'm to blame."

Bea: "Kay, when you feel unimportant and bad you don't think of anyone else."

Therapist: "I think this is all very important. Those of you who have attempted suicide see how the others feel. Kay, you also can be aware that the person who attempts it does not necessarily think at the moment of hurting someone, though that's what happens. It is a very angry act, though it does not seem that way."

Lou: "My father is still alive, and I can't get along with my mother. She is always sitting on his lap in front of me. I get very upset. Is it because of what happened?"

Therapist: "You feel angry that she reminds you that she is his wife. You also feel guilty about ever having become involved with him. When you steal and get in trouble—and you notice you make sure you are caught— you are punishing yourself and them at the same time, much as Kay's father did."

DISCUSSION

This small portion of a group session demonstrates the easy transition of a discussion of a girl's feelings of unimportance to an uncovering of all the guilt over an incestuous relationship and the father's suicide. The drama of Kay's hysterics is difficult to describe, since the whole group was electrified. Her feelings that her father suicided because of her were upsetting to those who had made the attempts. They had to face the hostility in their own behavior. In succeeding sessions this was worked through many times. In addition, Kay and Lou have had to work out their guilt to their mothers and their deep wishes to keep the fathers. Both girls are now dating and making a healthier adjustment. At the time of this session, neither could be comfortable with a boy friend on a date. Lou has stopped her stealing.

CHAPTER 8

"Turning On" the Turned Off: Active Techniques with Depressed Drug Users in a County Free Clinic

Priscilla A. Slagle, M.D., and
Dianne S. Silver, M.A.

SOMETIMES PEOPLE JOIN GROUPS when no other form of therapy is available to them. This paper will discuss this type of group variously composed of young adults, ages 16 to 30, seen at a county-supported free clinic serving a transient, essentially "hippie-like" population. All came seeking individual treatment but were referred to the group because of limited personnel. They often begrudgingly entered the group, feeling disappointed they could not get individual therapy. The therapists were two women in their late 20's, a psychiatrist and a psychologist. The group had been in existence one year with weekly sessions lasting 1½ hours.

During the life of this group, several significant issues emerged:

1. A drop-in group can be frustrating to both patients and therapist. This is particularly true if the patients seek the depth of insight which may enable them to behave and relate as they desire.
2. Depressed, withdrawn, passive-dependent and often drug-using young people offer serious resistances to consistent confrontation and attempts at understanding of behavior. Certain activating or provocative techniques are often necessary and can be of some value.
3. One of the important resistances in these patients is the reluctance to acknowledge and to express appropriate anger. The pervasive "love" facade facilitates and requires repression of anger, which

With assistance from Terry Peacher, M.D., and Irving H. Berkovitz, M.D.

then fosters depression, self-defeating behavior and avoidance of mutually respecting intimacy. Group therapy and provocative techniques can help to free the anger.

THE FRUSTRATIONS OF A "DROP-IN" GROUP

Originally, we planned to have a "drop-in" group. Anyone who came to the clinic with emotional problems was screened briefly by a social worker for suitability to enter group therapy. They were told of the group and invited to come on the night of the meeting. Some returned; some did not. Many of these people wanted on-the-spot magical cures from the social worker and were unable to follow through to the extent of returning. Others returned only once or twice, disappointed that the therapists and other group members did not undo their Gordian knots and remove them from their entanglement, once they were in the "magic circle" of the group.

Typical of this population was difficulty delaying gratification, or establishing and achieving goals. Many seemed to be drifting through life, with the waves never washing them to the same place twice. This was one of the problems the group faced and had to solve. We found it difficult to establish specific goals for the group or individuals, because of this lack of goal orientation. Most came in during a crisis, i.e., trouble with the police, disturbing drug experiences, impending drug addiction, tumultuous heterosexual or homosexual relationships and a general fear of people and of involvements.

They had marked difficulty expressing what they hoped to gain from the group experience, at times with bewilderment bordering on pathos; yet all shared common feelings. All were suffering from an overt or underlying chronic depression, manifest in numerous ways. All were glaringly, silently angry, in desperate fear of these feelings. All were in an identity crisis, and none had specific plans for the future. There was a seeming lack of relatedness to the past and apparent disregard for the future. Each was concerned with his life today; each had Herculean existential loneliness. Each longed for emotional sustenance but was unable to accept it, because of self-annihilating feelings of unworthiness.

Some of their goals, often stated in only one or two sentences, were as follows: "Want to get out anger"; "Want to be able to talk to people"; "Want to be able to think more clearly"; "Want to be able to stand up to girlfriend!"; "Want to stay out of jail"; "Want to be able to accept self." A few were vague as to any goals.

Throughout the year of the group, 20 individuals came in at various times. A sorting and sifting process occurred, leading, after 5 months, to a 7-member "closed non-drop-in group." An original nucleus of one male and one female remained throughout. Another female has been in the group almost since its inception. The other 4 present members have been in the group 8 months. Thirteen "drop-outs" came and went. Eight of these came only once or twice, and the other 5 stayed from one to four months. Because of these repeated abandonments, the core members became less and less accepting of new people coming into the group. Some had come in a genuine crisis; others had come "bullshitting," monopolized the group, took from them, then never returned to reciprocate. Some continued coming and talking for a while, then quit when they could no longer remain the center of attention. It must be remembered that all of these people wanted individual therapy and came to the group expecting, craving and coveting special attention from the therapists. When they failed to get this, they often did not return. The males were less interested in, and more frightened of, group therapy. Altogether, 9 males had attended the group; only 2 remained. Eleven females came to the group; 5 remained.

After 5 months of this drop-in, crisis type of group, we felt there had to be a change! A person could not get enough "crisis therapy" in a few visits to really help him unless the others were totally ignored. Also, a few of these "drop-ins" were bordering on psychosis and were entirely unsuitable for group therapy. They were disruptive, requiring strong intervention and control by the therapists. The group members were amazingly tolerant of the kaleidoscopic parade of people passing through, possibly because they were comfortable with a convenient exogenous excuse for not working seriously on their own problems. No group identity and trust could be formed. The more consistent members were wary of revealing parts of themselves, lest these be forever carried away by those passing through. The therapists were perturbed; should they continue to allow people to drop in and engross the group or should they obviously reward the stable members by directing more time and attention to them? Even with interpretations as to their resistance and the encouragement to participate, the more quiet, persevering members continued to allow this monopolizing by the transient individuals. The therapists could not expect the newer members to take less, since the older participants clearly allowed this.

THE GROUP BECOMES STABLE!

During the 5th month, the group consisted of only the 3 nucleus members, owing to a temporary lull in referrals from the social worker. These 3 were Mike, Lynn and Shelley. Mike was a 17-year-old high school boy, living at home with his parents. He had a past story of serious behavior problems, fire-setting and drug abuse. After periods of individual treatment with several psychiatrists and psychologists, he was now functioning better than previously in his life. He wanted further therapy, in order "to learn to stand up to my girlfriend." He had been intimately involved with her for 2 years and gave her credit for his "moral and social salvation." He was unable to relate to his emotions and viewed everything with an abstract, detached, intellectualism. Occasionally, he had feelings of depersonalization. He was extremely angry but unable to express this even with considerable provocation. The most he could manage was a languid, smiling "fuck you." He struggled against sadistic impulses and feared loss of control.

Lynn, age 20, had been in weekly individual treatment with one of the group therapists for 12 months during the life of the group. She had come to the clinic severely depressed, suicidal and was approaching heroin addiction. Lynn had deteriorated from being a scholarship university art student to being jobless, shoeless, aimless, a drug user, and sexually promiscuous while living in various communes. She initially presented herself as "a piece of shit."

Shelley was an obese, 16-year-old girl, who had severe difficulty relating to anyone. She presented herself as being ultra self-conscious, unable to talk to people, cringing and fearful of being seen. It was painful for her even to sit in the group—let alone talk. She was the silent member. Shelley was entangled in a dependent relationship with her mother, thereby receiving extensive secondary gain from her illness. Her mother had abandoned her in childhood but recently had become more willing to care for her. Shelley periodically contemplated suicide, usually as a reaction to a disagreement with her mother. She was excruciatingly agoraphobic. She had stopped attending school because she could not tolerate anyone looking at her.

Mike, Lynn and Shelley were understandably uncomfortable when they suddenly were alone—forced to talk or encounter silence. Lynn sewed patches on jeans throughout the meeting. Mike took advantage of the opportunity to affectlessly berate himself, saying "my head controls my emotions, except for occasions when my emotions are totally uncontrollable. There is no in between. My mind is fucked up. I want to hit myself over the head when I feel angry. It is always my fault, not other people's." We used a Gestalt Therapy technique to elicit his feelings. Noticing a clenched left fist, he was asked to exaggerate the squeeze. Then he gave both hands words. His inner fury and self-hatred quickly rose as his left hand spoke of beating him while the right cried out to break a bottle over his head. After a few minutes of violent dialogue, Mike became sad. He turned off his feelings and wanted to quit talking. When attention shifted to Lynn and Shelley, Mike said he was angry because he wanted more attention. "He wanted to leave happy." Lynn wanted to hug him; he refused. He took a hug from one of the therapists, then sat down, saying, "I have no feelings." Lynn and Shelley talked of their feelings of emptiness and inability to give. All 3 had clearly participated more than ever before.

There was no group meeting the following week, but Lynn came for her individual therapy. They found the small group too frightening. Lynn came and was on time for the next meeting. Mike was 15 minutes late. Shelley did not return for 5 weeks. Perhaps she had learned that the group had again enlarged. Mike monopolized and commented that he was angry when Lynn got any attention. She wanted recognition. We encouraged them to argue over their desire for consideration. Lynn did this effectively, but Mike was compromising and condescending. Only Mike returned the following week. He reveled in having two therapists to himself and did some work on his personal problems. We mentioned the possibility of terminating the group, as there had been no new referrals. During the ensuing week, both Mike and Lynn called us, requesting the group not be ended.

Mike hurriedly did some recruiting and brought 5 friends to the next session! Only one of these remained. Also, 4 new referrals were sent to this meeting by the social worker. Three of these remained. Mike's friends were understandably dazed and even more obtuse about their expectations from the group than the previous tourists. Anxious and concerned about what was to happen, they used the session to criticize the therapists and the Establishment. Remarkably, this had never occurred before.

The next week a group identity did blossom, with members interacting and expressing interest in each other. They did not want to stop after the 1½ hours. Their response to this closeness the following week was one of anger and distance. Expressions of interest in other members were met with rebuff. A few were clearly angry and "wanted to do something physical." We used some hand-slapping Gestalt techniques. This escape of suppressed angry feelings was threatening, resulting in mutual timidity and disinterest the following week. They also seemed lost, wanting direction, "not knowing what to talk about," "wanting to be asked questions," "afraid to talk, because afraid of criticism," "afraid to ask anything from the group." The following week they were defensive and intensely preoccupied with us and our reactions. They were afraid we would "pick apart and analyze." They felt we "didn't have feelings and weren't people."

Even with encouragement, they were unable to say more, but clearly used us as their defense against further dealing with each other and themselves. Finally, we sat in a separate part of the room with our backs turned, to enable the group to talk about us. We had repeatedly encouraged them to express their fears and feelings concerning us. Yet, only when we resorted to this distancing technique of leaving the group circle could they reveal themselves. We had come to an impasse beyond which further work could not be done until they could see that reacting to us would not precipitate rejection or criticism of them.

They "wanted more feelings from the therapist," did not like our ending the group at the designated closing time and were uncomfortable with us looking at them. However, they were more comfortable with us when we returned to the group circle. At the end of this meeting Mike asked for a marathon. They were closer the following week, revealing secret, detailed fantasies of their suicides and reactions of others to their deaths and funerals. A few had frequent thoughts of violently beating someone. They were intimate, sharing and supportive, as these sadistic and masochistic feelings emerged.

Silence prevailed at the beginning of the next session, until Mike was smilingly "pissed" at a group member who was going on a trip and would be absent for a few weeks. He felt "deserted and abandoned." When these feelings were related to his past problems, he became evasive and refused to say more. The group was annoyed with him. Lynn cried and screamed that she had been trying to talk but no one was paying any attention to her. This shocked the group. One member hugged her; another cried. Shelley, as usual, was aloof, vague and non-giving. The members stood up and joined hands, making a circle. Shelley was to try to break into the circle. She made pathetic, indifferent attempts to do so. We then put her inside the circle where she made desperate attempts to get out. The group expressed frustration with her. Through the above 4 meetings, the group had an essentially constant composition, which was a new development. All but one still attend the group.

It was interesting to note the *evolution from the drop-in group to the "closed" group*. Obviously, there was an element of chance in this development. Certain members came regularly because of a wish to do so. Only after 5 or 6 months of the drop-in group did they feel irritated and secure enough to actively define the group and indicate a wish for constancy.

Finally, they began to complain about the "drop-in" nature of the group, especially their repeated acceptance and loss of others. They extracted from each other a pledge to attend regularly or to stop coming. A few were unwilling to be firmly committed and chose to stop. Furthermore, the group wished to be closed to all newcomers. Eight members remained after this resolution. One left to pursue individual therapy, also admittedly to avoid her fear of releasing aggressive feelings in the group. Those remaining after all this sifting were the needy, passive-dependent people, who are more comfortable being given to than giving. This was particularly so since each felt that he had little to offer. They also had immense difficulty experiencing anger, generally directing it inward in a chronic, self-destructive manner.

In addition to Mike, Lynn and Shelley, already described, the group included the following members: Andy, a 24-year-old American Indian, who feared he had brain damage from drug abuse. Judy, 16, joined the group because she was "Andy's old lady" and wanted him to get help, but she later admitted to wanting help for herself. Susan was 17 and came to group to "learn to let out my anger." Alisa, 22, the only remaining one of Mike's recruits, initially complained that her boyfriend, with whom she was living, mistreated her and she was fearful of losing him. Andy and Judy dropped out after about 5 months when Judy's anger at Andy became a focus of the group discussion.

ROLE FORMATION

After these 7 individuals had been together for about 5 months, they developed a strong group identity, with consequent individual role formation. *Mike* gloried in the role of provider, leader and innovator by controlling membership (recruiting), seating arrangement (often suggested we move closer, sit on the floor, etc.) and length of time (request for marathon). He also frequently provided transportation for some of the others, thereby gaining a sense of controlling himself through structuring the environment. It was he who often mentioned and feared loss of control. He wanted desperately to be controlled and cared for, thus through reaction formation he did this for others. He sometimes acted superior and arrogant, particularly toward Andy (the only other male), with whom he was in obvious competition. He disarmed others with a winning smile, a flirtatious manner, a seductive voice and twinkling eyes, while softly saying, "Fuck you." In approximately half the sessions he characteristically briefly left the room, particularly if anger or violence was being discussed. He frequently sat next to Alisa and would quickly touch her if he felt anxious, as if to undo the anxiety aroused in him as others discussed aggression. He often giggled to attract attention.

Andy, alternately dense, stupid or profound, was the finder of quick solutions. He inadvertently challenged Mike's position as "leader," getting attention and directing discussion with frank comments, such as "If anyone said that to me I'd fart on them," or "I can just imagine someone full of shit and exploding all over the place," or "I've got pee on my leg, but it's drying. Does anyone else have that problem? I just can't stand there and shake it off all day." He was one of the few group members who frequently encouraged Shelley to participate.

Lynn was the inquisitor and "semi-coleader." She equally interacted with all members and the therapists. She was constantly self-depreciating and focused on the problems of others with many comments about wanting to talk and work. She used the group to displace her transference feelings from the therapist she saw individually to the other therapist. Thus, she was able to ventilate her feelings and discover there would be no untoward consequences. Her fear was that her therapist would reject and abandon her if she revealed herself.

Shelley was the silent one, allegedly through fear. She sat huddled, waiting to be addressed, yet blushed and seemed to become confused if the attention shifted to her. Her silence gained a special place for her, as she was the only one getting frequent, special invitations to talk. In this way people had to prove their interest in her. She was often flushing, and responded to their interest with "that's all" or "I don't have anything else to say."

Alisa was a superior-acting, pseudo-consoler who boasted in presenting herself as having few problems. She had always just solved problems mentioned by others, was invariably just one step ahead of everyone else. She talked of irrelevant topics in detail.

Judy expected to be victimized or to annihilate someone else. She generally alternated between angry pouting and criticizing.

Susan's tactic was to make several incomplete starts on a subject. When the therapists or others responded to this bait, she gained full attention for a detailed non-productive story. She was the extremist, alternating between total silence and complete monopoly and was rarely helpful in any insightful way.

Unlike reports of other adolescent groups, these teen-agers did not try to overcome and defeat the leaders. They seemed to have a *preoccupation with and deference to authority*, reacting in a strangely non-rebellious way. There was a conspicuous near absence of the testing operation described by MacLennan and Felsenfeld (1968): ". . . griping against authority; complaining and blaming others; verbally attacking the leader, directly or indirectly; seeing whether he will permit things which they know are not allowed; trying to use him as a tool against other authorities; trying to make him angry; seducing him into delinquent acts; trying to make him disapprove, proving they cannot trust; trying to get him into a power struggle, where they can defeat him; seeing whether he will betray them; scapegoating and attacking others, seeing if they can drive a member out of the group; testing whether the leader will play favorites or be pushed into defending and protecting the weaker members, thus emphasizing their weakness and infantilizing them."

On the contrary, *they needed to see the therapist as "perfect,"* ideal parent, feeling that they "can't be helped by anyone who isn't perfect." Thinking we were so helped them to distance up, providing an excuse for not directly relating. When we, unfortunately, had to say we were not perfect, they became anxious, partially out of a fear they had the power "to pollute us with their badness." They asked for more structure and response from us, yet were frightened when we reacted as "people."

In the tribalistic organization of this group, *loving feelings were overemphasized and aggression was denied.* We might say they had a communal reaction formation against aggression, modifying each other's anger by often laughing or quickly changing the subject when the anger emerged. Afterwards, they censured, restricted and inhibited the person who had been honest in his expression. All were extremely vulnerable to any supposed critical statements from others, and they were prone to see the most innocuous rmarks this way. All were afraid to respond to each other, lest there be a retaliation. We theorized they projected their critical natures and hostilities onto each other and particularly onto us, then used this as an excuse not to reveal themselves. It was hard to get them to recognize that the difficulties and differences were natural, that they could be concerned for each other and willing to stay with problems to work them out. They clung to the fear that disagreement would destroy the group. MacLennan and Felsenfeld (1968) emphasized that members need repeated reassurance that they will not be permitted to disrupt the group completely. We were definite in giving this reassurance, though it did not give the expected security for many months. Finally they began to change their belief that expression of anger was synonymous with destruction.

Another common resistance was *allowing someone to monopolize*. They took turns, so that no one person traditionally took this role. The monopolizer usually talked about a significant problem but often only wanted to relate to it superficially, saying "I'm not yet ready to face it"; "I don't know what else to say about it" or "there isn't enough time to really get into it." Yet they repeatedly asked for a marathon implying they had important agenda but were afraid to get into their problems and then "be left hanging for a week."

When someone discussed a difficult problem, the others seemed almost vanquished, particularly if they had had similar experiences. They felt burdened, obliged to help the other but utterly impotent. They responded with "I hear you, but I can't do anything to help you," or "what do you want me to do about it?" We agreed with them. They certainly couldn't change the dolorous past; neither should they feel so helpless. We tried to show them the importance and necessity of relating to the person's feelings at the present time. They became better able to do this. The reason for their frustration and sense of impotency became clear; when they related a problem they expected instant cures from the others, so why shouldn't it be reciprocal? They expected themselves to proffer the same remedy. When feeling unable to help each other, they collapsed into an apathetic impotence.

Strikingly, there was a *reluctance to ask personal questions* or to ask for follow-up from other members, even though significant work had been done the previous week and such inquiry seemed warranted. It was as if they were afraid to hear that circumstances had not changed, reaffirming their shared sense of helplessness. Intensifying this was the fear of being expected to make changes after working out a problem. If they didn't ask for follow-up from the others, perhaps they would be shown the same dubious courtesy, thereby avoiding possible chastisement if the tortuous status quo were self-maintained.

Unlike most adolescent groups, they had a *high tolerance for silence and the silent members*. They said they felt "to talk to her was equivalent to attacking her." When someone reacted on a feeling level, the group responded on a concrete, factual level, to distract, lest too much be discovered. They set up cliques outside the group and then tried to use group time to talk unproductively about outside mutual activities. Another resistance was their concern with equality and sharing, so that "everyone would get something from each session." This prevented further exploration in depth for those who were most eager to work. Yet this could have been a feature of their communal way of life. We sensed the need of each individual and his inability to ask. We responded maternally by also feeling "everyone should get something." We were acutely aware of the pervasive, unspoken, subtle vying for recognition. This was partly illustrated by an unspoken pact. If anyone were interacting with the therapist, the others would not interject, lest they "take away some of the milk." Various members intermittently continued to ask for individual therapy; others sought it through the original referring social worker.

At times their *willingness for others in the group to refrain from participation* was marked. They also didn't want to take too much themselves, fearing nothing would remain and the others would hate them. To their own detriment, they understood each other's needs, denying their own. They were not mature enough to see relationships as mutual and reciprocal. At times they used their concern for each other to avoid learning more about themselves. They did not allow drug discussions, feeling this was a waste of time. They seldom spoke of their everyday lives, jobs, school or anything "mundane." It was almost as if they were too desperate to spend time reviewing what they already knew. Their basic feelings of unworthiness demanded prime attention.

Discussion of everyday events was strikingly sparse. In one session which occurred the night following a major earthquake, no one mentioned the earthquake. After the second tremor during the session, one of the therapists felt the need to mention it. The members were displeased that *even here* we would mention "what we have heard about all day!" We did not consider this phenomenon resistance, but rather an indicator of their internal distress and wish not to spend time on external trivialities.

They were stultified by their own terrible feelings about themselves, saying, "If I do this or that, I'm afraid he won't like me." Therefore, "I will behave in a constricted, proper way, to avoid that catastrophe." However, some gradually became more able to express interest in others, acting at times even as a parental superego, disapproving of another's promiscuity, drug taking, self-abuse, etc. Some were able to express kindness, warmth and consideration more freely.

They seemed extraordinarily meek, considering their somewhat reckless, impulsive life styles and often manifest sociopathy. They did not show the normal assertiveness of adolescents who are struggling and rebelling. This was suppressed but emerged self-destructively, disabling them in school, relationships and living conditions. They often changed homes, living from week to week, anchorless, passively searching for meaning. No one talked of college or adult aspirations, with the exception of Alisa, who briefly stated that she would like to get married. They seemed lost, without identity, except for the important identity they gained from being group members, boyfriends or girlfriends. The use of the group as a family seemed at times to make them more afraid to express negative feelings, for fear they might lose whatever they had.

DISCUSSION

We have attempted a description of a group of "hippie-like" adolescents, different, in some respects, from previous groups with whom we had been involved, as well as from some described in the literature. Our therapy could be considered eclectic, with the use of psychoanalytic, encounter, Gestalt and psychodrama techniques. Basically, our goals were to show these people how they set the stage for and participated in many of their own difficulties. As with most schizoid behavior, they acted on expectations in interpersonal relationships, which may have been a useful protective device in their past but which was harmful when used in their current life situation. This behavior precluded knowing others as individuals, as well as receiving acceptance and friendship from them. They all attempted to ostracize themselves from meaningful, mutual personal interactions. While attempting to be physically close (for example, wanting to sit in a small circle, with chairs close and knees almost touching) they were isolated and emotionally separate. We were trying to bring them together in a changed and more secure way. Encounter group techniques were most useful in effecting this.

While previously we had not interfered when they had appeared unresponsive—a facade when frustrated—we began to encourage, then almost to insist they share hitherto secret feelings. We were unable to use these techniques until they had developed a strong group identity and felt accepted by us, i.e., they did not get the criticism they feared. When we had tried these methods earlier, they withdrew, became confused or intellectualized. After the formation of a stronger identity, we searched for the truth when we sensed someone was hiding a response. Later, the group members took over this function, with the resultant marked increase in emotional responsiveness and interest in each other. They moved from seeing interest in one another as an "attack" to seeing it as sincere interest. We also strove to help them lessen their diffuse self-destructive aggression, by increasing their self-esteem.

Their need to express anger appeared less urgent than the wish to be cared for and to have affiliative feelings. Suppressed anger had become a looming obstacle, which hindered their receiving security and support from each other. The increase in responsiveness among participants, described above, was directly related to their *increasing ability to show negative reactions and anger without fear.*

There were additional important aspects of doing therapy with this group. We had to be flexible and innovative in helping these people to mobilize themselves toward positive changes. This involved varying our techniques with the situation and using a more active therapeutic approach than is used in the usual "neurotic" group. Their directionless lives were dramatically highlighted in their directionless group attitude in the earlier sessions. Only with prompting, support and active guidance from us were they able to interact and grow in the group. In working with this type of person, we had to curb our expectation of quick changes in their everyday world. We also needed to avoid being over zealous as those who remained after the sifting process of the "drop-in" group were primarily passive-dependent and easily frightened. This was in contrast to the apparent needs of those "drop-ins," who wanted "crisis treatment" and individual psychotherapy. We came to doubt the value of a "drop-in" group when it became apparent that the three "core" group members, who had wanted an ongoing involvement, did not really talk about their problems until we stopped having "drop-ins." They needed the comfort, security and personal relationships of the more stable type of group.

A LAST LOOK AT THE MEMBERS' STATUS

Mike's intellectual passive stance became more active as sadness, loneliness, even feelings of happiness repeatedly came forth. Despite an ever ready rationalization, he could stop, focus and feel, with help from the group. He began to move toward initiating changes in outside relationships rather than just believing he was victimized.

Alisa, the most verbal in the group, related primarily by reciting activities or conversations with her boyfriend. Following an intensive session, in the

9th month, revealing a distorted idealization of and symbiosis with her boyfriend, she began the process of individuation leading to self-identity. In the remaining months, she recounted her extra group experiments in self-mastery and definition. These helped liven the other members, who gradually informed us of their progress outside of group.

Susan had been involved in an incestuous relationship with her stepfather. He was jailed. She went to live with her real father for "guidance and protection." Through exploration of her soon obvious incestuous motivation for living with her possessive, jealous father, she managed to leave him and return to live with her mother. Inappropriate affect continued to surround this area and further work is needed.

Lynn blossomed outside of group, becoming totally self supporting, enjoyed her artistic talent and regained her self-respect. These major changes were minimally revealed to the group by increased questioning of others, eye contact, attentiveness, criticism and compliments to the therapist.

Shelley had returned to school on a regular basis. Yet, she remained essentially unchanged in the group, retaining the title "the silent member."

REFERENCES

BERNE, ERIC, (1966). Principles of Group Treatment. New York, Grove Press, Inc.

CRUTCHER, ROBERTA (1961). The Usefulness of Group Therapy with Character Disorders. *International Journal Group Psychotherapy*, XI, 431-439.

PERLS, FREDERICK, S. (1969). Gestalt Therapy Verbatim. California, Real People Press.

JOHNSON, JAMES A., JR. (1963). Group Therapy: A Practical Approach. New York, McGraw-Hill.

MACLENNAN, BERYCE W. & FELSENFELD, NAOMI (1968). Group Counseling and Psychotherapy with Adolescents. New York, Columbia University Press.

ROSENBAUM, MAX, & BERGER, MILTON, eds. (1963). Group Psychotherapy and Group Function. New York, Basic Books.

SLAVSON, S. R. (1964). A Textbook in Analytic Group Psychotherapy. New York, International University Press.

YALOM, IRVIN (1970). Theory and Practice of Group Psychotherapy. New York, Basic Books.

CHAPTER 9

Activating a Group of Passive Boys

Harold B. Enns, M.D., and
Irving H. Berkovitz, M.D.

OCCASIONALLY A PARTICULAR GROUP of youngsters has qualities in common which can impede the beginning interaction in a group. Such a situation might occur in a group of primarily shy, inhibited, or passive boys, especially in an outpatient setting. In this situation, sorely taxed, frustrated therapists may well feel the need to employ a variety of procedures, or parameters, in the hope of activating the discussion, and facilitating the therapeutic process. On the other side, the careful therapist would wish to avoid whimsical and abruptly introduced parameters.

This paper presents the description of a group where the therapists did feel this need to activate the pace of the group interaction. The group consisted initially of four young men, 16-17 years old, all approaching the senior year in high school. The group sessions, one hour-fifteen minutes in duration, took place around a large table. The members sat at one end and the two male therapists* sat at the other end. The first parameter was introduced in the first session. The therapists explained that films or tapes would be used for the first half of each session, "to stimulate discussion,

---

*The therapists were the senior author and Frank S. Williams, M.D. Dr. Williams is currently Senior Psychiatrist, Dept. of Child Psychiatry, Cedars-Sinai Medical Center. The group described here was one of the early groups in the group therapy program at the Thallian Clinic, Cedars-Sinai Medical Center, Los Angeles.

122

since it was often difficult for adolescents to start talking together in such a group." (In retrospect, this statement may have added to any difficulty which might have occurred anyway.) Part of the stimulus for this parameter came from an experience with an earlier group, where the therapist felt that the silences had not been useful and had been poorly tolerated.

The therapists used well-known mental health films, "The Angry Boy" and "A Family Affair." There were some sophisticated criticisms, as well as discussion of the concepts and attitudes in the films. Because the members objected and because sufficient numbers of films were unavailable, the therapists then introduced recorded readings from J. D. Salinger's book, *The Catcher in the Rye*. It was the therapists' impression that very quickly Holden Caulfield, the hero of the book, took over almost as peer leader in the group. He was able to express the group's feelings in peer language, so that there was a disinhibiting effect.

These readings took up the first 30 to 35 minutes of six sessions, and covered about half the book. The subject matter of this part of the book covered several age-appropriate issues: 1) various phases of group life were brought out in the experiences in the boarding school, 2) there was a fairly rich description of oedipal ties in relation to some of the older women discussed in the book, 3) the highly sexual description of the visit to New York opened the door for the exploration of many heterosexual and homosexual topics.

After six sessions, the group discussed the issue of whether or not to continue use of these recordings. In a sense, this could be regarded as an attempt to depose the artificial leader and have someone in the group take over this function. It was probably more than coincidental that the first member of the group to show a tendency to take over this function was Jim, who had had the experience of an early, partial oedipal victory in his own family. The other three members of the group readily agreed with him that the use of recordings should stop and that they should have all the time to talk with each other.

For several subsequent sessions, then, Jim did a great deal of the talking. He had recently terminated individual therapy (with another therapist) and conceivably still needed to speak out some of his anger and pain surrounding separation from this therapist. Much of his talking was directed toward the therapists, in an attempt to establish an individual therapy relation with them. As well as being more useful for Jim, this also set the example for a more interactive discussion between the members of the group. After about 25 sessions, there did develop a greater degree of interchange. Whether this might have developed without the initially presented material is speculative. Possibly, the material helped to mobilize Jim's assertiveness, since he had known another kind of relationship, where he had been the more active.

A second change now occurred. New members were introduced. This was discussed in the group for several weeks and opened up many sibling issues for the boys. George, who had been very silent up to this point, talked of how he felt at age 6, when his younger brother had been adopted. Following this, his previous objections to having members added disappeared. He gave an interesting statement of his narcissism when he was able to say that he did not feel so much that he lost his parents at this point, but rather he felt that 'they lost me."

The idea of having girls as the new members was discussed in the group. This aroused a flurry of issues and, initially, resistance from the boys. One point mentioned in favor of the idea of having girls come into the group was the possibility of being able to date them. This naturally opened the subject of dating and the matter of the boys' possible lack of aggressiveness toward girls.

A third coincidental change now occurred. It was decided that one male therapist* would withdraw from the group to be replaced by a female co-therapist, at the same time that the girls entered the group. Preparation had already been made for this change by the less active participation of the withdrawing therapist and by occasional absences on his part. This change produced dramatic reactions. Jack, whose family had been disturbed by one of its members' leaving under unhappy circumstances, brought up many fantasies equating death and separation. George became convinced he would never see the departing therapist again, despite reassurance that the therapist was not leaving the clinic. After this, George had a dissociative reaction on the way home from school one day. His mother found him walking home, not knowing where he had been or what had happened to him. He quickly recovered from this and was able to accept interpretations pointing out his underlying separation anxiety.

A week before the girls joined the group, a student social worker entered as co-therapist. She was accepted quite readily by the group, although there were still numerous references to the previous therapist's absence and some fantasies that she had aggressively replaced him. The group continued henceforth with four boys and three girls. The boys' very solid commitment to the group was not shaken, apart from some occasional latenesses. The

---

* Frank Williams, M.D.

girls, however, experienced difficulty in integrating themselves into the group. It may well have been that they were at a disadvantage, coming into an already cohesive group.

It did become much easier for the boys to discuss sexual issues in the now heterosexual group. Possibly, homosexual fears had interfered with more active interaction, initially. In this mixed group, there was more opportunity for a realistic exploration of sexual attitudes, with opposite sex members available to give some answers. The boys frequently attacked the girls for what are generally considered acceptable narcissistic expressions on the part of girls. This attack diminished to some extent when the boys were reminded of a previous discussion, in which they envied the social acceptability of certain female narcissistic expression. Perhaps more than coincidentally, following this some of the boys did let their hair grow longer.

A surprising development was that the boys who had been most passive before the girls came, behaved quite aggressively with the girls, while continuing to avoid conflict with the other boys in the group. This allowed greater insight into the sources of their passivity, especially as it related to aggressiveness toward other men. The struggle for leadership in the group became more complex. There appeared to be a contest for leadership between Diane, one of the more verbal girls, and Jim, who had been the early leader in the group. In some ways this situation reminded many of the group members of marital conflicts that they had observed between their parents. The matter of whether either the man or the woman should carry the authority at home was discussed.

In summary, this paper discusses some of the experiences in an adolescent group which ran for about a year. For the first nine months, the group consisted of four boys. In the last three months, three girls were added. It appeared that the introduction of films and recordings in the initial sessions was of some help in the stimulating and the establishment of strong group leadership and interaction. In the later phases of the group, the introduction of several changes definitely helped to initiate meaningful discussions of vital issues. One of the most significant changes was the addition of girls. This experience, as well as reflecting the difficult flow of interaction in a group of passive boys, may reflect the inadvisability of forming an outpatient group of only boys.

CHAPTER 10

"Playing It by Ear," in Answering the Needs of a Group of Black Teen-Agers

Dana B. Stebbins, M.S.W.

ADOLESCENCE IS SUCH a difficult time for most. How satisfying it must be to have parents who are cognizant of this, and who can offer appropriate resources to help deal with these times.

The group we'll be talking about is without those resources, without the cognizance of caring parents. They are, at the beginning, almost totally unaware of the helping process known to us as therapy. They may, of course, have some vague conception of a scholarly man with a pipe, in whose office you lie on a couch, and for fifty dollars an hour learn that you have problems with your father, your sexuality, things like that. We must then, begin with the reality that we will need to adapt our clinical skills in some way to bring closer to these boys and girls the experience of group psychotherapy.

I first came to the agency where I am now employed exactly one week after I moved to Los Angeles to live for the first time. I realized during my first weeks there how little I knew about the community in which I worked. This disturbed me, for I wondered how I could be effective in my work with the patients of this area without knowing anything about the realities of their living environment. About this same time, a colleague discussed with me her concern about the lack of positive activity available for youth in the area. It was then that I decided to set aside time to meet the area's residents, and to attempt to get a view of their thoughts and feelings and life style.

I began by walking the streets. I found many of the residents, young and old, justifiably skeptical about my motives in coming into their neighborhood. However, I focused my efforts on mental health education about the service where I worked and its use as a resource for the community. I also visited recreation centers and playgrounds, where I found many idle youths spending their free time. After about three and a half weeks of regular appearances in the neighborhood, people began to talk to me as a friend. I began to learn a great deal about the problems, the joys, the frustrations, and the satisfactions of living in this area. I was finally introduced by a mother in the area to her 15-year-old daughter, who was having trouble in school. I believe this meeting to be the turning point and the key factor in my efforts to reach the youth in this community. By becoming a trusted friend of this young lady, I gained the opportunity to meet many other youngsters also living in the neighborhood. I then made it a regular part of my weekly schedule to visit with these youngsters and listen to their thoughts and feelings. I was tested frequently about the use of the information I was gaining, and I suppose it was only after passing this test that I was asked to come to a meeting of a neighborhood social club, where the request was made of me to give regular planned assistance to the group. I sensed that this was an important test. This was the test to determine my sincerity. Would I offer my assistance and be of some real use to the area's residents, or would I, as others had, use them for my own benefit and information? I responded by asking them to call a meeting of all the youths in the area who were interested in receiving some kind of assistance from me. I stated that I hoped at this meeting we could talk about just what they wanted and just what I was prepared to offer.

The meeting was held. They wanted to know about me. Who am I? What's on my mind? What am I going to do? Why am I working for "the system"? Often, with difficulties with authority figures contributing largely to their adjustment problems, these teen-agers spontaneously react negatively to any person they see as an authority. They wondered: Am I on the same side as the other authority figures? Am I closer to their parents who usually don't know and sometimes don't care about them? So *they strive to qualify me*. Will I have a direct bearing on their future? Can I seriously affect their lives? Can I do them any good? My response is that I'd like to help them in any way they like. They'll need to examine me closely and to give some thought to the possibilities of forming a group. If they find this unacceptable, then I'll quit. I use no words about "patient," "therapy," "group psychotherapy," etc. It's harder for me to explain the helping process without using these words, but it's necessary. These young adults have no true conception of the process of therapy. Using those terms may only confuse some of them, and surely "turn off" most of them.

Many people are reluctant to ask the girls in this group a question requiring a straight answer. If they do, they don't expect to get one. I do. I expect them to tell me by the end of this first session whether they're with me or not. If they're not sure, they are free to wait until they've made up their minds. But wait outside of the group; don't come to the group meetings and "play a game." It is through the simplicity of this confrontation that we arrive at a fundamental understanding of each other. "I've heard many of you have problems. I'd like to help; I think I can. You can either admit some problems, or offer to come until you're able to admit some. It is not acceptable to cop out, to say, 'I'm here because the principal says I must receive some sort of help or be suspended,' or 'I have no other choice.'" I offer companionship and friendship to start, hopefully, later, insight and help in alleviating difficult conditions. I won't quit on them as long as they want something and need it, but I won't force anything on them either.

Through this somewhat relentless, very direct process, we managed to work through the *establishment of trust,* a crucial issue in the first session especially, but also in many of the subsequent sessions.

Then there are the "who are you?" type questions. "Can we call you Dana instead of Mrs. Stebbins?" "Where is your house, where do you live?" This may be an identifying symbol of where I am on the social status. "Do you live in Inglewood, West Los Angeles, or Watts, or Compton?" and "If you do, do you have a house, or an apartment? Do you own your own car?" These questions are status-oriented. They don't mean, "Can I come and see you?" The needy youngsters may get to that eventually. But others are trying to put me into some place, like I've been to college. That automatically says to them, "She's up there someplace! But, just where is she?"

Now where do we go after we've made the commitment, or signed "the contract," so to speak? The girls who singled themselves out initially talked briefly about school problems, boyfriend problems, family problems, but there was very little depth to our discussion. I must begin by considering their verbal ability. These young women don't use standard English. They don't speak it, and they don't conceptualize in its terms. Some observers say they are handicapped "in verbal aptitude." I do not see it this way. This group of Black people, poor people, communicates differently than other Americans, but not less capably. Thus I expect and find less of the

verbal communication and interpretation characteristic of group psychotherapy. We begin, nonetheless, by talking. I truly believe that the "glue"
holding our group together at this time was the "realness" of our relationships. They found neither contempt, nor massive acceptance. They were
able to be themselves. I was able to say, "I can't dig that" about some
part of their behavior without labeling that behavior wrong. I hope to help
establish an atmosphere where each of us can be honest about ourself and
others in the group without giving in to the need to judge one another's
behavior. It is this kind of atmosphere we struggled to maintain, and which
prompted each girl to critically examine her behavior and her own fear
of life choices.

Towards the *middle of the process,* with this framework for the group
sessions, I began to notice personal satisfaction as members reached towards
resolution of conflict. We talked about reality-based problems such as poor
housing, crowded living conditions, scholastic deficiencies. We talked about
the psychological basis for much of their behavior (promiscuity, drug usage,
chronic truancy). We strove to differentiate between learned patterns of
antisocial behavior which could be changed if so desired and behavior
symptomatic of deep seated conflicts which could be changed maybe only
after examination and understanding of these conflicts. We looked at role
models, at me. I've struggled to keep from becoming an idol. I believe, and
hope to help them to see, that my life style is but one of many. It is not the
ideal. I do not want to be the symbol of The Black Woman who "made it."
I feel that by doing this one runs the risk of allowing a subtle kind of
value judgment to creep into the group value system: "TO SUCCEED AND
BE A GOOD PERSON, YOU MUST TAKE A, B, C, D STEPS."

Depending on the age group, the girls are often looking for not a role
model but somebody who can become a significant other person in their life
because they are lacking the older mother, older sister, aunt, with whom
they can have just friendship and closeness. We were able to incorporate
the philosophy that the lives of one set of people have no more validity
than the lives of another. What's important is to be able to have some
choice about your life; to be able to weigh alternatives, to think things
through, and to make choices which satisfy us and those who matter to us.
For example, there was Vivien, age 13, who was extremely promiscuous.
She's never been pregnant, but she'd had venereal disease so many times
that we can't even remember how many times now. In one session, the group
members started joking and laughing, which had become a symbol that
they're getting ready to get into something pretty deep, and they would

like me to be aware of it. They frequently started off with, "She's breaking
the school record" . . . then there would be the joking. At this session somebody's comment hit Vivien. She said, "If I could get attention any other
way, I would, don't you think I would?" The whole room got quiet. Vivien
continued, "If I could be maybe an A student, or an athlete, or a cheer-
leader, then I could get to be a teacher, or a psychiatrist." And I said, "Why
couldn't you just be a girl who didn't just jump into bed with every fellow,
but when you did, you were good at it, and you didn't catch VD." They
looked at me. I don't want them to think that their road is a bad road, and
that the only way to get their lives straightened out is to make a complete
switch and go in the entire opposite direction. Just being a therapist doesn't
give one the option to establish a scale for priorities of life styles. It's
just bad to have VD because you're sick and because this isn't a consequence
one relishes.

Vivien started the discussion very puzzled, saying, "Well, why would
you say that?" I started off with, "What does VD do to you?" And, she
said what it does to her. "Does it make you feel good?" "No, it makes me
feel bad." "Do the fellows like you afterwards?" "No, they don't like me
afterwards." "Do you enjoy sex?" "Yes, I enjoy sex." "Would you like to
have one man, or a couple of men?" "Well, a couple, I'm not ready to settle
down." She'd answered her own thing. She didn't want VD. She didn't want
especially to be promiscuous, but she didn't want to have a boyfriend, at
the moment, and be the little "true-blue" type girl. So, there I was. She
wasn't asking to be Miss Puritan, nurse or missionary, or whatever. She
was asking just for a way out of the situation she was in at the moment,
which would be a little more acceptable to herself and others. This is not
a ventilation group, this is an action-oriented group. The repetitive question, "What are you going to do about it?" which follows any serious revelation of a difficult situation helps keep it that way. I think there are many
well meaning, but off-target helpers working with people in this socio-
economic group who see a dead end in offering therapy when there is vir-
tually no hope of improving the environment impinging upon these individuals. They are horrified and gravely concerned about the "misery," the
poverty, "the stigma of being a member of a minority group."

I reject that attitude! I despise it! Let's look at the realities. Most of the
people with whom I work have very little chance of moving out of their
social strata. They may improve the sanitation of their houses or neighborhoods, acquire a car, or get a stable (not high paying) job, but their life
styles, the socio-economic status, the roles they are assigned by the rest

of society are not, for the most part, going to change. Thus, to reinforce the feeling that they are living sub-anything from anyone else is gravely detrimental to their whole self-image! What I try to do, and what I feel anyone who wishes to work effectively with oppressed groups, especially youth, must do is to say, "Yes, part of your life experience is difficult. It could be better in terms of self-satisfaction, but there is a lot there. You're not sub-anything. You're *different* from other people. You live a *different* life style than other people."

I don't think you can afford to reinforce in any way the feeling that they are below somebody else, because then they constantly fall into a thing of using that as an excuse. "I can't achieve because I live in this neighborhood." "I can't do this because I haven't so much money." "I can't get a job because I graduated from such and such a school rather than such and such another school." I don't want to do that, so I say, "Yes, you're different, I'm different. But different is no worse or no better. Different is just different." The trap here for the therapist may be giving in to the guilt that one may feel about having come from a different life style, or being college educated and somehow a step removed. You're never going to be exactly like your patients, I don't care who it is you're seeing. To want to overidentify with them, or jump on a cause, gets the roles messed up.

Then there is the *naive defense.* They also may play the game of the little wide-eyed innocents in the beginning. I tell them, "Don't hand me all that crap." They ask me little, stupid questions, like, "If you feel two pulses on your neck, does that mean you're pregnant, when you feel more than one pulse?" Now, that's absurd? For these girls a question like that is absurd. They know all the ways of telling they're pregnant, and this is not one of them. They just like to "put me on." They do that to anybody who's from the outside. They want to know where you are, really where you are. "Are you really hep?" Do you just throw around the terminology, or do you really know what their life style is all about. I could have spent hours saying, "Well, I don't know. Do you feel two pulses? What does it feel like?" It would have been a long discussion and, afterwards, they would have had a big laugh, and I might have widened the distance between us.

About this time a *definite communication system and group structure* began to emerge. The girls, like most poor people who are in contact frequently with public agencies, at first felt very little for the concept of confidentiality. Unfortunately, privacy is not one of their life's demands. Week after week people in the neighborhood would make comments to me about our group discussions. We worked on that for awhile. Part of the problem was that the girls lived in the same apartment complex and it was rather difficult for them to separate group "business" from the day-to-day social "business" which still confronted them.

As the girls worked on learning to keep the content of our sessions out of their lives for the rest of the week, I gave a great deal of thought to ways in which I might help them. I thought it especially important because, if accomplished, it would help them understand the therapeutic process better. I decided to experiment by suggesting to the girls that we hold work sessions (analytic, verbal therapy) only every two weeks with only half of the total group. They liked the idea and decided to try it. One of the girls who was fantastic with numbers worked out a rotation system where there were five girls in one work group and four in the other. However, every three weeks a different girl replaced one of the original members. This way, each member had the opportunity to interact with each of the other members in a work session for at least three weeks. The remainder of the month, the entire group participated in activities, taking trips, etc. We've gone to plays, read books, held psychodrama sessions and experiential sessions. We found that, by separating "therapy" from other group activities, we provided the closure, the specialness necessary for effective psychotherapy. The "non-work" sessions also helped build interpersonal skills, coping skills, and assertive techniques which many youths in this socio-economic bracket lack. The combination of both in a rotation system provided a nonthreatening place to unload, with the freedom for each individual to choose the exact time, and still feel very much a part of the group process.

We have, at this moment, been meeting for eight months. Our original contract calls for ten. Recently, the girls and I have begun to share our satisfactions in reaching individual and group goals. It appears that this group will end in June as planned. We will remain friends, and I anticipate a great deal of continued informal communication. But what we had set out to do has, to a large degree, been done.

These are now more confident, more aware, less hostile girls. They are willing to risk being independent. They are committed to governing their own lives. And I am closer to youth, and totally enthusiastic about the burgeoning potential of working with youth in spontaneous creative ways. I urge those who feel that same enthusiasm to come on in—the water's fine!

CONCLUSIONS

1. Adolescents who are completely unaware of the process known as "therapy" can learn the "patient" role as easily as many other people in-

volved in psychotherapy. For those youngsters whose emotional problems are compounded by reality problems, it is better to curtail this. It is not advisable to encourage ventilation and insight production as the sole purpose for group activity. It is more rewarding for both adolescent and therapist to place primary emphasis on action *resulting* from an intrapsychic focus. There can also be some experiential recreational, social, and informational values to groups for teen-agers.

2. Persons whose value systems and cultural patterns do not emphasize the importance of time can, perhaps, better be reached by working within time periods natural to them. A semester, a quarter, is often good for students. Learning to structure and use periods of time is easier when using elements of time familiar to them.

3. Crisis-prone people can be reached most effectively when they are in crisis, and by going to them to offer service. This requires somewhat regular contact (outside of the office) with the population served.

4. Not always, but many times, in a minority community, the peer group or the neighborhood group is a stronger group than the family group. This peer group then becomes a more natural group with which to work. In this way, the individual appears to be more able to satisfy his needs and build the skills he lacks. The transition of these skills to other groups and to non-group life situations appears to be facilitated by working with whatever group is natural.

5. Privacy and closure are especially important in working with youths whose day-to-day lives bring them in constant contact with each other. For psychotherapy to have any value, or to be respected at all as a helping process, it must allow for this privacy.

6. A therapist offering help to a group of oppressed adolescents must have more to offer than his clinical skills. Commonality of background, life style, or mode of communication helps greatly. But if just as one human being who has some realistic perception of the pitfalls encountered by other human beings, you must offer something for these young men and women to hold on to. You must extend yourself, your time, and your mind. This increases greatly your chances of receiving reciprocal sincerity.

CHAPTER 11

"Two Gray Cats Learn How It Is" in a Group of Black Teen-Agers

Charles O'Shea, M.S.W.

THE FOLLOWING ARTICLE and epilogue describe three years of work with eight young men who were delinquent, drop-outs, from disrupted homes, and Negro. The word Negro is used last because of many complex conditions which contributed to massive displacement of human resources and talent with these young men. Each knew his share of human tragedy, each could feel for another person, each worked hard to change his "bag" and each dealt with the human problem of attempting to change human patterns. With the changed emphases and events in Black-White relations (especially in Berkeley), perhaps this group experience is important as an example of an experience that could have taken place only in the middle sixties. Fixed thus in time though it will be, still there are certain timeless lessons derived.

The remarks which follow and any learning that anyone can take from these comments are due to the work done by Brooklyn, David, Eddie, George, Raymond, Robert, Jerry and Junie, and that of the therapists. We believe the work was very successful.

Let us start with the final meeting in January, 1967. The atmosphere was relaxed as Eddie and George, awaiting induction into the Army, and

Done at School of Social Welfare, University of California, Berkeley, California. The first cotherapist was Hubert Coffey, Ph.D.

Judy and Chuck, the therapists at that time, joked and recalled how it all started, who said what, and when. Eddie said, "These two cats, gray studs from the University, came down to offer "discussions" at Cal., and we stood 'em up, and we tried to shock them. And it lasted this long, Christ, three years, and without it, I don't know where the hell I'd have been." Several of the original members moved away at the end of the first year. The remaining eight stayed for approximately the full three-year run.

In the beginning, each member of the group was in attendance at a continuation high school, a special part-time school for high school drop-outs. Of the eight members who stayed in the group, one later enrolled in junior college and received tutoring through the University. Five joined the Army, specifically to make themselves eligible for the G.I. Bill of Rights. Two boys graduated from the high school in the city in which the group experiment was conducted. This indicated functional change from "school drop-out" to "school drop-in" for three members, and career choices with educational goals via the Army for others. Above and beyond this was the growth in pride in themselves. Each recognized some of what he could do and how far he had to go, and developed an approach to life that was more flexible and workable.

Both therapists were white. All group members were Negro. It is our opinion that the race of the therapist was not a crucial issue to the success or failure of the work. The race or personality of the therapist became grist for the mill of the group process. Problems arose and were viewed as resistance to the therapeutic work and as part of the non-trust transference. As any experienced clinician knows, a true therapeutic relationship is difficult to establish for anyone. No histories were taken except as they evolved in the process. Attention was on the here-and-now transaction and extended to exploration of history as such exploration became needed in context.

The start of the group was, therefore, very informal. The word was passed along through the Dean of Boys at the continuation high school that two men from the University of California Psychology Clinic would offer a discussion group if a number of students were interested. There was some screening done by the Dean of Boys. He stated, "Well, I will not give you 'our worst,' but, at the same time, neither will I give you 'our best.'" So, some place between "our best" and "our worst," the selection for this group was made.

Twelve boys met for our first interview in the basement of the continuation high school. The therapists introduced themselves to all the boys and stated that they were here to propose a discussion group at the University of California Clinic to help with the school "foul-ups" that had forced them to the continuation high school. Specific, pointed questions were raised with each boy as to what "foul-ups" he had experienced. This was a pointed start and began with the admission that being at continuation school was not good. It implicitly recognized that they might wish to change, and, should they, we would offer discussion as a way that might help them to figure out a better deal. Each "volunteer" was specifically asked in the first and subsequent sessions what it is that got him in trouble and what he wanted for himself. *"Where do you want to be in five years?"* is a confronting, rather provocative question that was used. This question served to focus the work by getting each member of the group to define his aspirations for himself. The answers were later used, within the group, to point up resistance to work toward the goals. When resistance occurred, i.e., when the horseplay got too thick, anyone of us could then say, "Hey, what has this got to do with where you want to be in five years?" It was an effective technique.

It was very important to be blunt and "gut" honest. Things got bantered and joined rapidly. One did not make this social, nor did one use the fish-eyed approach to "the patients." One must relate with the therapeutic prejudice from the start. Students trained in their idea of the psychoanalytic model were quite shocked by the technique when observing. It started with relationship treatment and only later became uncovering.

The following week a frightened, loud, noisy group of ten boys burst upon the Psychology Clinic. "Burst upon the Psychology Clinic" is not an overstatement! The boys arrived, loud-voiced, running up and down the hall, popping in and out of classrooms or interview rooms, picking up the phone, putting it down. The group brought almost frantic activity to the place where they were going to be treated for "craziness." The early anxiety and extreme activity had to do with the fact that this was a psychology clinic and "these guys were going to psych you out, get down on your case, and find out how crazy you are." These particular constellations of feelings are brought to any therapy situation by any patient. It is just that this particular group of patients graphically and intensely acted out their anxiety.

We found the first problem. Should we try to change or directly forbid this kind of behavior? One professor noted after his class had been "raided," "You haven't quite gotten them University-broke yet, have you?" The point was that the therapists decided not to attempt to "break" them to the decorum that is usually acceptable in a University clinic. Instead, each person connected with the clinic who was to have contact with the boys was encouraged to say to any boy exactly what he wanted, or believed indicated. As a result, the head of the clinic would enter upon the scene and ask for quiet in the halls. The secretary would say, "No, I will not, and will you please hang up the phones." The role of the therapists was to treat the encounters, when mentioned in the group, by saying, "Well, what do you expect? Where is your social awareness? Didn't you think that this kind of thing would happen if you acted that way?" This, in turn, was interpreted, or questioned, "Where is your radar with people? Why aren't you thinking ahead?"

The resistance was high and attacking. Derisive shouts greeted any therapist's comment. Mimicking of the two therapists accompanied the noise. Any specific comments by therapists were denied. However, bit by bit, the behavior in the clinic became more mature and markedly modified. The clinic became a home to many of these boys. They would come to the clinic, sit in the waiting room, join the graduate students in the coffee room, and use it as a kind of special settlement house. The group, in twos and threes, explored the University: the first stop was the gymnasium, additional stops were the various restaurants and gathering places for the college students, and, over the three-year period, individuals began to take on a college-like identity. By the end of three years, the new role of "college student" had been adopted. Now they all hoped for advanced education. The clinic became home away from home during its open hours.

Two visiting experienced therapists observed the beginning sessions. Their comments were mainly directed at the tremendous hostility demonstrated at everything by the group. Questions such as, "How do you take it?" characterized their remarks. Later hostile outbreaks were limited by the group itself. But the question, "How do you take it?" is of interest. First, one must answer what is "it." The anger was there, but it was a form of relating. It was not real. It was called "Bogarting," and was part of a way of life that lets fly and doesn't mean much. "It" is hectic but the kids were weaned on "it." "It" tore the hell out of an identity.

The next answer had to do with "take." We did not feel we were personally "taking" anything. It was part of the process. At a deeper level, all the therapists knew their own anger pretty well and were not too worried about it.

The therapists fell into two stances intuitively. One therapist took the role of questioning the group interaction, asking how this one felt about what that one had said, wondering why Junie or Moose or somebody had very little to say, in effect encouraging them to look at their participation per se. The other therapist developed group process around whatever was presented in session. He asked others what the group felt about a topic, asked what they thought, what they would do, generally *calling for the group to consider the actions of others as representing actions of themselves.* He questioned when were they going to get serious, and whether they would or not. It was about three months before the transference became verbalized. The therapist who concentrated on the interaction, person-to-person, was referred to as "Dr. Creepy." He was always writing down names, or writing down notes, and there was a great deal of wonderment as to what he did with these magic words that he put on his note paper. The other therapist was seen as "The Swinger." He was hep; he knew what the jive was. He could understand, and was more or less "with it." There was a question as to whether these "gray cats" could possibly understand.

The group proceeded in a rather random fashion, only sometimes serious, until about the *fifth month*. Then we had a *crisis*. Eddie had been in a fight in the streets. He and a partner had been attacked by a group of twenty-year-olds, pushed around and told to "get your ass out of town before you're going to get killed." He came to the group session frightened and agitated, and sought partners to "go down with him to get 'em." This, in turn, made for a tense first forty minutes as Eddie would question from one to another as to who would go with him, and where they could meet, and what they would carry, knives, chains, etc. He was frantically trying to develop his allies when he turned to one of the more quiet, withdrawn members of the group, who responded: "I am very afraid to say what I am going to say. I have to say it. I am not going down with you. You got yourself into this mess, you get yourself out. I am afraid to say this. I'm afraid what you're going to do. I'm afraid to say no. But I have to say what I say." This was greeted by Eddie with a direct, hostile, calling out, "I'm going to beat your ass right now, or as soon as session is over." He went on taking him apart verbally, up one side and down the other, at which time the "Swinger" therapist entered and raised the question, in an interpretative, confronting way, that Eddie was perhaps really more afraid than anyone else. This was turned down silently by the group. Then, Eddie said, "Yes, that's where it's at. I am scared stiff." After he had said this, each member of the group mentioned how afraid he was and now they were able to talk as a group about how they didn't want to fight at all. They wanted to avoid it if it was at all possible. The question was then introduced by the therapist that perhaps the other gang was equally afraid. He went back and examined the content of the original fight, and Eddie changed his story quite noticeably, bringing out his provocativeness. It was finally decided among the group that the fight could be avoided, that it really ought to be avoided. Eddie was "rapping" to get partners because he felt that he needed them, but this wasn't the answer, and this was the end of the "fight." Now the group was able to recognize that this was the first "gift" of treatment: that resolution is one of the aims of discussion, that this is the "good stuff" of coming to the psych clinic. And so, the "gift" was known, the goal was felt, and we were able to return to this process for resolution of trouble.

Another crisis followed. The boys, in their wanderings around the University campus, had become conspicuous. They did not look like University students, the dress was exaggerated, the "process" jobs on the hair were extreme, they had an extreme "thug" appearance. One day, three of the boys arrived a few minutes late to the group therapy session to be followed immediately by a uniformed University policeman and an off-duty, part-time University student policeman, who sought to protect the integrity of the alma mater. It was a general roust. The police were immediately ushered out by the therapists, at which time the matter was turned back to the group for discussion. The boys, in effect, took it passively. This kind of thing happens all the time. It always will happen. Both therapists verbalized that they were furious, that this shouldn't happen, that the therapists will make sure it won't happen. The police here, at least, cannot float in to question without specific charges. This anger and defense of the group by the therapists later proved to be crucial in the formation of deeper trust. This intervention, in which the righteous anger of the therapists was visible, was taken by the group as a second meaningful "gift." One can leave interpretation of its significance to the reader.

Both of these phenomena gave the opportunities for intervention that occur by chance in any treatment situation. Had Eddie not gotten into a fight, had the policeman not come into the therapy room, it would have been a longer time before the group got serious. But *these crises expedited two things*: (1) the self-realization and self-resolution that were possible, and (2) the good faith and deep trust which resulted. After this, "Dr. Creepy" and "The Swinger" became Chuck and Hugh, who were treaters, the group leaders of discussion, and a group bond was shared.

And so the group got serious. Bit by bit we spun out the historic, dynamic information. The interpersonal roles and statuses began to stand out in sharp relief. No information was gathered except as it appeared in context. To us, this is the meaningful way to catch the attitudinal constellation and parameters that accompany a fact of a father's departure, a mother's illness, the death of a brother, or being dumped from school.

To an extent, the account which follows is classic for any good working group; however, the intensity of the emotion struck us. A boy doesn't have a fight, he has a violent epic. He doesn't love, he has his nose open and it's painful. He doesn't get depressed. He gets so blue and so "up-tight." It's as if every feeling he has is experienced rawly, vividly, intensely—the joys, the sorrows, the loves, losses, the disappointments of life cut very hard, cut very deep. The happy moments of life are grabbed at frantically. "Catch it now before it's gone" becomes the mode. You appear charming, attractive, humorous, but border on panic and desperation.

Technically, we employed good teacher models to deal with the tremendous amount of superstition and the vast misinformation upon which these boys were building their lives. It was fantastic! Talk of white witches, owners of Africa, myths, and all sorts of misinformation filled the conversation. From time to time, on the blackboard in the room, specific new information was reinforced and described visually, somewhat as a teacher might do. On the blackboard we began to illustrate our interpretations, our clarifications, and our points of learning. Thus, five major themes became the work areas for the subsequent 24 months: (1) "Trust Nobody"; (2) "Nigger"; (3) "Fuck It"; (4) "Lover Boy"; (5) "Who, Me?" These themes are comparable to other work in the long-term, intensive groups. They ebb, they flow, they cross and recross each other, but they came up again and again. From the conflicted depths, things come roaring, seeping, or oozing back until they are done.

1. "Trust Nobody"

This is a theme you will see in any normal, healthy, suspicious person, a theme which is not that different with these kids, but has the particular racial quality and heightened intensity, as mentioned before. Its first verbalization began in the transference situation when "Dr. Creepy" became Hugh and "The Swinger" became Chuck. It also began as one or another member of the group talked about how he would like to say something serious, but that he would "trust nobody" in this group. It bubbled up again and again. It appeared initially as acting out, and was then verbalized each time a crisis arose. When we were about to enter into a new, more emotionally loaded area of work, it appeared. Its arrival became recognized by the group as a prelude to hard work. When *"Trust Nobody"* is called, something is being hidden, something that must be observed, something that must be talked about. The group itself could recognize its use and would confront the speaker with its use and significance.

It was about the *10-month point*, at the time of the *Watts riots* in Los Angeles, that the nature of the therapist as white and the trust then meshed. Whether to put the major therapist into their white stereotype or to exempt him as a man became the issue. As it was resolved, *"Trust Nobody"* led to *"Nigger"* as an identifiable conflictual area.

2. *"Nigger"*

"Nigger" was a very derogatory theme. It spoke of the negative identity which was hidden, and broke out at times of stress and anxiety when the crisis situation yielded the recurrent, impotent, fruitless reaction. If one can't fight it, and can't identify with the aggressor, one turns it in on oneself. It's done in classic, self-maiming terms, and he calls himself *"Nigger"* and his friends *"Nigger"* and laugh-cries about it. Done with high humor, loud voices and Bogarting, you push right down to the end. Ironically, one courted black disaster by harassing your brother yet maintaining a frantic, sadistic position of strength just this side of catastrophe. The degradation, the humiliation which was inflicted (on each other) was the essence of this tragedy. It was emphasized with the word *"Nigger."* Again and again, the word *"Nigger"* and every other negative white man's stereotype term was used to slice a partner; *"Kinky," "Liver-lips," "Black-ass," "Nigger."* The word *"Nigger"* was occasionally used lightly, but the bitterness and rage were visible, even in its lightest use.

This theme was noticed by the therapists, at first, at times of stress when the seriousness of some work was disrupted. *"Nigger"* was used to head off someone from saying something that would be revealing, meaningful, or possibly tender. At this time, the personal *"Nigger"* attack would begin. The therapists picked this up and highlighted it, noting that when the anxiety became quite high, "up-tight," or when some one was headed for a point that someone else didn't want to talk about, this *"Nigger"* game began. In a questioning tone, the therapist wondered what it meant that this *"Nigger"* game was used at this time. Gut honesty fired at a peer explained it: "If he is a *'Nigger'*, he is no good, you know?" Implied here was, "I am no good, because I am black and a *'Nigger.'*" Denying, hysterical humor accompanied the explanation. In our eyes, *"Nigger"* was a defense. Slowly we were able to lift the rage. Under the rage was longing and depression.

Accompanying the *"Nigger"* theme was a *"punk"* sub-theme. This represented the *homosexual fear,* and/or the pseudo-homosexuality of adolescence. Much of the sexual identity crisis got confused in the *"Nigger-punk"*: whether the "Nigger fucks better than the white man," whether the "Nigger can do anything else but fuck." This kind of statement accompanied the evolution of the theme into the "punk" crisis. This was particularly related to feelings evolving toward the Swinger therapist. "It's all right to feel the way I do about you about a broad, but I don't want to feel this way about you."

Homosexual fears haunt affectional ties with anybody. Love or friendship creates threat. Love and affection, tenderness or warmth, are not to be trusted. This in turn is linked to specific traumata. In all of the individual histories of these boys, and in the group history per se, direct personal violence at the hands of a parent was associated with being black and with fear of love. The violence was viewed as happening only with Negroes, i.e., the clubbings, beating of mother by father, the arrests, the murders, the lynchings, the burning of one child by its mother, all of this was seen by these boys as happening only to Negroes. This was reinforced when the child became aware of the differences between the races. In an intricate series of associations, love, tenderness and being black became antagonistic for these boys. They wanted to love, trust, and be loved and trusted, but the blackness got in the way.

One specific report narrated by a member of the group highlighted this whole complex issue. The group worked from the *"Nigger"* theme, through the *"punk"* sub-theme, to the depression, at which time one member of the group, who was an extremely big, rough individual, recounted the following harrowing experience from when he was age seven.

> He and his brother, age five, were playing on the railroad tracks, in and out and under the freight cars, when the train began to move. As the train moved, he rolled free of the wheels, but his young brother was pinned on the tracks, cut in two and killed instantly. The boy stood there, awestruck, not knowing what to do. He slowly walked back to his house, and told his father that he had better come because something had happened. The father ran to the tracks, saw the horror, and, as reported in the memory of this boy, turned on him, cursing, *"You, Nigger."*

In complete shock, father was unable to give then, or subsequently, any tenderness; was unable to meet the boy's needs in the situation. As a result, again and again the boy used *"Nigger-Killer-Violence"* as a specific reinforcement for the whole cultural degradation and his own denial of need for love by a father. To be Negro was to be *"Nigger,"* violent, thuggish, unfeeling, hard, suspicious, and cruel. Feelings that ran contrary to this, anything that we later termed as soft feelings, were suspect and labeled homosexual.

As the work pressed in this area, the most crucial sessions occurred. These were the *"beat"* sessions, and the stage was set before the therapists entered: all lights but one were turned off, and two or three members would be beating out a slow, intricate, contrapuntal rhythm on a file cabinet or table. "I've gotta spill it," or words to this effect, signaled the depressive, thoughtful, catharsis that was to come. And it came! Fear, guilt and grief characterized the mood and tone as their acting-out was reviewed in terms of themselves as guilty agents. Two killings in which members were involved were explored. The damage done by one to another human in a street stomping led, in association, to the harm that they had each done to their mothers. A deep, longing pain for an idealized mother, who never existed, was cried about in accompaniment to an appropriate rhythm. The rage reaction to the mother they had poured out, as well as the disappointment, the being not fed, the sadistic punishment from her. Their parents' failures, along with some forgiveness and understanding of their parents, were touched upon.

The dependency that develops as one works through these difficult areas is intense and expected, but it pays off. You will be called on day and night by odd-hour phone calls, contacts at the clinic, just happening by the therapist's home, etc. These are repeated contacts with the therapists, and are needed to be sure they know there is somebody still interested in them. One really doesn't have to do anything when such a phone call is received. Just be there and listen. We believe this was a necessary part of working through the depression that came on as they began to change the identity.

3. *"Fuck It"*

This is a denial theme. It has to do with the inability to bind tension and the need to act-out with impulsive behavior which is self-destructive whenever anxiety, either internal or external, appears acute. Initially, *"Fuck it"* arose while the kids were waiting to hear somebody else talk, waiting to hear someone else express forbidden material, waiting for someone else to make a mistake and then recover from the mistake. "Fuck it, man, don't worry about it, don't stop, don't think, keep moving, keep acting," was the mode. Particularly true around school, with the academic failure and caste failure, the response was, "Aw, fuck it!" Run off, run out, deny, play around, destroy yourself further.

The attempt was, of course, to allay the anxiety that came with the frustration of working through a task, intrapersonal or external. Work assignments were difficult. There was reality here. Reading of two of the boys was at the second or third grade level, and pride was involved in even trying to start to work this through. In order to get any help, it was necessary to bind the tension of being the slowest reader in the group, seek help, and work it through. This was accompanied with a great deal of embarrassment and anxiety. The siren song of acting-out is very seductive; it's easier to say, "*Fuck it.*" Working through was difficult. The therapeutic gambit was to circle back again and again to clarify and interpret the acting-out; circling back to try to find a way to bind tension, work it through, and come out with a different solution than "*Fuck it.*" At approximately the *year-and-a-half point* in therapy, one member of the group made a massive effort to change. It was his first move to stop "screwing around," as he called it. He sought a very fundamentalist, rigid, religious experience, and joined a hard-shell, evangelistic Negro church. He gave up smoking, drinking, and everything else. The group made a massive attack on him, and he took it week after week for about six weeks. They delighted in taunting him, "Aw, fuck it, c'mon, quit that. C'mon, we'll fix you up with a fine broad, we'll fix you up with a little taste of liquor. How about some pot." In a cruel, vicious way, the group attacked him and his attempt to change. Months later, the group talked about the fact that if he changed, if he could change, then they would have to change too.

In trying to describe this, all one can do is to hope to approximate the intensity of the investment in defense. If you know what you are, no matter how poor, if you know what your defenses are, no matter how ineffective, how destructive they are, at least they are yours. They are old, tried and predictable, even in their failure. "*Fuck it*" served this purpose in relation to the boys. It was only through a great deal of time, a great deal of patience, that we were able to slowly modify it. I think it has moved from "*Fuck it*" to a verbalized "*Oh, screw it!*", at this point. The intensity and proclivity are still there, but some of the fire and unthinking responses have diminished. The defense has been modified to this level. There is some freedom for employment of more life-sustaining defense operations. This is indicated by reports from outside judges in the schools.

4. "Lover Boy"

Great credit for the development and the exploration of this theme must go to Miss Judy Heavenrich, Psychology Intern, who joined the group at the beginning of the second year, and stayed with it during the second and third years. The transference reactions toward her, a woman, were the major elements responsible for the particular evolution of this theme. Its course started out very hard, and became very soft, and ended with a reasonable colleaguality which characterized the transferences at the end of the third year.

When Judy entered the group, she was confronted with an immediate dilemma. The boys were extremely polite, extremely courtly, and very glad to have her because she brought "a little sex" to the situation. In the first meeting, she was chosen "It" in a game where everybody was in a bomb shelter with only enough food for six people. She, therefore, had to kick out three people. Which three would she kick out? She was on the spot. Whom would she get rid of, or whom would she choose? She stalled and passed the test.

Miss Heavenrich became the focus of talk about boy-girl relationships. She was used to try out, dramatically, techniques of dating, asking a girl to a dance, and seduction. Each question was handled very directly and openly by her. She discussed the particular technique, proposed for its good and bad points. Through her, it was pointed out that there was no consideration of her as a woman in any of the particular approaches used by the lover boys. She was a thing, not a person, and the problem of object relations to women was evolved. She became alternately big sister and advisor, was subject particularly to the mother transference and sexual love object, then she became Judy. One of the boys fell in love with her. He acted this out by attempts to get close to her, by meeting her, carrying her books, showing up at her apartment, though never able to talk about it. The other members of the group would, and the group talked for him. His tender feelings for Judy were referred to as "having his nose open," a very vulnerable state. Could he be accepted by her? What were the problems and appropriateness of this? The fantasy of relationship of the male therapist and Judy, classically Oedipal, was the working through point. As this phase progressed, the boys brought their girls to the group meetings. For a while, we couldn't tell how many were going to come to the meetings as various casual sets of boys and girls would arrive (top was 22) for information about sex, for contraceptive information, and, particularly, to work through the problems of caring for each other. The boys fell in love and out of love. It was still very rough, but more than the beginnings of meaningful boy-girl relations started. Having a woman in the group, the sexual difference, not the racial difference, became important. By the same token, the boys could further explore the transference to the male therapist and their wish to identify with him. It was as if, by having a woman present, it was all right to deal with the friendship and affectionate feelings which were directed toward the male. In the end, the male therapist was used as an identity figure on an interim level. Everyone was going to be a social worker.

5. "Who, Me?"

This theme corresponds to the *reality-testing* in several stages in any treatment. "Who, Me?" has to do with the new choices made. "Me," the high school graduate, "Me," the sedate straight, "Me," with a five-year future, "Me," a person with some self-esteem, "Me," a man. This came about from the experience of accomplishing for the first time, and shifted the basic way six of eight of these young men thought of themselves, and acted accordingly.

A new "Me" was tested in a summer program in the last year of the group. Through an Economic Opportunity Program, the boys worked with younger boys and community leaders on concrete problems, and found themselves functioning in a different status role. But, the "Who, Me?" ended, and the group suspended meetings until after Army service.

College was the goal for five of the boys. The other three definitely wanted jobs which had some future for them. The Army was seen as a way to obtain a college education paid for under the GI Bill. All was not perfect. "Who, Me?" represented the beginning and the continuing question about themselves with a new identity.

CONCLUSION

The three years of hard work with these eight Negro delinquent high school drop-outs did work. This type of approach cannot be done on a short-term basis, but it can pay off with long contact. Sixteen or seventeen years of untold deprivation cannot be undone in any short set of interventions.

The group did not get involved in civil rights, nor did the group get involved in social acting-out. Underpinning the work was an eclectic application of Freudian, Sullivanian and Role theories. The actions or presenting conditions were viewed as psychosocial pathology, with treatment emphasis on the psychological component. The distorted perceptions, the fears, superstitions, misunderstandings, conflicts, rigid defenses, the lack of information, and the emotional blocks which these boys brought to adult life were monumental. The work which was done here was to enable these young men to take part in the opportunities which existed. We believe this work was essential and effective.

Within the therapeutic prejudice, the technique used was economic, with early emphasis on a developing process. Once the idea of therapy was accepted, the boys were encouraged to do their own therapy and, to a limited degree, they developed this capacity. They finally could say, "Wait a minute! Why is this happening to me? Wait a minute, why am I getting up-tight?" "Wait a minute, I gotta psyche out my case." This, in our opinion, was good.

After the initial phase, the therapy was not that much different from the therapy known and described by others. The key point in the technique was the *initial period* in which there had to be *extreme openness on the part of the therapist,* an attitude that he was going to be successful, and a focus upon psychological reality in whatever way it was presented.

The dynamics here were described as themes, others might call them complexes, still others games. These terms described the dynamics of the way the fears and tensions of living were expressed. Each theme represented only a variation of the greater human theme. It was important to realize that these young men could not be treated as sociological problems. The treater must be realistic in his own resolution of his questions about race. In the sound and fury of the moment, in the ebb and flow of crisis, political, sociological, racial, hysterical, societal, let us not forget that society is a collection of persons. The persons are responsive to other persons, and it is only through human contact and undoing that human damage can be undone. But this contact is not simple, nor is it magical. It's nitty-gritty work, and takes time and discipline. You get as much as you give, qualitatively and quantitatively.

This brief overview provides more than a worm's-eye view of the apple. Anyone but a fool could appreciate the coping that has been done by these young men. Only a fool would say all is now "cool" for the eight. The damage that was done was done exceedingly well, but through this particular part of social work, we can get a handle on the specific distortions that yield so many distorted lives of all races. We can then do it from the specific. After we have achieved the social millennium, we will still have to deal with the internal consequences. At the very least, it is in our enlightened best interest, professionally, personally, humanistically, to do both.

CHAPTER 12

A Drop-In Group for Teen-agers in a Poverty Area

Martin Reiser, Ed.D., and
Sylvia Kushner-Goodman, M.S.W.

IN 1965 THE San Fernando Valley Child Guidance Clinic opened a branch clinic in the part of Los Angeles known as Pacoima. This is considered a poverty area. The area contained the largest percentage of families with income under $4,000 in the San Fernando Valley—approximately 22.4% (Meeker, 1964). The population included approximately 50% Negro and Mexican-American. In order to avoid the usual waiting list situation and to counter some of the resistances to traditional clinic services, a drop-in service for parents, adolescents and younger children was made an essential feature. Persons could drop in and be seen almost immediately for screening by a staff person. The screening took from 20 minutes to an hour and might be with one parent or a whole family. When there was a heavy load, an applicant might be scheduled for the initial screening several days later. In an emergency, they were seen immediately. A recommendation was made at the end of the screening, unless collateral information was considered necessary. One possible recommendation was to enter a short term, crisis oriented, drop-in therapy group, one for parents and one for adolescents.

These drop-in groups met weekly for an hour and a half. Members attended as they felt the need. A short term problem-centered approach was utilized. Although the limit was ten visits, flexibility was exercised. When additional sessions seemed indicated, these were usually available.

The attempt was to avoid the usual on-going, long term treatment situation by keeping it brief and crisis-oriented (Parad, 1965).

Following the initial screening, the drop-in group was the first exposure to a helping process for most of the teenagers who composed the group. Each used the group in his unique way, depending upon readiness for involvement or need to defend against it. With growth, a more mature member often come through as a strong leader and performed the task of "enabler" to the more hesitant.

Readiness to trust quickly became evident in the group. For the most part, the members had arrived at a time of crisis and the primary purpose was to help resolve the crisis. Mutual acceptance and reciprocal support among the members seemed to be important towards achieving the benefit of this approach.

The Pacoima teenage group involved silence, verbalization difficulty, open resentment and hostility toward authority figures, including the therapist. We attempted to facilitate interaction by potato chips and soft drinks at the beginning of the session. Role-playing techniques, "going-around," and in certain especially resistant groups, starting off with a discussion topic were used (Reiser, 1963). Many of the youngsters had questionable motivation for attending, feeling forced to come by the school, probation authorities or parents.

The drop-in group occasionally served as the sole needed treatment. For example, a rather dramatic situation was that of Brenda, 13, who had been a reported run-away. The oldest child in a fairly comfortable home, the former obedient and cooperative daughter "suddenly" became obdurate. Her grades dropped in school and an enormous chasm of hostility developed between mother and daughter. The girl had a step-father who had been in the family since she was a small child. The natural father had only sporadic contact with her. In the first session, she was quiet and seemed surprised at what she was hearing. Members had been telling of car thefts, of taking pills, etc. In her second meeting, she responded to a member's query and told of her run-away episode and of being suspended from school. She seemed comfortable as she felt that she was matching the tales of the other members. Her behavior received insightful discussion. She did not return, however, to subsequent meetings.

A few weeks later in the parent group, her parents related that Brenda was again her former cooperative, bright, achieving self. She had shared with her mother that being in the group had opened her eyes to how deeply in trouble she could get unless she "straightened out" now. In hearing the description about other members' parents, she became aware that hers were not so bad after all. She had tested her parents and they had come through as concerned and caring. But she also recognized that adolescence was not an excuse for license. Her ego was strengthened as she began to see that her concept of the world was really based on fantasies. This kind of immediate behavior change was not the rule.

Initially the drop-in group concept was designed as a brief crisis-oriented group treatment modality. It soon became apparent that in addition to brief services, the extreme environmental deprivation and affectional hunger of many of the adolescents in the poverty area required greater flexibility of the initial design. The drop-in group gradually evolved into a multi-purpose group which retained its brief service orientation on the one hand, but on the other, tended to become more stable and on-going by providing to the very deprived youngsters acceptance, affiliation and security which were not available to them in other social group contexts. The group also was a force towards super-ego reinforcement of a kind not usual in the ordinary social group. Two examples were Maria and Roberto. They would often drop in, either to socialize or briefly speak to the therapist. With Maria, the topics would range from sharing a recent date to her feelings towards her mother.

Maria was a well-developed teenager, the youngest in a large family. Her siblings were either married or out of the home so that she lived with her aging mother. She was experiencing problems around controls at school. She was involved in physical conflict with other girls and was sniffing paint. Raised in a Spanish-speaking home, part of her strove to identify with the Anglo community. In the group she related, particularly at the beginning, to a blonde, blue-eyed Mexican, Roberto, the offspring of an Anglo father whom he never knew and a Mexican mother who identified with her own people. Each saw reflected in the other the problem of duality, the Mexican and the American society.

The symptom which had brought Maria to the clinic, in addition to school difficulties, was her paint-sniffing habit. She would often arrive giving off a heavy odor of paint. Gradually, she became less defensive and more verbal, finally sharing with the group that she had given up the habit. Significantly, she was also becoming more eloquent, particularly in supporting others who were on the "habit" (paint, pills and marijuana). As her self-image improved, she was able to test out successfully her ability to be independent. She felt comfortable in the group in her self-appointed role of questioner and confronter, especially with newcomers. She often helped the process of beginning self-awareness in the newcomer. Conversely, her openness had the effect of encouraging confrontation by the group around her comments concerning her activities, or frequent lapses into Spanish, which the group insisted she translate. This she would do without feeling affronted, responding to any member of the group in order that she not be excluded.

Roberto would drop in occasionally to discuss with group members his latest adventure, and his excitement over school graduation. En route to the school commencement Roberto came in, for example, to show off his new suit, and he glowed when the therapist congratulated him. When termination from the group was broached to either youngster, each would come up with a variety of reasons ("where else will I go?") for continuing the affiliation. Roberto's ambivalence about staying in high school and entering the Job Corps extended over a period of numerous weeks. His use of the group, particularly over this time, served to carry him through a very difficult decision which, eventually, led him into the Job Corps. When last heard from, he was enjoying the experience and happy in his new surroundings. The sustained use of the group by Maria helped her to work through her decision to return and complete high school, then hopefully to enter nursing school.

For the majority of its members, inclusion in the group experience was the first opportunity to be listened to. The cross-cultural nature of the group presented a unique opportunity to clarify cultural and ethnic misunderstandings. Members worked toward acceptance of the differences of others, learned during the heat of emotional interchanges. In the group, they were provided the setting for testing out each other's strengths and weaknesses in a unique, non-threatening environment. When crises were presented, intensive work was done with some success. In a large proportion of cases, however, the problems were really of a more chronic nature, an integral part of the environmental fabric and, therefore, much more difficult to influence in a short time period. While many of these chronic cases realized gains from the immediate drop-in approach, several felt the need to continue in the group on a more sustaining basis.

REFERENCES

MEEKER, M. (1964). San Fernando Valley Profile. Van Nuys, Calif.: Welfare Planning Council.

PARAD, H. J., (1965). Crisis Intervention: Selected Readings. New York: Family Service Association.

REISER, M., & WALDMAN, M., (1963). Group Therapy in a Work Adjustment Center, *Int. J. Group Psychother.*, 13:300-307.

CHAPTER 13

Family Group Therapy for Adolescents

Saul L. Brown, M.D.

ADOLESCENCE DOESN'T JUST HAPPEN to the adolescent. It happens to his whole family. Even those viewing adolescence from a fairly conventional psychoanalytic perspective have been onto this for some time. Eugene Pumpian-Mindlin's article, "Omnipotentiality, Youth, and Commitment," published in 1965, is an example. Pumpian-Mindlin points up the subtle interplay of parental-adolescent fantasy systems in relation to omnipotence. He observes also how coupled with "omnipotentiality" is the adolescent's tendency to be cavalier about day to day commitments. The sheer energy and momentum of omnipotent fantasies in their adolescent children may revive long dormant ones in parents. Old defenses are revived and new ones emerge. Pumpian-Mindlin notes that therapist reactions to these aspects of their adolescent patients may be somewhat similar to parental reactions. To Pumpian-Mindlin's comments about revived omnipotence and the defenses it provokes in parents, I would add other dynamisms such as envy, competitiveness, fear of change, identity shifts, separation anxiety, etc. All of these are potentially pathological elements in the intricate network of parent-adolescent relationship (and of therapist-adolescent relationships).

Fictional literature has always been ahead of us. In "Death of a Salesman" written in the 1950's, Arthur Miller dramatized the crisscross of father-son expectation and self-doubt, and the inexorable movement toward

Reprinted with permission from *Psychiatric Opinion*, February, 1970.

a crisis for both in the striving-suffused American urban middle class with its peculiar identity problems. We are all aware that Shakespeare knew better than any of us about the torment provoked in upper middle class families by their irrepressible and sexed-up adolescent children—like Romeo Montague and Juliet Capulet. Although the Greek myth about Oedipus is mostly about him, his mother Jocasta and her husband were by no means free of their own error and pain when they received the news. What was the ultimate fate of their relationship? And in our most recent times, *The Graduate* and *Portnoy's Complaint* have each come crashing down on us as not so subtle reminders of how sexuality in an adolescent boy evokes and is evoked by the interpersonal maneuvers of the adults around him.

While fictional literature portrays the interaction of individuals within families in cause-effect sequences, these emerge as inevitable consequences of what preceded them. In contradistinction, the interactions that we clinicians work with provide us the opportunity for redirecting what might without our intervention follow an inevitable pathologic course. From therapy with groups, family and otherwise, we are learning how affective inputs organized with appropriate timing and skillful communication technique can bring about new awarenesses and new action-choices for the members of a family. The constructive results of our efforts may not be immediately measurable however. In meeting with families we free up and also catalyze developmental processes which may not bear fruit until much later in the lives of the participants. The language of symptoms and psychopathological classifications derived from the medical model is therefore not always adequate to describe this. The language of ego-dynamics comes closer but may be insufficient without the addition of conceptions and terminology from general systems theory and from role theory. Lennard and Bernstein's recent volume, *Patterns in Human Interaction* (1969), explicates this very well.

Although phenomenology of middle class adolescence has undergone fairly radical changes under the impact of recent social movements (Keniston), underlying dynamics may not be very different from what has been long described (A. Freud, I. Josselyn, P. Blos, J. Kestenberg). Beneath the surface phenomena that are so dramatically presented through fanciful clothes, nudity, long hair, psychedelic experiencing, communal experiments, etc., lie the somatic-sexual changes of puberty with associated sexual fantasies and drives; newly awakening cognitive and perceptual processes which reorganize identity, self-imagery, self-expectation, etc.; rapidly changing role functions; revived oedipal rivalry; imminence of separation from the nuclear family with accompanying ambivalence about dependency and autonomy; preoccupation with peer status, with heterosexual submission and dominance, with companionship and loneliness, etc.

What is going on in other members of the family at this time? In general this seems to have been left implicit in the clinical literature—as if everyone really knows about it anyway. How the ever-evolving parental-marital relationship interrelates with the unfolding phenomena of adolescence, how the shifting sexual functions and fantasies of the parents as well as of the siblings connect or rebound from those of the adolescents in the family, how the career or economic or existential stresses of father or mother connect with the adolescent's preoccupation with dependency, autonomy, challenge to conventionality, etc., have all tended to be placed in the background of clinical discussion. Traditional clinical focus has been on the psychodynamics of the youngsters themselves. Supporting this has been a certain clinical mythology which declares the inviolability of the therapist-adolescent relationship. Parents keep out! I have often noted that the awkwardness and anxiety and reticence manifested by beginning therapists toward the parents of their adolescent patients become elevated to a virtue by their overly cautious supervisors and teachers. What should be simple, easy, straightforward exchange between therapists and parents of adolescents becomes obscured behind mysterious C.I.A.-like manipulations, all under the heading of 'necessity." Skillful family interviewing demonstrates over and over that there is much to be openly talked about between adolescents and their parents. Common sense is needed of course. (Sensitivity on the part of a therapist is always a desirable quality!) There is a time and a place for everything. Family interviews need not violate this bit of human wisdom. Most important is that even in deciding what is appropriate for discussion, the well guided family interview introduces new family communication. It is quite possible for some families to decide in a family meeting what reactions and feelings ought to be shared between the generations and what should be kept "private." The content of what is "private" becomes thereby less prurient and less significant as a medium for pathologic relating.

Clinical Reality

In psychotherapy of adolescents, contacts between therapist and parents of the adolescent need to be well-timed, appropriate, well-considered, and even, at times, nonexistent. This ought to be a mutual therapist-family decision evolving out of the therapist's direct interaction with the family. It should not simply be imposed as dictum. In other words, how the situational reality of the adolescent affects his *clinical reality* needs to be assessed. The best way to do this is for the therapist to sample his patient's situational reality by experiencing it for at least one or two therapy hours with the whole family present. Ideally this should occur in the family's household but sheer economic practicability limits this.

Clinical reality is a relative state. Some of its elements are the degree of family cohesion; the parental openness to psychological thinking; the pressures—both supportive and destructive—arising from school or relatives or social group or peer group; the degree of consensus between the parents that help is needed; the general level of ego maturity of each family member, including the presence of manifest behavioral patterns that reflect fixation or regression; the obtrusiveness in the family life of major psychopathology in certain members such as alcoholism, thinking disorders, sociopathy, etc.; the status of the marital dyad and its dynamics; the nature of familial communication systems, the characteristic modes of affect expression, and the role designations; the family myths, the family secrets, the family image of itself; the socio-economic-ethnic realities surrounding it; recent or ongoing crises; major familial traumata of the recent and the long past, etc. In short, the immediate ecology of the family.

All of the preceding represents a multifactorial diagnostic perspective which, although not in conflict with traditional clinical theory, has often tended to be put aside by traditional clinicians in favor of an overfocused approach to the adolescent himself. The profusion of factors just listed has tended to be viewed as discouraging encumbrance and hindrance in the way of psychotherapy with adolescents. By contrast, the work of the pioneers in family therapy (they can be identified by reviewing the editorial board of the journal *Family Process*) has demonstrated these many factors can be incorporated into the therapeutic process. This requires not only a multifactorial comprehension, but an altered system of clinical management (Brown, 1969).

Clinical Management and the Developmental Perspective

What is important for clinical management is not the notation in a clinical record that various of the phenomena just referred to exist, but rather an understanding of the ways in which their existence limit developmental progress in the life cycle of the family (Fleck, 1966). Thus, the first step in the new system of clinical management derived from family diagnosis and therapy is to discover what the potential for change is and, simultaneously, where the resistances to developmental change lie for this particular family. This requires of the clinician a developmental perspective in which the adolescent and his family group are viewed as progressing through a steady flow of existential changes from day to day. The advent of adolescence in one or several family members becomes a nodal point in the flow of developmental change (Lidz, 1968).

How the developmental phase of adolescence is integrated (or fails to be integrated) into the life cycle of a given family becomes the target of clinical thinking. Mere existence of a particular kind of psychopathology in the family—viz., alcoholism in father or recurring depressions in mother, or even recent situational crises such as economic reversal or racial tension at school—may or may not be of significance for clinical management *at a given time*. Through one or several family interviews the perceptions and comprehension and feelings of various family members become evident. Thus it may become clear that in a particular family an adolescent's obesity is intertwined with her mother's recurring depressions. The latter in turn may be related to chronic marital frustration. The fluidity to change in this family group needs to be tried out by participating in some interaction with them. If it turns out that the marital dyad is rigidly fixed in its dynamics, the regressive mother-daughter relationship and the inhibited developmental individuation of the obese girl may need to be approached through extended therapy with her alone. Conjoint meetings with her and each of her parents may be useful from time to time to deal with separation anxiety and depression in all. If on the other hand the family meetings reveal some readiness for change in the marital relationship, a few family interviews may facilitate a fairly rapid loosening of the mother-daughter relationship. Siblings who are not directly caught up in the pathologic dyads may help move this along. Individual therapy for the girl may still be indicated but the working through of her separation conflicts can occur simultaneously with a progressive working through of the dysfunction in the parental relationship.

However the therapy becomes organized (individual, family, conjoint alternating with individual, etc.), open discussion by all family members with the therapist about why one or another course is chosen has its own powerful impact on them. Being invited to participate in the decision making about the next steps to be taken vitalizes the therapist-family interaction. Thus the very nature of clinical management introduced by family interviewing re-shapes therapeutic process and what the participants expect of it. Also mutual involvement and decision-making about the clinical process (who is to be seen next and why) demonstrates to all who are involved that productive communication between the generations is possible.

Therapist exchanges with family members often include clarification of intrapsychic dynamisms but often this is set aside in favor of clarifying here-and-now exchanges between family members. It is the latter that may more immediately reduce resistance to developmental change. Loosening of the rigid dynamics of a particular dyadic relationship, such as mother-daughter, may not occur until new things get said between them in presence of father or directly by them to father and vice versa. For this to occur the therapist may need to actively demonstrate or at least invite possible ways of talking. Again sibling participation provides additional fuel and impact.

The full weight of the therapeutic action need not however rest upon the family interview per se. This is never my own expectation and I believe such an expectation was only a transitory one early in the history of the technique. Boszormenyi-Nagy and James Framo now indicate that contrary to what appears in their volume, *Intensive Family Therapy* (1965), they no longer hold exclusively to family interviews in their work. (Personal report.) Ackerman has long emphasized flexibility in clinical management (1956).

Resistance to Developmental Change

In the effort to reduce the complexity of phenomena that occur in family therapy, and in order to teach principles of clinical management, I have settled upon *resistance to developmental change* as an organizing and unifying concept (Brown, 1966). This notion is a practical one for cutting through the conflicts of priority that arise out of commitment to various frames of reference such as communications theory vs. interpersonal relations theory vs. psychoanalytic-psychodynamic theory vs. learning theory, etc. Developmental change used as the dominant frame of reference includes all theories. Resistances to developmental change in any group may lie predominantly in one or several factors *at a given time* in the life of the group. For family groups these might be the marital dynamics, the psychological naivete of the parents, a recent trauma, major psychopathology in certain members, rigidity of the family's socio-economic situation, leaderlessness within the family, etc., etc., etc. At a given time, priorities of clinical management and selection of specific approaches are made in accordance with where the resistance to developmental change seems to be most active. Thus, direct educative comments, direct confrontations, psychodynamic interpretations, psychodramatic playing out of role reversals, task assignments, use of anxiety allaying drugs, or whatever, may each have their time of importance. The guiding question is, ". . . what is the current locus of resistance to change?"

Apropos of this kind of assessment I have found that my own "countertransference" responses to a family group provide a crucial gauge. When I meet with a family I try repeatedly to feel what an adolescent in the family needs to do to "make it" i.e., to keep maturing in that family. Simultaneously I judge, through my own reactions to the parents as they interact, what the limits for psychological change are for these people (at least if I am to be their therapist). This is in the category of intuitive-diagnostic appraisal of resistance to change. It helps avoid fruitless psycho-therapeutic endeavors of a traditional psychoanalytic type when these may be irrelevant.

Adolescence precipitates disequilibrium in a family system. Adaptability of the family members and of the group per se to this developmental phase may be limited in a few or in many areas. The locus of the resistance to progressive developmental change for both the adolescent and the whole family group needs to be defined. From his work described in *Multiple Impact Therapy* MacGregor (1964) views adolescent dysfunction as a reflection of the limited developmental maturation of the parents. While this is an oversimplification, it implies much about the pragmatic aspects of clinical management because it defines some kind of therapeutic-educative task re the parents. A much more complex set of formulations comes out of general systems theory which attempts to define, in communications language, how the sub-systems of a family interrelate so as to maintain steady state homeostasis and also how they perpetuate pathology once it evolves (Grinker, 1967).

Some Crises of Adolescence

Using the psychodynamic genetic frame of reference, Robert Counts in an article, "Family Crises and the Impulsive Adolescent" (1967) describes how the precarious equilibrium of the adolescent and the peculiar form in which his conflicts emerge revive latent parental conflicts. These now become masked in the family through scapegoating or through unwitting provocation of the adolescent by the parents. Thus the very behavior that is characteristic for adolescence invites dysfunction in the intergenerational sub-system. Parental resistance to the changes evoked by adolescence lead to malfunctioning of that system and to pathologic reaction in both the parental and the adolescent generation. A vicious circle is now in danger of perpetuating itself. Effective clarification and modification of all this through family meetings are often possible and prevent a freezing of further developmental progress.

Suicidal attempts by adolescents are often a response to overt or subtle family disruptions. Morrison and Collier (1969) describe their work with 100 families in a child psychiatric emergency clinic. 34% of these involved a suicidal threat. Three-fourths of those seriously threatening suicide had experienced significant object loss within prior weeks. In most of their cases familial equilibrium was quickly reestablished through a few meetings in which the separation-loss theme was dealt with. Character change is not claimed by the authors for the adolescents involved. What the family meeting clearly achieved was a reduction of the progressive isolation and alienation from others that would ordinarily occur for most adolescents who have attempted suicide. Ultimate reworking of deeper psychopathology requires something more but it becomes clear from their experience that many families, and adolescents, are not ready for this.

SUMMARY

The endless variety of problems and contexts which comprise the "clinical reality" alluded to earlier make it plain that a general statement about the effectiveness of family therapy for problems of adolescents is futile—and even misleading. Whatever is said needs to be set in the context of an ecological frame of reference, a developmental perspective (with resistance to change as a guiding notion), a general systems comprehension of the family unit (including concepts of homeostasis, role functions, equilibrium-disequilibrium, the nature of communication loops within the system, etc.), and psychodynamic understanding. With all of these concepts before us, the use of family interviews becomes not a cheaper way out of the challenge to mental health clinicians, but a more complex and yet a more relevant one. The reports of many family therapists demonstrate that it is quite possible to carry out productive, enlightening, even exciting interviews with adolescents and their families in any number of contexts: guidance clinics, ghetto clinics, middle-class private practice, in-patient services, delinquency programs, residential settings, etc. It is possible for many adolescents to become quite open about themselves in family meetings and for all the family members to enter into genuine and anxiety-relieving and guilt-relieving exchanges. Psychological curiosity, empathy, and the self-observing ego all grow. Specific clinical advances can often occur in a fairly short time but my own experience teaches me that emphasis should be placed not so much on immediate change but rather upon the lessening of inappropriate and self-defeating resistance to developmental and existential change. If all the family members evolve a deepened respect for the life cycle of each human being, the adolescents in the family automatically progress.

REFERENCES

ACKERMAN, N. W., (1958). The Psychodynamics of Family Life. New York: Basic Books.

BLOS, P., (1962). On Adolescence. The Free Press of Glencoe, Ill.

BOSZORMENYI-NAGY, I., & FRAMO, J. L. (Ed.), (1965). Intensive Family Therapy: Theoretical and Practical Aspects. New York: Harper and Row.

BROWN, S. L., (1969). Diagnosis, Clinical Management, and Family Interviewing. Science and Psychoanalysis. Vol. XIV. New York: Grune & Stratton, Inc.

BROWN, S. L., (1966). Selective Variations in Family Therapy in the Light of Resistance. Presented at American Orthopsychiatric Association Annual Meeting, San Francisco, Calif.

COUNTS, R., (1967). Family Crisis and the Impulsive Adolescent. *Archives of General Psychiatry*, 17: 1-7.

FLECK, S., (1966). An Approach to Family Pathology. *Comprehensive Psychiatry*, Vol. 7, No. 5.

FREUD, ANNA, (1937). Ego and the Mechanisms of Defense. London: Hogarth Press.

GRINKER, R. R. (Ed.), (1967). Toward a Unified Theory of Human Behavior: An Introduction to General Systems Theory (2nd ed.). New York: Basic Books, Inc.

JOSSELYN, IRENE, (1952). Adolescent and His World. New York: Family Service Association of America.

LENNARD, H. L., & BERNSTEIN, A., (1969). Patterns in Human Interaction. San Francisco: Jossey-Bass.

KENISTON, K., (1963). Social Change and Youth in America. The Challenge of Youth, Erik H. Erikson (Ed.). Originally published as Youth: Change and Challenge. New York: Basic Books, Inc.

KESTENBERG, JUDITH, (1968). Phases of Adolescence: With Suggestions for a Correlation of Psychic and Hormonal Organizations. Part III. Puberty Growth, Differentiation, and Consolidation. *Journal of the American Academy of Child Psychiatry*, Vol. 7, No. 1.

LIDZ, T., (1968). The Person. New York: Basic Books, Inc.

MACGREGOR, R., (1964). Ritchie, Agnes, Serrano, A. C., Schuster, F. P. Multiple Impact Therapy with Families. New York: McGraw-Hill Book Co.

MORRISON, G. C., & COLLIER, JENNY, (1969). Family Treatment Approaches to Suicidal Children and Adolescents. *Journal of the American Academy of Child Psychiatry*, Vol. 8, No. 1.

PUMPIAN-MINDLIN, E., (1965). Omnipotentiality, Youth, and Commitment. *Journal of the American Academy of Child Psychiatry*, Vol. 4, No. 1.

CHAPTER 14

Mediation within a Group of
Multiple Families

Lillian B. Vogel, Ph.D.

INTRODUCTION

TODAY, MANY SPEAK with great expertise of the generation gap—that never before has it been as it is today. Others say it is a new term for a phenomenon existing since time immemorial. In the 8th Century B.C., Hesiod wrote:

> "I see no hope for the future of our people if they are dependent on the frivolous youth of today—when I was a boy, we were taught to be discreet and respectful of elders."

Even though generational differences have always been with us, the fact is that today's adolescents are living in a world where in the few decades before and during their lifetime drastic changes have occurred. This, coupled with their ongoing biological and psychological changes, makes it exceedingly difficult for them to adjust to values of a society which they will shortly inherit.

Those of us who work with adolescents and their families are aware that each member has a longing (overt or covert) for an atmosphere of warmth and mutual concern; for congeniality, consideration, and acceptance; hoping at the same time for the freedom to express negative as well as positive feelings. But we also know that for most families this is far from being

162

achieved. Adolescents have difficulty comprehending why their parents get so "uptight" with them, while most adults find that having been an adolescent is not much help in understanding their own young son or daughter.

Parents often feel themselves manipulated and become angry; at other times they are overcome with feelings of guilt and remorse. They will lambast the teen-ager with "after all I've done for you," "what about your studies," "the kids you go with are unworthy of you," "why must you always be away from home." Thus, the young person feels himself harassed and under stress. He is striving for separateness from his family, at the same time being dependent upon them. He is aware that he should be making decisions as to his future and is frightened to do so. There is a pull to identify with his peers; or the opposite, depressed feelings because he doesn't relate. In addition, he is troubled by sexual impulses and conflicts.

The parents may lay great stress only upon the child's behavior. They see and hear the anger, the defiance, the defensiveness, the provocativeness. They are not sufficiently sensitive to the underlying feelings, and are usually not aware that unless the feelings are considered, the behavior will not be modified easily. The young person, because of his characteristic ego-centricity, hears only the critical remarks, the ridicule, cynicism, and martyrdom. He is unaware of the parent's deep concern over drugs, violence, lurking dangers, or his future.

As the cycle of distance develops like a broadening spiral, the generational gap widens. We know these phenomena occur in middle class American families. Whether this gap is any more or any less extant within American Jewish families than in the general population, we do not know. We do know however, that there is often much conflict within the Jewish families encountered in the Community Centers.

PROCEDURE

It was suggested at the Valley Cities Jewish Community Center that several families with teen-agers, in the presence of a mediator, meet for a limited number of sessions. The goal would be to improve communication. Hopefully this would create sufficient momentum to start a growth process which might better realize the potential within each family. Because of the composition of the group effective help might be derived within a short period of time. Since parents have much to say and adolescents have much to say, it was felt that it might be of value to create a setting in which the two generations could talk and try to hear what each was saying. The uniqueness of this project was to have a number of families meet together with the idea that each generation might derive some valuable experiences in communicating with his own family members as well as with others than his own.

Referrals to the group were made by the worker at the Center. Where it had been observed that young people had personality problems manifested by difficult social relationships, over-defensiveness, over-aggression or passivity, or where there were implications of difficulties within the family, an invitation was given to the family to join the group. There was also publicity in the Center newspaper. In the initial invitations, the teenagers showed less resistance toward participation than did some of the parents. Excuses by the parents made reference to their card-playing night, possibility of working, travel, or the hopelessness of any approach. It was suspected that some of the reticence might be due to fear of exposure amongst acquaintances. However, after a few weeks, five families accepted participation in the first group.

Meetings were set for a period of eight sessions, one and one-half hours weekly. Invariably the sessions lasted over two hours and there was hall discussion following. Group I had five families which included seven adults and nine adolescents. Attendance throughout averaged thirteen per session. One father discontinued due to a class commitment; other absences were due to illness, school exams, etc. Group II was formed in a way similar to Group I and met the following spring. Four families attended—eight adults and four adolescents. Death of a relative in one family and serious illness in another prevented attendance from being as consistently high as in Group I. Both groups have been combined as to description, observations, and evaluations.

PROCESS

To facilitate participation and encourage feelings of acceptance, the mediator spoke briefly regarding the fact that in usual discussions of generation differences, alienation of the young is emphasized, while that of the parents may be generally overlooked. It was the hope that within this group the young people would be listening to what the adults had to say and the adults would be listening to what the young people had to say. The importance of confidentiality was stressed; to the best of our knowledge there were no repercussions in this area. The only other limit set was that only one person should talk at a time. It was anticipated that this might become a problem because of the size of the group.

As each family gave a capsule summary as to why they were present, members were encouraged to talk to each other directly rather than through the mediator. Very quickly discussion became active and mutually stimulating. The following vignettes from a few sessions illustrate the cohesiveness which developed.

Development of a sense of responsibility.

Nate's father: "He's so impetuous—it must be now—absolutely. He yells that he just can't wait."

Nora's father: "I know what you mean. She doesn't get what she wants and she has a tantrum. Like now—she wants a wig—NOW. 'Get it for me now and I'll pay you back later.' Sure, I know—it's happened many times. Then she refuses to do her chores and we have put out the money."

Nora's mother: "Well—you still do her homework. What do you expect?"

Dan: "Good God—I can see why you have no responsibility and can't wait for something."

Dan's father: "Who are you to talk? You spend $2 or $3 on candy bars and eat them the same day."

Dan's mother: "I threatened to have him pay for his dental bills and then it turns out he has no cavities. (General laughter.)

Nora: "Yeah—I guess they give me too much."

Insensitivity to the other's needs.

Pat: "Talk about kids not wanting to communicate. I can be all uptight from things that happened to me during the day with my friends and my teachers. I can hardly wait for her to come home— and then, she won't listen to me."

Pat's mother: "Sure—as soon as I walk in the door there she is with her problems. She bombards me."

Ned's father: "Look—she's giving you what we all want from our kids and you complain."

Pat's mother: "But what about my stresses during the day. What's wrong with telling someone when you are tense. Like—leave me alone—I'm all upset."

Jack: "I worry about my Mom's problems—she works too. But my sister—all she cares about is herself. Maybe you could at least wait till she gets her coat off."

Pat's mother: "Pat, you really do a lot of things for me. I guess I get too nervous sometimes."

Pat: "Boy—you sure do. Like it's my fault that you have to work. —I suppose in a way it is."

The need for acceptance and understanding.

Ned's father: "I can't explain what he means to me. I love him so much and want to give to him. But he's so demanding—like it's coming to him."

Ned: "Well—I do try to please you—but when I do, you don't notice."

Al: "Yeah—you're like that too, Dad. Nothing's ever any good— I don't do things like you. 'Be a good student—stop wasting so much time.' Always putting me down. When I think about it—I guess you mean well—but it sure doesn't sound like it."

Al's father: "I guess you're right—and I often feel guilty. But you get me so damn mad with your procrastination. —But I do want to be able to talk to you."

Linda: "My dad—he isn't like that—he's different. He only sees Carol and her problems. 'Be careful—don't upset her. She'll have an asthma attack again.' That's what goes on—all my life it's been that way. Our whole family has centered around her. I think she uses it but nobody believes me. I always get blamed."

Pat's mother: "Maybe that's the only way Carol can protect herself—because you're the good student—so orderly—always the good one. You sure are critical of her—I've heard it here—jumping on the few words she does say."

Linda's father: "That's not true, what you say, Linda. I do want to talk to you. I'm really proud of you. But if I try to get close, you kind of 'float' away."

Linda's mother: "Don't make yourself sound so good. When you talk to her you yell. She's right—how can she open up to you under such circumstances. All you ever talk to her about is Carol."

Linda's father: (Smiles sheepishly.)

The resistance to communicate.

David: "Penny, where do you plan to go to school next year?"

Penny's mother: "Oh, she doesn't know. We can't get a word out of her. I see her mail letters but she never tells us a thing."

Penny: "See how it is—they don't trust me. They give me no credit. Treat me like a baby."

Penny's mother: "That's not true. You know we love you. Whatever we say is for your good."

Nora's mother: "Just listen to yourself—you never let her talk. You answer for her before she even has a chance. I've heard it time and time again here."

David and Dan: "You sure do. You just did it."

Penny's mother: "If only she could be a little more tolerant. She jumps on me before she knows what I'm going to say."

David's father: "You say that Mrs. F., but you never give her a chance. You sure are intolerant of her."

Penny: "We've been through this before. Nothing will ever work. They tie me to them—then they complain that I won't do anything by myself. Nothing is worth it."

Nora's father: "Nora is like that too—just like your Penny. Only anger, that's all she can tell us."

Dan: "It's not hard to see why Penny gets so angry. I would be too. And I do get angry when you belittle me so much. 'You're a slob, you don't speak clearly, get to your homework.'"

Dan's mother: (Laughingly.) "Since coming here I've learned that you can think. You used to mumble and we never knew what you were talking about. Now I can see how articulate you really are."

A gamut of feelings and attitudes were evoked. One could note poignancy, hostility, humor, projection, rejection, anxiety, emancipatory strivings, remorse, guilt, hopelessness as well as hopefulness expressed. The following comments, even though out of context and in no particular sequence, convey emotional expressions which elicited many interactions similar to those described above.

Adolescents

"I've improved in my grades this year—and they still keep bugging me about the guys I hang around with."

"I have no freedom at all—they just won't leave me alone."

"I want to do my thing—I have the right to be an individual."

"You can do better—not that you can do well—that's what she always says."

"I do want your approval—."

"Dad gives in to every wish—as if he has no power."

"We never go deeply into things—like nobody cares about how you feel."

"Everything has always centered around her because of her illness . . . never me. . . . I'm always supposed to understand."

"If my voice gets strong—then I don't think I'm as bad as they say I am."

"If I don't act, I'm blamed—if I show initiative—whatever I do they're critical."

"I went through a period of arguing—just for the ducks of it."

"We sure know each other's sorespots."

"I don't feel I know you and Dad at all."

Parents

"I say one little thing, and she blows up."

"You're a conversation stopper—you'll give me a one word answer."

"I resent being pushed around by you. You matter so much to me—and all you have to say to me is 'I want.' Never a 'thank you' . . . like it's coming."

"Just no responsibility . . . messy room . . . leaving things around."

"I didn't really know how to say 'no' or 'yes.' . . ."

"She came in late . . . glassy eyed . . . it really had me worried."

"I can't believe she doesn't know that I love her."

"We never talk about the things that hurt."

"You must be ashamed of your friends, so you won't bring them home."

"I never realized you are as intelligent as you are. I guess I just never listened to you before."

"You think you can talk to us any old way—angry, vulgar, obscene."

The mediator remained generally non-directive, primarily encouraging intercommunication. At times, when discussion was very stimulating and there was side buzzing, a reminder was made that we are all interested in hearing what was said. Although this remained a mild problem throughout, it was never sufficient to create disruption, nor did it appear to quell anyone's continued participation. Occasionally there was an attempt to control a more verbose member, sometimes in a humorous way. Less reticent members were at times turned to in order to encourage responses. Following a discussion within a particular family, the mediator would clarify or confront when appropriate. When deep feelings were released, support was given. In a few instances it seemed important to interpret what meaning these feelings might have.

EVALUATION

During the last session members were asked to fill out an evaluation form. Combining Groups I and II, thirteen adults and twelve adolescents

TABLE I: SELF-RATING

	Parents—N=13			Groups I and II combined. Adolescents—N=12		
	None	Moderate	Much	None	Moderate	Much
Improved communication within family	2	8	3	2	9	1
Your improved listening	2	4	7	3	7	2
Your improved self-awareness	2	7	4	2	4	6
Your improved expression of positive feelings	2	7	4	2	10	0

were present. In Table I, participants rated their own change. It can be noted that parents and adolescents both indicated that change had occurred. The differences between the generations is not significant. Combining *moderate* and *much* in each of the four areas, 11 of the 13 parents reported change (87%) in a positive direction. In three of the four areas 10 of the 12 adolescents reported change (83%) in a positive direction whereas in "improved listening" only 9 of the 12 (75%) did so.

In general, more parents than adolescents indicated that *much* change had occurred. The greatest difference was in the area of "improved listening." Seven of the parents reported *much* (54%) whereas only 2 of the adolescents (16.5%) did so. As to "improved communication" 8 parents (62%) reported moderate while 3 (23%) reported *much*; adolescents were close, with 9 (75%) reporting *moderate* and 1 (8%) reporting *much*. To summarize, in all of the areas of self-rating, a high percentage of the participants felt that *moderate* or much *change* had occurred.

Table II shows ratings by the mediator of the descriptive comments made by the participants in answer to four self-evaluations. This table does not include the total group since four parents and three adolescents did not make statements clear enough for rating, or they omitted the item entirely. The adults, in each of the areas, described many more *much* and *moderate* changes than did the adolescents. Possibly this was because the adults who did answer were much more articulate in their descriptions than were the adolescents. Whatever the reason, the adult responses, were weighted decidedly in the direction of positive change, whereas the responses of the adolescents showed considerably greater distribution. In spite of felt improvement, all of the parents who responded indicated greater awareness that the family problems could benefit from further exploration.

TABLE II

Groups I and II combined. Ratings made by mediator
from comments in response to question.

(Describe)	Parents N=9*			Adolescents N=9*		
	None	Moderate	Much	None	Moderate	Much
Improved expression of hostile feelings	1	3	4	3	4	2
Changed expression as to nagging, condemning, indulgence (parents)		6	3			
More awareness of problems in family that could benefit from more exploration			9	4	2	3
Changed behavior as to demandingness, cooperation, friends, leisure, procrastination (adolescents)				5	2	2

* Four parents, and three adolescents did not express descriptive statements clearly for rating so they were omitted.

Under "additional comments" many spontaneous statements were elicited. Most were laudable although two conveyed an air of hopelessness, both by adolescents. "I think the same things were discussed that have been brought out many times before; the situation and problems remain unchanged." This was from a very depressed girl, Penny, whose mother was most controlling and rigid. A very hostile boy, David, who had been rebellious and insolent but whose parents reported much change in him, wrote: "This is a weekly safety valve . . . the problems solved will recur in different ways when the sessions have ended."

No specific question had been asked as to the value of this particular kind of group, but the following statements by some of the parents reflect their feelings about this.

"I have had her to clinics and nothing has opened her up as much as this group."

"This program should be continued. It was very beneficial in that I never knew my son was so articulate—he talked about what he thinks and feels, and has demonstrated his self-control."

"We should have a group going like this in every room in this building."

Less specific but expressing their gains are the following:

"These sessions are helpful in making me more aware of other people."

"I'm able to think a little more about the other person's reaction to what I might say."

"Within this setting some clear vision of the other guy's feelings has come about and all of us appreciate this."

"I'm amazed at how much help it has been. We've all been stimulated to much introspection."

"I'm able to see that our family isn't the only one that has problems."

"I feel a deep relationship with all members of this group."

At no time, in any of the sessions, was it voiced by either adolescents or parents that this group format might be inhibitory. Rather, one might conclude that resistance was readily decreased and communication facilitated because of the obvious universality of the problems.

CONCLUSIONS

Most of the participants, adults as well as adolescents, indicated that these sessions had been a valuable experience. In eight of the nine families the evaluation of the mediator and participants were in agreement that change was in a positive direction. Tension and hostility were lessened, and the interpersonal interactions became more congenial. This of course varied within the families. We must keep in mind that our goals were limited for this kind of intervention. We were interested in facilitating improved communication, but perhaps even more than this, to activate the family to change by its own momentum. This does seem to have occurred in varying degree in most of the participant families.

Since the real measure of any procedure attempting to induce change is as good as its lasting quality, we must ask whether this momentum will continue or will the families who made gains gradually sink back into the mire of hostility, anxiety, and distance. Five months after the completion of Group I and two months after the completion of Group II, a letter was sent to each of the families asking for a brief evaluation as to the ongoing effectiveness of the sessions. Five families responded (by one parent) stating that in general relationships and communication were better than before the sessions. They added that there was increased awareness that there were still problems within their family that could benefit from further exploration. Since most of the adults had indicated the same need in the first evaluation, possibly they were conveying their anxiety that they were finding it difficult to maintain the felt gain without further support of the group. Four families did not respond to the letter. This may have been due to the fact that many staff members as well as families were on vacation at that time, and additional letters were not sent. In any case, this follow-up is obviously too incomplete for any conclusions to be drawn at this time. There is enough evidence from this pilot project, however, to conclude that multiple families in a group can explore problems together, and induce some change. Perhaps this can be done effectively in short term groups precisely because of the catalytic effect of the group composition contributing to more rapid action. In our search for new ways to intervene in averting family breakdown, this multiple family group may be a preventive procedure to be utilized in centers, churches, or schools.

REFERENCES

ACKERMAN, N. W. The Psychodynamics of Family Life. New York: Basic Books, 1958.

Group for the Advancement of Psychiatry, Comm. on Adolescence; *Normal Adolescence*. New York: Charles Scribner's Sons, 1968.

LATTIMORE, R. Hesiod. Ann Arbor: University of Michigan Press, 1959.

MEAD, M. Culture and Commitment—A Study of the Generation Gap. New York: Natural History Press, Doubleday, 1970.

WHITAKER, D. S., & LIEBERMAN, M. A. Psychotherapy Through the Group Process. New York: Atherton Press, 1967.

YALOM, IRVIN. Theory and Practice of Group Psychotherapy. New York: Basic Books, Inc., Publishers, 1970.

ZUK, G. H., & BOSZORMENYI-NAGY, I. Family Therapy and Disturbed Families. Palo Alto: Science and Behavior Books, Inc., 1967.

POSTLUDE

The Transference Dynamics of the Therapeutic Group Experience

Martin Grotjahn, M.D.

I. *Some General Dynamics of Transference in Groups*

The transference aspects in the therapeutic group situation are experienced similarly and at the same time quite differently from the transference neurosis in psychoanalysis. In the psychoanalytic group experience, a three-fold transference development can be observed: the transference relationship to the therapist—or central figure—is patterned according to the transference neurosis as it is known from psychoanalysis. A second important transference relationship develops between the members of the group to each other. According to all clinical experience it is this peer-transference which exerts the greatest therapeutic pressure in groups of adolescents.

A third transference relationship develops to the group as a pre-Oedipal mother. This third transference relationship is of decisive importance in groups of adolescents since the central conflict of adolescence takes place between the need for dependency and the drive for individuation and identity.

In the transference neurosis of psychoanalysis, the infantile neurosis is experienced, interpreted and the insight is integrated; in the psychoanalytic group experience, the equally important family neurosis is transferred to the group, re-enacted, re-experienced, interpreted and worked through. This is of decisive therapeutic, educational and maturational importance. If this insight from general clinical experience of the group process is compared with the behavior of adolescents in groups, it becomes obvious once more that the analytic group is probably the treatment of choice with the overwhelming majority of young people.

The analytic group experience is not an analysis of an individual in the presence of a 'board of lay-analysts." It is an experience in which the central figure needs all his analytic training, insight and knowledge in order to consistently interpret the group transference phenomena. Such an analyst working with a group will be surprised at the influence of his group work on his style and his technique in analysis. Almost everybody genuinely suited for group work will experience growth and maturation himself and will make a decisive step in his development to freedom, spontaneity and honest responsiveness. Here again, adolescents are good teachers since they are sensitive toward the honesty and directness of the "real person," as they call it, in parents and therapists. They are, furthermore, honest, courageous and direct enough to say so clearly and without much hesitation. Any therapist who stands up against the sharp eyes of a group of adolescents has passed the baptismal fire. Young people of today have the sharp eyes of analysts. The next best test for a therapist, besides conducting a group of adolescents, is to conduct a group of his own peers.

The neglect of group-phenomena has led to many peculiarities of psychoanalytic group formations. While the individual analysis aims at liberation from the tyranny of the individual unconscious, the analytic group experience aims at the equally important liberation from the repetition of the family neurosis.

In individual analysis, a patient is—so to speak—the only child of the analyst; in group psychotherapy everybody is a member of the family.

II. *A Brief Note on the "Oscillating Transference" of Leaderless Groups*

I had the opportunity to observe indirectly and by consultations the group process as it developed in a leaderless group. It is of less importance here for our purpose to know that this was a group of experienced, medical therapists. Observations of this group helped me to understand the special aspects of group transference in adolescents.

I found it helpful to look at the leaderless, analytic group as if it was the "Ur-Horde" which Freud so graphically described in *Totem and Taboo.*

Every member in such a group offers himself as a father at one time or another, to be murdered, and as a son to be resurrected. Everyone is a mother, good or bad, loving or rejecting. Everybody is her infant: oral, anal, naughty or good. Everybody is a brother, older or younger, Cain or Abel, both or none. Everybody loves and hates, gives and takes, speaks, listens, experiences and interprets. It is not necessarily a chaotic situation, but it is a truly democratic one.

Every transference reflection may change, roles may be reversed, new ones may be assigned, fit or unfit for various different transference needs. The structuring influence of the central figure, this rock of Gibraltar, the pre-Oedipal parent, is not present: this is the prevailing transference of a leaderless group. The best term for this situation is, perhaps, for the time being, to talk about an "oscillating transference," or a multi-faceted one. The situation is therapeutic because there is always someone (or several) who feels called upon to interpret, offer understanding, to give and to gain insight and stimulate integration.

III. *The Specific Characteristics of the Adolescent in the Group*

The insights as described in the dynamics of the transference in analytic groups and in leaderless groups can be applied to the understanding of the transference in groups of adolescents as described in its various aspects in the different chapters of this book.

The one to one transference neurosis, most similar to that as found in psychoanalysis, is of least importance in groups of adolescents while the peer transference relationship moves to the foreground. It is understandable and convincing that this transference situation is of special therapeutic impact and strength in adolescents who in our times are quite resistant to accept the authority of parents or their representative by the central figure. How often have we heard young people of today say: "I cannot learn anything from anybody over 30." They do listen to each other and the group can influence greater pressure towards change than the "establishment" could exercise. The long term relationship to an individual analyst invites a strong resistance as another aspect of adolescent rebellion.

Furthermore, it became obvious that the central conflict of adolescents is the fight between the need for infantile dependency and the urge to independent individuation and identity. This struggle which is acted out in the reality of the home situation, and repeated in school and college, leads to the behavior problems so significant for our youth. It is re-enacted in the group since the third transference trend with the group as the pre-Oedipal mother shows all the features of this struggle which can now be re-enacted, interpreted, understood, and perhaps integrated in the interest of further maturation and growth.

When investigating and observing the transference dynamics of the leaderless groups, insight could be gained into the behavior of the "Ur-Horde" which after all was thought to be largely a group of adolescent sons. The "oscillating transference" as we call it is also quite obvious in the group of adolescents. All the traumatic features of the situation make the group process with adolescents so loud and lively, so equally near to reality and to the unconscious. A well conducted group of adolescents is no hour of rest but of drama and participation for all, including the therapist. The intensity of "the happening" is in direct relationship to the therapeutic impact. Any therapist who tries to remain outside of the process loses influence with the group. At least he must be able to join the group and at other times to retreat from it into his role and place of central figure. This leads to recognition of the importance of the co-therapist who is of special meaning in a group of adolescents.

It seems to be the consensus of opinion in all the chapters of this book, as it is also my clinical experience, that especially for adolescents in a group, it is advisable that the function of the central figure be divided between two people, preferably a man and a woman. This has two advantages: in the first place it stimulates further the similarity of the group with the structure of the family situation, inviting family transference and offering a chance to understand the variations of the family romance. The only child will try to behave like an only child; an older brother will be an older brother, but his behavior will be unlike in analysis and in contrast to the real family situation.

The therapeutic situation in the group is only an imitation and a reactivation of the family situation at home, but with better chances to understand, to interpret, to work through and to integrate. A team of co-therapists, especially when they are a man and a woman, invites such effective family transference. Since the young people grow up anyhow, there is naturally a chance in the therapeutic family to change behavior, to rethink, to mature and grow, so significant for the healthy family.

The responsibility divided between the co-therapists has a beneficial influence on the therapist's countertransference. From the pages of this book it appears certain that the group process is dependent on the active, honest, frank and spontaneous responsiveness of the central figures. This is of importance in groups of adolescents even though groups of adolescents are more peer directed.

The learning and maturating experience for the therapists is insight giving to the entire group. Their co-therapeutic relationship offers one great advantage for the therapist: in a group of adolescents the therapist must have the freedom and the opportunity to become at times "one of the group," one of the adolescents, in order to sharpen his empathy and understanding, to interact, and to be accepted. It is a necessity for any therapist to communicate freely with his unconscious. The group therapist needs an additional ability: to communicate with the group just as if he were one of them at times. At such times it is good for him to know that the other therapist remains in control of the situation. There is in all of us an adolescent left alive who is a rebel, who is longing for dependency and searching for identity, independence and individuation. There is in all of us a tendency to be "Mother Superior" and an infant at the same time. At times, tentatively testingly and sparingly, we have to allow ourselves such part regression in order to feel that way because it gives us strength, patience, faith and therapeutic impulse. This strength is sorely needed by the therapist when holding onto his position in a group of adolescents.

A therapist's countertransference can develop toward "counter transference cures." When treating adolescents a therapist occasionally feels more clearly and perhaps also more frequently than in the treatment of adults: "Here by the grace of God go I, and I have to cure me in this, my younger brother." It must be understood that such relationship should be of transitory nature only and should be known to the therapist. They help, however, to give an adolescent, lost in the turmoil of our times, meaning and direction for a while, until he finds himself. In this way he will come closer to find the proper medium between dependency, independency and interdependency; he will have advanced another step in the struggle for identity which is the central core of being adolescent.

SUMMARY

According to the evidence presented in the pages of the chapters here it can be claimed that analytic group psychotherapy for adolescents is a well suited instrument for psychotherapy, especially suitable for this age group. The clinical evidence has been given and the conceptual interpretation of the dynamics with special emphasis on the transference has been summarized in this chapter.

The time may come when the analytic group experience will be integrated in the education and training of most adolescents regardless of whether they are considered to be patients or not, but just because they are human, young and in transition. It is feasible to assume that psychoanalytic group psychotherapy for adolescents will become an integral part of growth and maturation in the education of free adults in the future.

BIBLIOGRAPHICAL NOTE

All chapters of this book have given the clinical evidence and have helped to formulate the conclusions as stated in this chapter, which is an attempt to summarize.

See also my essay on: "The Analytic Group Experience in the Training of Therapists," *International Journal for Group Psychotherapy*, Volume 19, July 1969, pp. 326-333; and also my chapter on "The Profile of the Group Therapist," in Kaplan and Sadock, editors, *Comprehensive Group Psychotherapy*, The Williams and Wilkins Company, Baltimore, 1971.

Several dialogues with Frank Kline, M.D., about his work in leaderless groups have given me insight as stated here in the text. His observations are scheduled to appear under the title: "The Dynamics of Leaderless Groups," in the *International Journal for Group Psychotherapy*, in April 1972.

Part II

EXPERIENCES IN HOSPITAL AND RESIDENTIAL GROUPS

EDITOR'S NOTE

In the previous chapters, various examples of experiences in outpatient and community groups have been presented. Groups in institutions or residential centers are necessarily of a different character.

A hospital or residential center, in a sense, is a group—albeit a large community group. The communal association in ward or cottage has provided a bond of common experiences which can facilitate the beginning of smaller groups. The initial, superficial getting-acquainted stage has usually already occurred, unlike the awkward inception of clinic and office "stranger" groups.

While this preliminary of involvement may be expedited in the hospital or residential community, repelling forces may have accumulated, as well. These will depend on the nature of the administration, the type of population, the physical setting, etc. The size and congestion of the particular social unit will make for obvious differences in the intensity of interaction carried over into any smaller group. A 24-bed ward in a large medical hospital building will foster different interpersonal tensions from those of a unit of 16 children living in one of several cottages on several acres of ground. Despite these differences in setting, experience in smaller groups can have special values in all settings. Notable would be the opportunity for a corrective group experience of intimacy, supplementing those which may be more or less available with house parents, staff, etc. These values may promote the growth of the individuals in the groups, as well as frequently improve cooperative living in the institution as a whole. The quality of these values will depend on the setting and other variables. Many of these are discussed in the articles of this section.

In the first chapter, the description of a ward group at Mt. Sinai Hospital exemplifies the values of such a smaller group within a larger ward group. The group allowed the adolescent patients to feel more securely their differences and individuality when confronting the adult population of the ward. The adolescent's anger and need to act out against the adult patient group, as well as the adult caretakers, was significantly reduced. In a sense, the "generation gap" became less filled with hostility.

I. H. B.

CHAPTER 15

Adolescent Group: A "Must" on a Psychiatric Unit–Problems and Results

Florence Blaustein, M.S.W., and Helen B. Wolff, M.D.

THIS ARTICLE WILL DESCRIBE: (1) the rationale behind the decision to institute a group therapy program for hospitalized adolescents; (2) problems faced in the group's initial stages; (3) the manner in which problems were handled; and (4) changes brought about by the program, in terms of its effect on the unit—some predicted and some unpredicted.

SETTING

The Mt. Sinai Hospital is a private, voluntary, nonprofit general hospital, located in western Los Angeles. It has 237 beds, 26 of which comprise its psychiatric unit, a locked ward known as "The Third Floor."* The ward population is composed of patients of both sexes and most ages, ranging from adolescence to old age. An attempt is always made to keep certain proportions of each age group. The very old and the typically adolescent often create management problems for nursing staff, despite the high ratio (one to three) of staff to patients. The unit offers milieu therapy, intensive individual psychotherapy, drug therapy and E. C. T. An energetic activity program includes patient-staff meetings, occupational therapy, work

---

* Dr. Stuart Turkel was Chief of the Inpatient Psychiatric Unit and Dr. Judd Marmor was Director, Divisions of Psychiatry, Cedars-Sinai Medical Center, Los Angeles.

therapy, discussion groups, supervised outings, psychodrama, dance therapy, games and cooking.

The "Third Floor" has a serious geographical drawback: it offers no access to the outdoors. Patients with no passes or privileges tend to feel "cooped up." Adolescent patients feel this confinement more intensely than others on the unit, since they usually stay for longer periods of time. Because they tend to run away, they are occasionally restricted to the ward by their psychiatrists for months at a time. These physical limitations exacerbate the usual adolescent explosiveness. Despite the need for adolescent beds, it was never practicable to have more than five or six adolescent patients at any one time. Starting an adolescent therapy group was thought to be a first step in determining possible value of this more economical treatment mode, whether used exclusively or adjunctively.

The physical limitation of the unit was not the only factor that made the teen-age patients hard to handle. Long years of behavior problems had rigidified patterns of relating to adults as "the enemy." Many adolescents recreated pathogenic family patterns on the ward, reacting to staff members as if they were "bad parents," and particularly female staff, as if they were "bad mothers." Healthy adolescents often live in states of rebellion and turmoil, which are manifested sometimes by acting up, sometimes by mute withdrawal. With sick adolescents, this turmoil is heightened by their psychopathology, whether the diagnosis be addiction, schizophrenic reaction, depression or attempted suicide. Usually, by the time they arrived on the "Third Floor," many other forms of treatment had been tried unsuccessfully. They often came half dead from drugs or in a state of rebellious defiance. Some were sent by the courts as an alternative to Juvenile Hall.

Staff members tended to be put in a bind by the almost constant defiance of most of the adolescent patients. On one hand, staff felt forced to be accepting, because they knew how acutely ill the teen-agers were, but they felt angered, on the other hand, because they saw these patients as "just plain ornery" or "spoiled." With staff often only a little older than the adolescent patients, rivalrous feelings and envy came into play. On occasion, nursing staff had difficulty in preventing negative countertransference reactions from interfering with professional stance vis-a-vis the teen-agers.

All of this added up to a long-time pervasive situation of chronic difficulties between staff and teen-age patients. Not only staff, but also older patients, became targets for hostility similar to that shown to parents on the outside. At patient-staff meetings, run by psychiatric residents, the adolescents acted up with such provocativeness and such rancor that constructive use of meetings was difficult for everyone. Still another intermittent adversary relationship was the one between staff and attending psychiatrists over the issue of control of their adolescent patients. Staff personnel were often put in the spot of having to be the disciplinary or "bad" parent to the teen-ager, while the individual doctor would often be "conned" into being the overindulgent or "good" parent by a teen-ager well schooled in such deception. This running tug of war between ward staff and the doctors tended to make the ward milieu further imitative of some of the home conditions which had contributed to development of the adolescents' problems.

Other authors have indicated that there might be values in having an adolescent group, aside from ward management considerations. Kraft (1961) has stated that the "adolescent is primarily peer oriented and his adjustments emphasize peer problems. Group therapy with his peers is often the device by which problems can be elucidated and worked out. The adolescent needs to let out the explosive feelings that beset him. This is often difficult to do in individual therapy, with its threatening adolescent-adult configuration, whereas in a group situation it is quite feasible and acceptable.

"The variable nature of adolescence is another consideration. For example, the adolescent may be withdrawn, which makes individual therapy difficult because of the traditional requirement of verbalization. He can be withdrawn in a group for meeting after meeting, however, and still be a member of this particular therapeutic situation. Under group conditions the adolescent can obtain strength from others. He can see himself by contrast in a way that is not critical or belittling."

We tend to agree with Kraft's opinions, rather than with those of Pattison, Briessenden and Wohl (1967). They reviewed the literature of the last 20 years and state that to date "psychoanalytically oriented group psychotherapy may not make any unique contribution to an intensive inpatient treatment program in which therapeutic group activity is already employed. Behavior in group therapy may be related to other treatment factors, instead of to group experience. Group therapy may even vitiate other aspects of a multitherapy program, although it may equally well have a synergistic interaction." In their own study of this problem they concluded that in "comparison with a control group, patients in group psychotherapy did *not* show greater improvement than control patients, although both groups improved."

Kraft's observations seemed particularly pertinent in terms of the acutely disturbed youngsters we treated. Our teen-agers appeared to feel especially isolated and alone. They needed their peers but were usually awkward and uncomfortable in groups. They tended to be suspicious and distrustful of adults and found they could relate to one another by attacking the adult world. All had past, present and, undoubtedly, future problems in dealing with parents and peers, as well as with life goals and reality choices. It seemed, therefore, that group therapy for these patients could have special utility: (1) as a place for the detailed examination of ways of relating to their peers (many adolescents avoided growth in this function, since drug taking obliterates the anxiety and pain which stimulate this kind of growth)* and (2) a place for an additional corrective emotional experience, with therapists providing a chance for a new kind of mothering.

In accordance with this last point, the unit director chose two women to act as cotherapists. It was felt that women could more directly fulfill the dependency needs of adolescents, and cotherapists might reduce the difficulty of one therapist's facing the defiance and hostility of the group alone. In addition, since most patients have male psychiatrists, it was thought that female group therapists would add an extra dimension to the total treatment process. Women therapists also would be likely to take a maximum amount of pressure off the female nursing staff. One of the women chosen was an attending psychiatrist who, for many years, had treated adolescent patients on the ward and was especially expert, both in ward and adolescent problems. Her cotherapist was the unit's psychiatric social worker, a person with several years of experience. She also served to improve communication and coordination of efforts, as she worked not only with the patients, but also with their families and individual psychiatrists. Simultaneously, it was planned for her to conduct one of the patient-staff meetings each week.

When plans for the new group were announced, there was "wait and see" neutrality from many nursing staff members but cooperative, optimistic attitudes from most of the attending doctors. We expected hostility, testing and resistance from the adolescents themselves. Regarding these reactions, Westman (1961) writes: "Because of deep-seated identity uncertainties in these patients, the importance of encouraging identification with the therapists and the difficulties in achieving this were of considerable significance. We unobtrusively offered ourselves as objects for identification, because explicit efforts to impress our attitudes or friendship upon the patients

---

* Our adolescent girls gave us a clue to their needs along this line by showing avid receptivity to a discussion group, called "Social Growth," run by the nurses.

would have been perceived by them as threatening and would have evoked enmity."

Ackerman (1955) points up the importance of the therapist's revealing himself and thereby being seen as a model for identification. To help motivate adolescents toward identification, the therapist must first achieve their respect and admiration. Shellow (1958) describes the inevitability of personal anxiety in the therapist, which creates an unusual burden for him, requiring that he not only withstand the skillful, provocative attacks of the patients, but also that he handle the attacks in such a way that he gain their respect. The patients test in a perceptive way. The task of the therapist is to pass these tests. Positive transference is achieved only after a long contest, which taxes the personal fortitude of the therapist. Schulman (1952) states that a benign authority-dependency relationship provides an optimal climate for the disturbed adolescent's identification with adults. Westman (1961) confirms this view and states further: "The essence of the therapist's acceptability as a model for identification appears to be reflected in his resiliency as he interacts with the boys or, in the vernacular, his ability to 'take it' and to 'dish it out.' If he is vacillating, tentative or vague, the patients' search for a stable figure is frustrated. Their keen, penetrating analysis of the therapist renders ineffective anything but a forthright approach on his part to the group."

THE GROUP BEGINS

Our initial group meetings, which took place once weekly for 1¼ hours, covered the whole spectrum of resistance. There was personal attack, "What are your qualifications?" "Why do you sit that way?" and angry silence, "We talk to our own doctor; we don't have to talk here." There was lateness, rudeness, an attempt at splitting the therapists, outright attempts at sabotage, private jokes to shut out the therapists, attempts to trap or subvert them into overt or covert winks at broken rules. "My doctor won't let me smoke on the ward, but here it's different; you won't tell." It took steadfast purpose, mutual support (one therapist alone might have been scorched by the "heat") tolerance and understanding to withstand the withering attacks. We began devising ways to break down some of that initial resistance. Food helped. Since the meeting took place at 9 a.m., we provided sweet rolls, coffee and milk as an alternative or addition to breakfast. For a number of weeks no one would touch our offering, but gradually a nibble or a sip bespoke the beginning of acceptance.

We attempted to present ourselves as models of both flexibility and firmness. When there was a request to skip exercises on group day, we granted it but then grew more insistent on punctuality. The issue of trust and confidentiality arose almost instantly. The patients tended to see the therapists as spies who would chart their behavior for staff and doctors, thereby jeopardizing privileges. Evidence of this concern was discernible from verbal content focusing on the discovery of high school friends that their most trusted buddies were "narcs," who turned them in to the police.

Gradually, *over a three- or four-month period, the resistance began to diminish.* The therapists simply had to endure the transition period, refusing to play any stereotyped role, whether stool pigeon or collusive parent. As the hostility was permitted ventilation and verbalization, without retaliation and without induction of guilt, the adolescents could begin to use the sessions fruitfully. The group began to have a firm place in the structure and sub-culture of the unit, as some adolescent patients left and others came in. Adolescents began to see themselves as part of a special "in" group within the unit. It became increasingly clear that the therapists would not be "conned" or corrupted, and therefore, they could be trusted. This provided a new and often corrective experience for adolescents accustomed to corruptible parents, who accepted antisocial behavior rather than risk teen-age wrath.

Within the nurturing atmosphere tender feelings were more easily expressed: feelings of yearning, loneliness and dependency, a desire to be cared for and protected by adults. It became possible to investigate the meaning of drug abuse—drugs served to mask anxiety around feelings of inadequacy and inferiority. From this we proceded to discuss anxiety about the future, how relationships with other people could help after hospital discharge, how goals could be set realistically and, therefore, closer to achievement. The group began to be a safe place for voicing doubts, perhaps because the dependency needs and fears were shared by peers.

Meanwhile, resistance and anger came from other areas. *The reaction of a number of ward nursing staff members to the initiation of adolescent group was unexpectedly negative.* We had predicted that the idea of group would be universally welcomed as a helpful addition to the total milieu. Our prophesy was inaccurate. Some staff reacted with overt irritation, "Tell us what went on in there," others with covert signs of anger, "We forgot to order the sweet rolls. Sorry." Some openly stated a feeling that something was being taken away from them. Reasons for staff resistance seemed to lie in an old ward tradition, that only the individual psychiatrists did therapy with patients. Relationships between the staff and the adolescents were often jealously guarded and overintense. We saw the antagonism as a function of that overattachment. When the group began, the therapists were not looked upon as collaborators within the milieu who might help share the burden of adolescent care with staff, but rather as interlopers. This was probably related to the role change of both therapists. Additionally, there was the factor that many staff people were themselves just past adolescence, resulting in a double-edged phenomenon. We observed staff competing with the therapists (as rival parents, perhaps) for relationships with the teen-agers, but also competing with the adolescents (as rival siblings) for the attention of the therapists.

Gradually, ways and means were found to integrate the staff into the new ward activity. The therapists instituted meetings with key staff members preceding and following the group therapy hour. Before adolescent group meetings the staff clued us in on ward feelings and events. Afterward we shared with them content relevant to facilitating their own dealings with group members. For example, if an adolescent patient were especially depressed, staff could be alerted to elopement or suicidal behavior. Communication was thereby enhanced. Furthermore, these corollary meetings seemed to help the staff to deal with their strong fears of being overlooked or supplanted. Gradually, some of the staff began to see that they themselves were reacting to their own early life problems related to mothering and perhaps felt some envy of the extra attention being given to the teen-age patients. Little by little, the adolescent group came to be perceived as a joint venture on the part of staff and therapists. Within a few months the staff became enthusiastic endorsers of our efforts, openly stating that the existence of the group made the adolescents more manageable.

Unexpected *resistance also was demonstrated by some attending psychiatrists.* It was certainly a break with ward tradition to have group therapists where previously only individual treatment had prevailed. Overtly the attendings endorsed the idea of an adolescent group but in covert ways seemed at times to sabotage it. For example, despite notification of group meeting time, doctors would schedule individual sessions at the same hour and take their patients from the group. Adolescents were sometimes given passes to leave the ward when our group was due to meet. One attending psychiatrist displayed open anger when the group's psychiatrist suggested to him a diagnosis that differed from his own impression. Another attending man commented it was no wonder the adolescents showed initial hostility toward the group when it was "being run by two old ladies." Psychodynamically, the resistance and anger were probably a function of competitive feelings toward therapists perceived as rivals, rather than as teammates.

Gradually this attitude changed, and the attendings, too, became cooperative and collaborative. Certain cases necessitated administrative edicts, stating that the group was to supersede all other activity, except for emergencies. In other cases there was no leverage, and the orders of the private psychiatrists prevailed. In one instance an adolescent patient felt so isolated because she could not meet with the group that she eventually pressured her psychiatrist into changing the time of the individual hour.

We tried to detoxify the situation and promote acceptance by sharing openly and assertively content from group sessions, to illuminate both interpersonal transactions and internal dynamics of adolescent patients. This was accomplished within the formal structure of the ward at scheduled meetings, and we actively arranged impromptu conversations on the ward.

RESULTS

By the time three months had passed, the adolescent group was integrated into the total milieu treatment program and was accepted fully by the patients, the staff and the attendings. At this point we began to examine over-all ward changes, with the idea of assessing the purpose served by the group on the unit and the value in continuing it.

We could observe phenomenologically that there was a *distinct change in the atmosphere on the ward*. No longer did adolescents battle with the staff in the old destructive ways. Old-timers among the staff recalled incidents of an earlier era, for example, when some teen-agers barricaded themselves in a conference room and hurled records against the walls until the room looked as if it had been under mortar fire. Of course, angry feelings still existed, but increasingly they were expressed verbally. Staff became less prone to see the individual adolescent as "an irascible, spoiled brat," but rather as a disturbed young person amenable and in need of help. There were still fluctuations of mood on the unit, but they seemed to be more a function of other variables, such as severity of diagnoses, arrivals and departures and staff vacations.

The relationships between adolescent and adult patients likewise became less hostile. In patient-staff meetings, some adolescents carried over gains from their smaller group meetings, becoming leaders in the larger group. This was a therapeutic boost for youngsters struggling toward new identity. Former angry attitudes toward parent figures among the older patient population altered, and many good discussions took place. We saw this not only as bridging the generation gap on the ward, but also as helpful to family relationships on the outside.

The attendings became increasingly supportive of the group, insisting that their patients participate. In addition, some have requested that an outpatient group be available for youngsters who have left the hospital. The adolescents themselves began to wait for each group meeting to start and were reluctant for it to end, even on days when they felt passive and depressed. There was relief when they learned of the plan for a post-discharge group.

FOLLOW-UP

After the first year one observable change has been our ability to meet (albeit in a small way) the ever-increasing need for adolescent beds. It is now possible to integrate into the unit two or three additional adolescent patients without overburdening the staff or disrupting the adult population. There is still no way to evaluate therapeutic gains for the individual patient, although it seems reasonable to speculate that an improved milieu makes for a better hospital experience. Whether the addition of a post-discharge group will facilitate maintenance of gains made in the hospital is a question for the future.

We are continuing to evaluate the idea of group therapy as a sole treatment modality for hospitalized adolescents as the need for adolescent beds continues to grow and as psychiatric care becomes increasingly expensive.

From the experience with our adolescent group thus far, we are impressed by this form of treatment as a way of reaching teen-agers. The stresses experienced by the adolescent patient in the intimacy of a one-to-one relationship seem to diminish within the group. Intensity is diffused, demands on the individual patient are fewer, and therefore, there is less need to defy for the sake of defiance. The result seems to be that dependency needs may be revealed and dealt with in a growth-producing way. There is the possibility of learning to talk intimately without use of drugs as a crutch, admitting to enjoyment of the spotlight, along with learning to share it, and talking openly with authority figures in a mutually respectful way.

The gains, in terms of interchange and harmony within the milieu itself, have been maintained. The network of communication has progressively expanded with new-found ways of using triangulation as a means of zeroing in on patient problems. Patients are viewed at different points by individual psychiatrists, staff and group therapists, or at other points they are observed in patient meetings, family sessions and in adolescent group. Feedback is an on-going and proliferating process. The over-all understanding of each patient, both psychodynamically and transactionally, seems to grow geometrically. The adolescent group has become such an integral part of "The Third Floor" that it is difficult to recall the time when it did not exist.

REFERENCES

ACKERMAN, N., (1955). Group Therapy with a Mixed Group of Adolescents, *International Journal of Group Psychotherapy*, Vol. V, pp. 249-260.

KRAFT, I. A., (1961). Some Special Considerations in Adolescent Group Psychotherapy, *International Journal of Group Psychotherapy*, Vol. XI, pp. 196-203.

PATTISON, E., BRISSENDEN, A., and WOHL, T., (1967). Assessing Specific Effects of In-patient Group Psychotherapy, *International Journal of Group Psychotherapy*, Vol. XIII, No. 3, p. 295.

SCHULMAN, I., (1952). The Dynamics of Certain Reactions of Delinquents to Group Therapy, *International Journal of Group Psychotherapy*, Vol. II, pp. 334-343.

SHELLOW, R. S., WARD, J. G., and RUBENFELD, S., (1958). Group Therapy and the Institutionalized Delinquent, *International Journal of Group Psychotherapy*, Vol. VIII, pp. 265-275.

WESTMAN, J. C., (1961). Group Therapy with Hospitalized Delinquent Adolescents, *International Journal of Group Psychotherapy*, Vol. XI, pp. 410-418.

EDITOR'S NOTE

The next article describes a group at The Westwood Hospital. Here the group had both a peer authority and activity orientation. It shared and facilitated some hospital administrative decision making pertinent to the adolescent patient population.

Undoubtedly, hospital groups at both Mt. Sinai and The Westwood shared many similarities, all of which could not be detailed in the articles themselves. The physical features and staff orientation of each setting played a part in the differences. Both hospitals, at the time of these reports, served a similar middle class population. However, the Mt. Sinai unit was a locked facility on the third floor of an eight-story hospital building. A more directed control by staff was therefore possible. The Westwood Hospital, on the other hand, was a one-story, rambling, ranch style building, with many doors opening onto an acre of green, grassy field. The sense of containment and proximity to fellow patients was considerably less than in Mt. Sinai. This comparative lesser feeling of containment may have benefited, therefore, by an adolescent group which provided greater administrative structure. At Mt. Sinai the closeness of the ward arrangement undoubtedly created a tension which was benefited by a group, which allowed for some discharge of feeling. Some administrative decision making occurred in the Mt. Sinai group, as well as some discharge of feeling in the Westwood group, but the proportion of both these ingredients may have varied, owing to the setting.

I. H. B.

191

CHAPTER 16

The Value of a "Youth Group" to Hospitalized Adolescents

L. James Grold, M.D.

THE RAPID GROWING ADOLESCENT sector of our community has had a profound effect on the psychiatric hospital. There has been increasing community pressure to admit more psychotic adolescents and young adults with severe problems of social adjustment, such as drug abuse, delinquent behavior and sexual promiscuity. Many private hospitals have figured that from one-third to one-half of their total census is composed of disturbed adolescents. This influx of young adults affected staffing, budgeting and treatment programing of psychiatric hospitals. The Westwood Hospital, a 60-bed, private, psychoanalytically oriented hospital, had its composure shaken by this type of pressure. Modification of the traditional hospital structure was necessitated.

Each patient at The Westwood was admitted by his own psychiatrist, who prescribed a specific treatment plan, according to the understanding he obtained from individual psychotherapy and from the patient's behavior in the milieu. The doctor's goals were translated by the directors of nursing and adjunctive therapy into an organized schedule of recreation, work and social activities, which permitted the maximum amount of contact between patients and staff members in a variety of different situations. The entire hospital was organized into a work-therapy program, from the kitchen to

Dr. Grold was Medical Director, 1966-69, of the Westwood Hospital, Los Angeles, California 90025.

the maintenance department, from the switchboard to the garden. All these areas were available for therapeutic assignments, conducted by the non-clinical staff in collaboration with one of the nursing or adjunctive therapy staff.

A meeting of all patients and staff was held weekly, to discuss and vote on the problems encountered in group living. Since all members, including the medical director and director of nursing, had only one vote, the staff were obligated to state their opinions before the proposal had been decided by a majority vote. Committees composed of patients and staff members, such as the Welcoming Committee, the Week End and Evening Activities Committee, the Library and Executive Committee, met weekly with their staff advisors. As the patients progressed they were given, and assumed, increasing responsibility in their committee work and other planned activities.

The hospital, which had been functioning on this basis effectively for some time with primarily adult patients, entered into a crisis in November 1966, when the staff suddenly realized that one-third of the patients were adolescents. Harried staff members were functioning more like policemen than performing any therapeutic functions. The frustrations and anxiety of the staff and of other patients were mounting as the adolescents became increasingly destructive. An emergency staff meeting was called to discuss the problem and to find some effective means of dealing with the mounting tension. It became clear that the staff members were uncertain as to what constituted normal teen-age behavior and were inconsistent in controlling behavior which exceeded reasonable bounds.

It was decided that the adolescents needed a regular meeting, in which the everyday problems of adolescence could be discussed on a group basis. As a result, The Youth Group was instituted as an integral part of the hospital's milieu program. Staff members especially interested in working with teen-agers volunteered to be advisors to the group. The first meeting was held with the medical director and director of nurses. They directly confronted the entire group of adolescents with their destructive behavior, admonishing them to begin conforming to the hospital's rules and regulations or of necessity be subjected to administrative discharge, if the behavior continued. In consonance with each adolescent's physician, it was stated that attendance at The Youth Group's meetings was *mandatory*. At the following meeting a tense, subdued group of teen-agers appeared. The staff advisors discussed the purpose of the meeting and the structure to be followed in future meetings. An election of officers and other arrangements were made at that time.

One of the major themes which was repeatedly explored and interpreted to the group was the adolescents' attempt to test limits and thereby discover external controls for their impulses. The adolescents constantly tried to outwit and outmaneuver the staff, often by very subtle techniques. The mood of the meetings fluctuated from a resistant, hostile silence to a total unwillingness to participate in any kind of constructive activities.

Several events were crucial in developing a more collaborative relationship between staff and patients. It was suggested by one of the teen-agers that *a car be bought as a project* for the boys to rebuild the engine. A group. of adolescents and staff scoured the used car lots and bought an old jalopy for $50. Working on the car together created the most enthusiasm and involvement seen for many months. A *cooking and sewing group* was scheduled *for the adolescent girls*. This was greeted with considerable interest and participated in actively by many of them. Out of this regular weekly meeting came plans for improvised music sessions, a Youth Group dance night and off-grounds shopping trips. In order to pay for the twice-weekly outings, the Youth Group organized a car wash.

A more collaborative phase was emerging. One of the adolescents suggested that a specific study hour be set aside for those attending school and those involved in private tutoring. Also, the group itself decided on methods to govern misbehavior and appropriate punishments, such as exclusion from youth activities for one week.

What was now becoming progressively more obvious to all concerned was the dramatic lessening of destructive behavior. Testing of the limits of the staff advisors continued, but to a considerably lessened degree. As time went on, the Youth Group became an integral part of the total hospital milieu program and was accepted as routine by all newly admitted adolescents and their staff psychiatrists.

Because The Westwood Hospital treated many different age groups, the adolescents were obliged to work out their relationships with adults in a variety of different settings. Adult patients often helped reduce the panic experienced by the adolescents as they attempted to cope with their impulses. Transient relationships were established with adult patients, who provided models for identification, often without the intense ambivalence experienced in relation to staff or to the patient's own parents. Oftentimes adult patients were able to point out unrealistic and destructive behavior in the patient-staff meeting. This often exerted group pressure on the adolescent, resulting in effective modification of behavior. Thus, pressure, or persuasion, toward more realistic interaction with others was exerted from three sources: therapist, Youth Group and patient-staff meetings. Consequently, an optimal corrective resocialization experience, with appropriate attention to intrapsychic components, could take place.

EDITOR'S NOTE

The third article demonstrates a different need of the adolescent population, again related to the structure of the setting. On an adolescent ward in a teaching hospital, such as U.C.L.A., group therapists are frequently changed, undoubtedly leading to some anger in the group members. This anger could be easily displaced from the frustrating, potent, senior caretakers to the less potent, more transient, resident psychiatrist group therapists. The homogeneous population would provide more peer group security than a ward that also contained adult patients. The special, smaller group then would be less necessary as security, compared to the situations in the previous two adult-adolescent hospitals. Separate administrative ward meetings were held, and a smaller group did not have to deal with special administrative decisions pertaining to adolescent patients, as did the group at The Westwood Hospital. The absence of sick adults, on the other hand, deprived adolescent patients of perspective and the possibility of helpful attachments to sympathetic adults. The lack of this older population may have encouraged concentration of anger at the caretaking adults, since displacement was less possible. The paper of Constas and Berkovitz exemplifies a type of hostility to the therapist not described in any of the other papers. It may have occurred in other settings and been included under the category, "testing the therapist." The type of "bugging" described here, however, seemed to be stronger and more ritualistic, perhaps for some of the reasons stated above.

I. H. B.

CHAPTER 17

"Bugging" of the Therapist in Group Therapy on an Adolescent Ward

Robert L. Constas, M.D., and
Irving H. Berkovitz, M.D.

THIS PAPER IS A COMMENTARY on how the "generation gap" can be deliberately fostered in an inpatient setting and how it can be at least partially resolved, with mutual benefits for both the generations. The Adolescent Inpatient Ward in the U.C.L.A. Neuropsychiatric Institute is an open ward, located on the third floor (of six) with the Children's Ward. Four adult wards are located in the same building, but on different floors. The ward contains both girls and boys, with the age range from 13 to 17. The girls and boys have their separate sleeping quarters along different corridors. The average census is 22, with 16 to 24 beds being occupied at any one time. The NPI school was then located on the same floor as the wards. This material was written in 1967, and situations to be described may not have prevailed in subsequent years.

An adolescent subculture is encouraged on an all-adolescent ward. It has been our experience that, indeed, such a ward is difficult to manage and expensive to operate. However, careful selection will be helpful.

Best results have been achieved with those adolescents who have generally been excessively shy, inhibited, obsessive-compulsive or borderline

The groups described took place in 1967-8 when the senior author was enrolled in the Child Fellowship Program. No reference is intended to groups now in progress at U.C.L.A. Neuropsychiatric Institute.

With assistance from David Albin, M.D., and Larry Newman, M.D.

psychotic. Those with anorexia nervosa and frank schizophrenia at times have improved. Poorest results on the ward were with severely sociopathic, severely delinquent types. A few mildly acting-up patients on the ward do help to "spark" things along and encourage the inhibited types to risk confronting and challenging authority. At times the staff was "secretly" happy when an inhibited patient "split" (ran off for a while) or became more self-assertive. Obviously, such an approach is not useful for severely delinquent adolescents.

All patients were seen in individual psychotherapy by either second-year residents or child psychiatry fellows. The ward psychiatrist supervised all residents and fellows assigned to the ward at the time. The number of therapists seeing patients on the ward at any one time could have ranged from five to eight.

GROUP THERAPY STRUCTURE

All patients attended group therapy once a week for 45 minutes. Attendance was compulsory. Boys and girls met separately. The group size ranged from five to eight. Thus there might have been two girls' groups and two boys' groups. The therapist was either a second-year resident, rotating through the service for four months, or a first-year child psychiatry fellow, rotating through for six months. Nursing staff members also usually attended the groups, a female with the girls and a male with the boys. There was an effort to avoid the therapist's having his own patient in the group. In addition, troublesome combinations of patients were separated, if possible. The patients in any particular group remained the same, except for new admissions and discharges. The nursing staff member also remained the same. This made for a sense of on-going group unity, often a problem for the new resident or fellow, since this unity was initially always against him. The nursing staff member was usually noncommittal during sessions.

Both boys' and girls' groups were characterized by a general atmosphere of permissiveness. Anything was allowed, except breaking things and physically hurting someone. Frequently, the therapist entered the group room and found the patients lying on the floor, reading books or turned away from him. There was group pressure to remain silent toward the therapist or to gang up against him and other adult authority. This pressure seemed to help some inhibited and schizoid adolescents toward more typical adolescent challenging of adult authority. However, this influence at times made some very frightened and silent youngsters even more so.

The therapists generally settled on trying to get the group to talk about anything. Interpretations were rare, and the group rarely talked about the issues which had led to hospitalization. There seemed to be an unwritten code about privacy.

BOYS' GROUPS

On the average, the boys were younger than the girls. A new therapist was always harassed and verbally attacked. Foul language was used freely in addressing the therapist, but this occurred only in the group and not outside on the ward.

In the boys' group, especially, there was frequent hazing of members. The older, or larger, characteristically attacked the younger, weaker and more effeminate group members. Those who were mentally retarded or neurologically handicapped were very threatening to the others and became victims of scapegoating.

Although there was group pressure to remain silent, boys could not indefinitely contain themselves and invariably brought up things pertaining to castration and homosexual anxieties. There was much talk of their fear of being sexually attacked at night while asleep, as well as dreams of "cock sucking" and that "so-and-so is a queer." Talk about girls and heterosexuality was lacking.

A major theme of discussion was that of being threatened by the hyper-masculine Negro male nursing staff. Invariably, there was some complaint that a particular male staff member had been too harsh with one of the boys in setting limits. This was one of the few situations in the group in which the resident psychiatrists were asked to help the boys. If the issue of male staff "brutality" assumed serious proportions, the adult in question was invited to come to the next group meeting for discussion of the matter. Usually, this reassured the boys regarding the therapist's concern for them. In the meeting with the male staff member present, the situation was reviewed, and almost invariably, the boys acquiesced and stated that the measure was not as "brutal" as they had made it out to be. There seemed to be an unwritten code that the therapist had to take whatever the group dealt out. Once, when a therapist walked out on a particularly unruly meeting, the group was astounded and commented, "You can't do that; you've got to stay." This agitated them considerably, and the next week they were rather quiet. It could be they were afraid restrictive measures might be imposed upon them if the unruly behavior continued.

GIRLS' GROUPS

In contrast to the boys' groups, there was no hazing of either a new girl or a younger or weaker girl. In general, they were rather protective of each other and seemed to want to draw out the more passive, timid girl, acting like nurses. Very often, even the worst-behaving girls might try to protect the weaker ones.

Unlike the boys, they talked freely about heterosexuality. There was an air of pseudo-sophistication, in which they readily talked about alleged sexual experiences with men. This might involve relationships not only with boy friends, but also with stepfathers, foster fathers and relatives. There was considerable joking about boys. However, there was equal, if not more, emphasis placed on "bathroom" talk and "baby" talk. There was less expressed anxiety about heterosexuality and little or no anxiety voiced about homosexuality.

The girls were noticeably messier than the boys. During a meeting they might spill cigarette ashes on the floor, scatter magazines or other material lying on tables or chairs. This usually occurred within the context of discussing bathroom scenes.

In "bugging" a male therapist, the girls used all the same techniques as the boys but, in addition, employed sexual seduction. One girl with a mild delinquent and sexual acting-out history would lie down "innocently" on the floor and spread her legs suggestively in front of the therapist. When he commented that this was not very ladylike, the other girls maintained "she only wanted to lie on the floor." Another girl, a very attractive blonde, once sat on the resident's lap and would not get off. The other girls hooted and made various remarks. This particular girl had had affairs with her stepfather and foster father. Sexually seductive behavior in the group was usually planned in advance by the girls.

In contrast with the boys, the girls could maintain silence for long periods. It is quite possible that if the therapist said nothing, a girls' group would go on for weeks without saying anything. This probably would never happen in a boys' group.

The experience in these groups encompassed a trying but valuable initiation of a therapist into group therapy with adolescents. Teen-agers have an uncanny ability to detect an adult's character armor and weak spots, and they invariably attack the most vulnerable chink in this armor. In the adolescent subculture of this ward, it was permissible to attack him verbally, although foul language was confined to the group therapy.

A new resident or child fellow, encountering a group already formed, might receive total silence, perhaps shifting to sarcastic remarks about his therapeutic authority and ability. Comments were frequently made, such as, "They are probably just the same as all the other doctors who come through." "Where did you read that one—*Mad* comics?" "You guys all read the same book. What page did you get that from?" "You're just like a computer." They might also begin to tussle about and behave in an unruly manner, testing out to see who was really in control. If this occurred, a particularly recalcitrant group member might be ejected from the meeting by the therapist. Interpretations were often met with booing or hissing. Various jokes were sometimes made about the therapist's name, appearance or sexual identity.

This "bugging" was really not a personal attack. It was an attempt to see if the new resident or fellow was truly mature, dependable and safe as an authority. This behavior illustrated that adolescents will not trust the weak adult. They test to see if the therapist can withstand an aggressive, verbal attack or sexually seductive "assault" without retaliating or taking advantage of the situation. In a sense, they strip away character armor and adult defenses to see if the therapist himself still has unresolved adolescent conflicts that would "hang him up" in dealing with teen-agers.

The therapist here was expected to "keep his cool" and not succumb to the "bugging." Teen-agers really do not want him to come down to their level. They do want him to be congenial, warm, understanding and firm, capable of setting appropriate limits and maintaining a sense of internal authority. In some ways, the "bugging" might be regarded as an active aggressive defense to counter their yearnings to be dependent upon adult strength. The therapist could learn much from the encounter. He could learn to relinquish more external control, without becoming overly anxious or angry. He could find out that teen-agers were really not so frightening. He could learn to cope with aggressive confrontation, not be so defensive, and emerge stronger than before the group experience, a baptism by fire, so to speak.

CONCLUSION

The group therapy structure on the adolescent ward described here was expressly designed for training residents and child fellows in the context of an adolescent subculture. This ward structure seemed to be particularly suited to the needs of the more schizoid, inhibited, and borderline type of patient. Experience in group therapy offered an excellent opportunity for teen-agers who have been unable to cope with normal adolescence to blossom out and challenge adult authority, to find out they can do this safely and, eventually, appropriately. For the resident or child fellow in charge of the group, this experience of being "bugged" and verbally attacked could serve to "initiate" him into a higher level of maturity, resourcefulness, inner strength and confidence in dealing with almost any behavior from future adolescent patients.

EDITOR'S NOTE

The next paper describes a therapy group also in a teaching hospital ward. Here the authors are more concerned with discussing an episode of countertransference on the part of the group therapist. The kind of "testing" described in the previous paper occurred only briefly and was handled differently. Here the way the therapist handled his own feelings seemed to provoke anger in the group members. The presence of timely supervision helped to rescue the group from what might have been a very damaging experience.

The comparison of these two papers offers some suggestions for design of training programs. The Barter and Buonanno experience occurred in a setting where the group had the same therapist for one year. Supervision was frequent, and the therapist had elected to do the group therapy. In the Constas and Berkovitz experience, therapists changed every four to six months, supervision was not consistent, and the therapists had no choice about undertaking the group experience. Possibly under these latter conditions, the group experience is more likely to become an angry, aggressive outlet for the teen-ager. The therapist fortuitously receives a distorted, even though toughening, experience in withstanding adolescent aggression. Another factor may have been that in an all-male group the intensity of anger is greater. The presence of females may well have tempered the type of anger at the therapists. These papers make no attempt to evaluate comparative therapeutic differences. It may be that both have important benefits for the adolescents, as well as for the therapists, in the long run.

I. H. B.

CHAPTER 18

"Should the Therapist Tell When He Hurts?": Countertransference in Adolescent Group Therapy

James T. Barter, M.D., and
Aurelio Buonanno, M.D.

THE PURPOSE OF THIS PAPER is to present a case history of a countertransference episode which arose in the treatment of an adolescent group. For a time this episode seriously impeded the progress of the group. It was recognized and worked through in supervision and then successfully resolved in the group.

Countertransference, as encountered in group therapy, has received less systematic study in the psychiatric literature than that encountered in individual therapy. Goodman, et al. (1964), in regard to group therapy situations, states, "We define countertransference operationally as a response or projection which is not in the therapist's awareness and which, on subsequent exploration, has proven to be evidence of a repetition compulsion which distorts the therapist's perception and has an adverse impact on the therapeutic movement in the therapy group."

It is easy to overlook such reactions when one is trying to understand the myriad transactions going on between members of the group and between the group and the therapist. There is some feeling that when a countertransference problem occurs in group therapy it is usually more intense, more discernible by the patients and more difficult for the therapist to handle than when it occurs in individual therapy [Hadden (1953); Loeser and Bry (1953); Grotjahn (1953); Mullan (1953)].

The countertransference problems arising in the treatment of adolescent groups are only briefly alluded to in papers on group therapy with adolescents. Kraft (1961) warns that "the therapist must understand his own adolescence well, because the urge to act out parental authority conflicts through the group is a very strong one."

SETTING

Group therapy with adolescents is an important aspect of the training program, as well as the total treatment program at the New York State Psychiatric Institute. Group therapy for adolescents provides a setting in which common fears and anxieties can be shared. Weak and primitive ego functions can be strengthened by the group. Needs for intimacy and sharing are met through the constant interaction of the group members in a safe, and protected environment. The withdrawn and isolated adolescent can benefit by observation of group interaction, even though his verbal participation is minimal. Problems with peer relations can be worked out in a potentially more comfortable situation than exists in individual psychotherapy, with its usually threatening adult-adolescent confrontation. Superego attitudes and values toward conformity with the expectations of society can be strengthened through discussion and exploration of "right" and "wrong" behavior and through group pressure.

THE GROUP

At the time of this experience, all adolescents in the New York State Psychiatric Institute were in group therapy, as well as individual therapy. Group therapy was compulsory and, as with other activities in the adolescent program, failure to attend meant loss of privileges or restriction. The groups met for an hour-long therapy session each week.

The therapists of the adolescent groups were either second- or third-year residents, who elected to do group therapy and were usually changed every six months. The therapist of this particular group was a third-year resident, with a major interest in adolescent psychiatry and group therapy, who elected to treat the group for a full year.

The group consisted of from six to nine adolescents, with approximately equal numbers of males and females in an age range of 14 to 18 years. These patients were admitted for intensive milieu-oriented therapy, and some had been in the hospital for as long as three years. Diagnostic categories ranged from schizophrenic reaction to adjustment reaction of adolescence to primary conduct disturbance.

The group had a previous experience with another therapist and were now reluctant to continue. The members displayed a great deal of testing behavior and resistance: tardiness at sessions and long discussions of the worthlessness of group therapy. Suggestions were made by patients to eliminate group therapy altogether, to have shorter sessions, make group therapy voluntary and have it outdoors. Some members attempted to read books or do their homework; others held disturbing secret conversations. The group had been accustomed to a very permissive attitude on the part of the previous therapist, but much of this negative behavior was seen as a testing of the new one. He responded by gradually instituting a number of ground rules to curb these resistances. His consistency in enforcing these rules was constantly tested, but gradually the group became more cohesive, and there were signs of a positive attachment to the therapist. At this point the patients began to talk with more freedom about their behavior and feelings.

In the fourth month of treatment a special episode occurred, which will be described in detail. The therapist had to be out of town for about a week, during which time one of his younger siblings committed suicide. His immediate reaction of grief was not readily apparent; however, over the next few weeks he became increasingly depressed, irritable and withdrawn. At first the group did not seem to pick up this reaction.

In a session during the fifth month of treatment, group members were talking about their experiences in running away from the hospital and helping others run away. The reasons for leaving seemed to be related to whether people cared for them or not. The proof that they were loved was obtained if parents came to look for them or if their therapist responded by restricting them upon their return. This led to a discussion of the fears of leaving the hospital, and they wondered about their ability to cope with the world outside the hospital. Deborah,* an older adolescent, asked, "Have I gotten any better?" The therapist did not respond to this question. Deborah began to banter in a seductive way, her usual mode of behavior in

---

* All names are, of course, pseudonyms. The quotations are accurate, and descriptions of the patients and their responses are as complete as was necessary for this paper.

the group when she wanted something. Her seductiveness had not been mentioned in group before, so the therapist chose now to discuss this manipulative behavior. Surprisingly, the group became angry at him because he had ignored Deborah's question. In a vigorous interchange the therapist tried to defend his action, and this culminated in acknowledgment that he had been threatened by her seductive conduct. As the session ended, various members expressed feelings of resentment because "doctors never answer a straight question; they always twist it around."

Retrospectively, it became apparent that this had been a crucial session. Deborah's query, "Have I gotten any better?" was aimed at securing the answer to another, more important, question, "How sick am I?" That is, if she knew the ways in which she had improved, then she would know the nature and extent of her illness. In a later supervising session it became apparent that this had been a threatening question for the therapist. At that time he was not prepared or willing to discuss illness. Certainly, a counter-transference feeling had been involved in the decision to explore Deborah's seductive behavior. At that moment it had been disturbing to the therapist.

This was a turning point. An attack on the therapist came in the next session. The patients placed special emphasis on the fact that the doctor should not express his feelings at any time. Some pointed out that possibly he was projecting his own feelings when he spoke of Deborah's seductiveness. One straightforward comment was, "You talk as if you wanted to go to bed with her." At the end of this session the therapist felt tired and discouraged.

The following week's session was replete with comments about the therapist's own health. "You have changed. Everybody has noticed it. We are all concerned about you." The doctor admitted that they were right in their observations, that he had been and was still feeling depressed. The youngsters inquired as to the reason but were told that it was a personal matter that did not involve any of them. A long period of silence followed this announcement. Finally, the therapist "jokingly" suggested that perhaps he was a poor group leader and should resign and turn the group over to one of them. Retrospectively, it was clear that this was an attempt on the part of the therapist to abdicate his role and assume the role of a patient, in order to meet his needs to receive care.

Members responded to this in a variety of ways. Joan and Chuck expressed the fear that the therapist might leave the group and they would have to get used to someone else. Mary, who was looking forward to her discharge from the hospital, was warmly supportive and expressed concern that the group might have harmed the doctor in some way. Joan, who was psychotic, reported a fantasy that she had killed the therapist.

In the days following this session, various members of the group approached the therapist and expressed concern for his health. Frequent encounters in the halls involved a reaching out with a half-serious, half-joking remark, such as "Hope you're feeling better."

At the next session, two new members were introduced to the group. They were not made to feel particularly welcome, and the therapist began to concentrate on the problems of group newcomers. However, this discussion was consistently blocked. Chuck began an attack on the therapist, claiming that he was "falling apart" and that he was "sicker than anybody in the group." Tom was concerned about himself and his fears of being hurt or maimed. Deborah was angry at the doctor, stating that she "used to like you a lot but now can't stand you," and calling him a "dirty old man" and a "fink." This session was in marked contrast to the previous one, in which the group had been so supportive to the therapist. At the time the anger was inexplicable. The group leader felt bewildered and hurt by this onslaught. That the anger was associated with feelings that the therapist had abandoned them and had not met their dependency needs became obvious only later.

The therapist and supervisor had been unable to meet during the period of these four sessions, for a variety of realistic reasons. The therapist was concerned with the negative attitude of the group, felt that he had contributed to this feeling but did not really see what he could do to rectify the situation. The patients' dependency needs seemed unreasonable, particularly at a time when he felt that his own needs for guidance and support were not being met. When these sessions were reviewed in supervision, the pattern of events did not seem to make sense. Then the therapist told the supervisor about his sibling's death and his own feelings of grief and depression, and the difficulty became understandable, in terms of a series of countertransference problems.

The first issue in the countertransference was related to the therapist's depression and guilt over his sibling's death. The therapist was the oldest of 10 children, and the family pattern had been to depend upon him, all during childhood and adolescence, for a variety of duties. His own adolescent rebellion had been to decline these responsibilities in favor of independence. He had often felt overwhelmed by various siblings' demands for help and also guilty about not having been able to do more for the family. The death evoked all these guilty feelings again, and the depression followed.

Thus, when Deborah asked about herself, "Have I gotten any better?" he did not answer because he could not. This was a sibling asking for help, and he did not feel able to help anyone at this time. The second issue was related to the question itself. There was something threatening about discussing illness. Certainly, the therapist was concerned for his own mental health at this time. He was depressed and did not feel up to discussing or dealing with the question of anyone's illness.

Finally, there was Deborah's seductiveness. The therapist had been aware of this for some time and could see it as being related to her own psychological needs. The girl was very attractive, and the therapist realized that he was being seductive toward her in return. The sexual feelings she aroused seemed quite unacceptable and further increased his anxiety about his own emotional conflicts. This accounted for the choice he made of attacking this defense, in part realistically and in part as a projection of his own unrealistic feelings, which could then be condemned.

The supervisor pointed out that the group felt the rejection of the leader and reacted by being angry at him. Group anxiety was increased further by his unwillingness to reassert his control and by their inability to do anything to change the feelings of helplessness engendered. Furthermore, by leaving the cause of the depression unknown, the therapist was fostering fantasy formation in the group.

The leader had to take steps to regain group confidence. The supervisor suggested that he inform the group that he had suffered a loss and, as was normal under such circumstances, he had reacted with grief and depression. He was also advised to point out that such grief and depressive reactions are limited in time, that he was now feeling better and was able to help them with their problems once more.

The next session started with Fred and Chuck seated on either side of the therapist, commenting that they would protect him from Deborah. Tom seemed uncomfortable, because of the size of the group, and commented that it seemed as if the group were starting anew. Fred offered the doctor a cigarette, to which he responded with "'How come you feel I am really so fragile that I need protection?" He then endeavored to review the previous four sessions, despite diversion by the patients at each attempt, and finally made the following review as a means of reasserting his therapeutic role. "It all started when I was asked, 'Have I gotten any better?' by Deborah. At that point I was unable to deal with it and talked about her seductiveness. Then you picked up my depression and had many fantasies about why I was depressed. Some of you even felt that you had been responsible for my being depressed." The therapist then revealed that he had suffered a loss, and he had been depressed, as one normally should be under the circumstances. He conveyed the feeling that he was now quite capable of helping them with their feelings and suggested that the group's task was to discuss their problems and not his own.

The general impression obtained during the session was that the therapist had begun reinstating himself in the role he had abdicated and that the patients again were looking to him for guidance and support. In subsequent sessions this impression was confirmed. Members responded to the leader's comments about the purpose of the group by an increased revelation of personal feelings. The ways in which various individuals of the group handled a variety of situations and feelings were discussed quite openly. In addition, the feeling developed that the group was in some way special. Comments were made about the difficulty of another adolescent group with a change in therapists. This group also became concerned with the ways one shows affection and caring. New members were made to feel that belonging to this group was something of a privilege, and it was implied that one had to work to belong—just coming to group meetings did not constitute belonging. A whole series of meetings dealt with problems of sibling rivalry, and there was much competition for the therapist's exclusive attention. The group had become a treatment group again.

DISCUSSION

This case history has been presented, not because it is so very unique, but rather because it illuminates a number of features of countertransference. More especifically, it points up some aspects of countertransference encountered in working with adolescents, individually or in groups. While concepts of countertransference were originally derived from work with individual patients, they do have pertinence to the understanding of countertransference in group therapy.

The influences on the therapist of his intercurrent life situations are also aspects of countertransference. The birth of a child, death in the family, marriage or other crisis situations can evoke feelings which may well carry over into the therapeutic situation. The effects of these events are more easily handled when one discovers the nature of the feelings. The question might be asked: *Are the countertransference problems which arise in the course of therapy with adolescents different in degree from those formed in working with adults? We feel that they are.*

For most adults, adolescence is a forgotten period of development. Childhood is often fondly remembered and seems so distant that one can successfully recollect it without fear of identifying the past child with the present adult. Repression of unpleasant childhood experiences is, more often than not, quite successful. Adolescence, on the other hand, is a tumultuous and painful experience of the recent past. One does not wish to be reminded of it. The gangly, ill-at-ease, unsure creature of adolescence is too uncomfortably familiar to the adult. Repression is much less successful in dealing with the unpleasant memories of this phase of development. In a treatment situation with a teen-ager or group of youngsters, all too many recollections of one's personal adolescence come flooding back. Often there is an attempt to work through, perhaps unconsciously, those unresolved problems of adolescence which persist into adulthood. This forms the nucleus of many countertransference reactions (Holmes, 1964).

In the situation described here, the therapist was confronted with some unresolved problems from his own adolescence. At a time when he needed support for himself he was faced with filling the dependency needs of a number of siblings (the group). As in the past, he tried to abdicate this responsibility by rejecting their demands for help and also by trying to change positions with them (role reversal). This attempt led to further frustrations.

The situation which arose in this group was uncovered in supervision. It may have been resolved eventually but not as successfully. Supervision was most useful in delineating the countertransference and, more importantly, in utilizing its positive aspects in helping the group achieve its purposes. For the group therapist out of training, peer group supervision, as described by Goodman et al. (1964), could serve a similar function.

Another aspect of the countertransference here was related to the fact that this was a mixed group. An adolescent girl can use her newly awakened sexual awareness in an aggressive assault on a male therapist in quite disastrous ways. Adolescent boys stimulate different responses in the adult therapist. With their increased size and muscularity they become quite worthy challengers to our adult prerogatives. Unconscious homosexual problems may be activated. Of course, if the therapist is female, then adolescent boys pose a problem quite similar to that which adolescent girls pose for the male therapist. Unconscious fears of sexual assault and bodily harm often lead to aggressive counter moves by the therapist.

One factor may be adult jealousy or envy of the adolescent's freedom from adult responsibilities. The adolescent has an ability to explore new experiences denied the therapist by age, role, convention, or just plain inhibition! Group therapy is a situation which facilitates the unconscious use of the adolescent for gratification of one's own unattained adolescent strivings. The young person's ability to fool us, let us down or use us may then generate aggressive retaliatory feelings.

Of course, the countertransference problems arising in a particular group will be determined by the nature of the group, as well as by the personality and character structure of the therapist. Cotherapists have quite special transference and countertransference problems which are beyond the scope of this paper. In this particular group setting, the intercurrent life problems of the therapist had a great deal to do with the countertransference. Perhaps it would have been better if the therapist had taken time off and had a substitute take over the group while he resolved his feelings. However, the group apparently benefited from an awareness of the therapist's grief and found reassurance in the fact that he was able to solve this human problem and then take care of them again.

SUMMARY

The development of a major countertransference problem which arose during the treatment of an adolescent group is presented. The initial effect of the countertransference was to impede therapy by creating confusion and role reversal in the group. However, a thorough analysis of the development of the countertransference enabled the therapist to restore himself to the role of group leader and, in fact, the experience became reassuring to the group. A discussion of countertransference in the treatment of adolescents is developed from this case sample.

REFERENCES

COHEN, M. B. (1952). Countertransference and Anxiety, *Psychiatry*, 15:231.

COHN, R. C. (1961). A Group Therapeutic Workshop on Countertransference, *Int. J. Group Psychother.*, 11:284.

FLESCHER, J. (1953). On Different Types of Countertransference, *Int. J. Group Psychother.*, 3:357.

FLIESS, R. (1953). Countertransference and Counteridentification, *J. Am. Psychoanal. Assn.*, 1:268.

FREUD, S. (1957). *The Future Prospects of Psychoanalytic Therapy*, Standard Edition, 11:139. London: Hogarth Press.

FROMM-REICHMANN, F. (1950). *Principles of Intensive Psychotherapy*. Chicago: University of Chicago Press.

GLOVER, E. (1955). *The Technique of Psycho-Analysis*. New York: International Universities Press.

GOODMAN, M., MARKS, M., and ROCKBERGER, H. (1964). Resistance in Group Psychotherapy Enhanced by the Countertransference Reactions of the Therapist: A Peer Group Experience. *Int. J. Group Psychother.*, 14:333.

GROTJAHN, M. (1953). Special Aspects of Countertransference in Analytic Group Psychotherapy, *Int. J. Group Psychother.*, 3:407.

HADDEN, S. B. (1953). Countertransference in the Group Therapist. *Int. J. Group Psychother.*, 3:417.

HOLMES, D. J. (1964). *The Adolescent in Psychotherapy*. Boston: Little Brown & Co.

KRAFT, I. A. (1961). Some Special Considerations in Adolescent Group Psychotherapy. *Int. J. Group Psychother.*, 11:196.

LOESER, L. H., and BRY, T. (1953). The Position of the Group Therapist in Transference and Countertransference: An Experimental Study. *Int. J. Group Psychother.*, 3:389.

MENNINGER, K. A. (1958). *Theory of Psychoanalytic Technique*. New York: Basic Books.

MULLAN, H. (1953). Transference and Countertransference: New Horizons. *Int. J. Group Psychother.*, 3:169.

ORR, D. W. (1954). Transference and Countertransference: A Historical Survey. *J. Am. Psychoanal. Assn.*, 2:621.

REACH, A. (1960). On Countertransference. *Int. J. Psychoanal.*, 41:389.

SLAVSON, S. R. (1953). Sources of Countertransference and Group-induced Anxiety. *Int. J. Group Psychother.*, 3:373.

EDITOR'S NOTE

The final two papers in this section describe groups in residential settings. An important feature for comparison in these two papers is the degree of institutional control. In the first paper a more open, less intense contact is involved, while in the second there is an enforced, close peer group contact. The increased peer group impact would have been useful in both but could not have been achieved in the Vista Del Mar experience. Involvement and engagement at Vista Del Mar had to be achieved by fortuitous or deliberate focusing on anxiety issues. Fortunately, the age-appropriate sexual issue provided this cohesion factor. This issue was not deliberately raised but in a retrospective evaluation was seen to have been significant. The discussion of sexual themes allowed for a useful improvement in sexual enlightenment, as well as in attitude. This aspect of adolescent group therapy is not often mentioned in the literature but probably does occur unnoticed in the abundance of material that occurs in any on-going group.

At Las Palmas, the walled-in structure physically decreased alienation between the girls but, without any additional measures, could have reinforced hostile, manipulative relating to each other. Here again the factor of openness of setting, as well as population, may have dictated the type of group and the values involved. Vista Del Mar is an open setting of seven cottages on several acres of ground, with 16 children per cottage. Las Palmas is a closed, maximum security setting, with 10 cottages on several acres and

10 girls per cottage. The first serves primarily neurotic children of both sexes, while the latter serves moderately antisocial girls. The article of Pottharst and Gabriel describes the changes in therapeutic milieu which occurred when the small group experience was moved into the living unit and increased from once a week to five times a week. The remarkable changes in peer group and patient-staff relating are fascinating to observe.

In this highlighting of physical differences of various settings and the differences encouraged in the groups, I do not mean to imply that these are the only variables which determined the type of group. Neither do I wish to suggest that any one of the experiences was superior to any of the others. The total set of circumstances is crucial. The contrasts, however, allow for live demonstrations of differing growth effects on teen-agers with varying needs and disabilities.

I. H. B.

CHAPTER 19

Groups Promote Maturation of Sexual Attitudes in the Residential Setting

Irving H. Berkovitz, M.D.,
Paul Chikahisa, M.S.W., and
Mary Lill Lee, M.S.W.

A GROUP THERAPY PROGRAM in a voluntary child placement agency was evaluated after two years. Although no focus or emphasis on sexual material had been consciously intended or practiced, it was found that discussion of sexual attitudes arose sooner and more fully in the group setting than in previous individual casework sessions. For purposes of this presentation, references to sexual material have been abstracted from the total group content, which may give the impression that mainly sexual topics were discussed. This, of course, is an artifact.

The agency involved is a voluntary child placement agency in Los Angeles serving Jewish children (ages 7 to 16) for whom placement is requested because of the death, divorce, illness or desertion of parents or because of conflicts in the family situation or within the youngsters themselves. One hundred fifteen children live in seven cottages; there are usually 16 children and two houseparents in each cottage, plus a part-time counselor. At the time of the groups described here, the cottage populations were coeducational. Group therapy was initiated as a way of increasing therapeutic contact with children who had not been successfully reached in the case-

Reprinted in part from the *International Journal of Group Psychotherapy*, 1966. (See bibliography, Berkovitz, et al., 1966.)

Ellen Mauntz Murasaki, M.S.W. was of important help in formulating some of the conclusions presented in this paper.

work relationship. The two therapists were psychiatric social workers on the staff. This was the first group experience for both. The senior author served as consultant in weekly meetings.

Cotherapists were not used. The groups were isosexual. The attitude of the therapists was permissive but did not stress uncovering. Limit setting was employed as group anxiety and disorganization required. Verbalization of feelings, including those about group interactions, was emphasized. Feelings about the therapists were not sought but were discussed when they arose. Educational and reality explanations were given when appropriate. Refreshments (Cokes, cookies and occasionally candy) were routinely provided at each session. Some group "sessions" (no more than once every one to two months) were held at a neighborhood ice cream shop. Sometimes games were introduced by the members, but a discussion format was encouraged. Selection of members was, in the main, circumstantial, i.e., the members were referred by the staff or were in the caseload of the group therapists at the time the groups were formed.

LITERATURE

Gundry (1956) mentions that in a group therapy program with delinquent adolescent girls at the Montrose School for Girls, "Sex was one of the topics most often discussed." However, she does not describe the handling of this topic in detail.

In a residential group of eight "hardened delinquent adolescent boys" (14¼ to 16 years of age), Epstein and Slavson (1962) describe how, after 12 sessions, "a few proceeded to brag about sexual orgies and use lewd language." The turning point in the group came when the therapist pointed out guilt about incestual masturbatory fantasies in one of the boys. Slavson (1962) describes in detail the development of one 15-year-old boy in a residential group therapy experience. Homoerotic panic subsided after the boy received help from the group in overcoming his guilt about masturbation and sexual urges.

Several articles discuss sexual themes in outpatient groups. Corrothers (1963) describes a group of girls whose median age was 13 years, 9 months: ". . . in the first year the girls were preoccupied with their own anatomy. They saw the female as a mutilated being. . . ." They projected or disguised their own sexual feelings. "The second year they revealed their rape fantasies and the fact that they were pleasurably frightened by them." During the third year, ". . . they could admit having sexual feelings, and their curiosity was no longer anatomic but sexual. At the same time they saw the 'female role' as exploited. . . ." There was little discussion of overt homosexuality. The therapists suggest that the group's heterosexual talk was possibly a defensive maneuver.

Schulman (1959), also discussing outpatient groups, states that ". . . contrary to one's expectations . . . the possibility for handling sexual problems in adolescents is enhanced in a mixed group. This applies to homosexual as well as heterosexual problems." He mentions that "spontaneous discussion . . . regarding concern about sexual identity and adequacy . . . is rarely encountered in a group composed of adolescents of one sex." (This point would seem to be contradicted by the experience described in the present paper, at least for residential settings.)

Spotnitz (1947) describes a group, consisting of six girls ranging in age from 15 to 17 years, in which there was much discussion of intimate sexual material. He concludes that ". . . their union into a therapeutic group served to intensify the force of these emotions, to bring them more readily to discussion, to make them more acceptable to conscious fantasy, and to make it easier for the individuals to act in harmony with these emotions." As feelings of inadequacy were handled, ". . . the individuals progressed in the direction of increased maturity." Ackerman (1955), in discussing a mixed group, states, "Four-letter words are used freely and casually, not to show off or defy social conventions, but rather because intense affects are often associatively tied to them. . . ."

MATERIAL

Adolescent Girls

Originally this group was set up to include all the girls living in one cottage. They numbered seven and ranged in age from 14 to 17. After eight sessions, one girl left placement, but the group remained otherwise stable through 36 sessions. One girl had both parents, living in an intact family; one had essentially no parents; one had only a father; and the other four had single, divorced mothers.

The majority of the girls were anxious and had felt threatened in previous individual sessions. All but one had the female group therapist also as caseworker. This group discussed sexual material less than did the other three groups. Relationships with parents and problems in the cottage living situation were of more concern to them.

Initially, there was much resistance to staying in the room for the allotted group time. Several would leave early to find their boy friends or for other reasons. One or two occasionally read books in the session. There was frequent discussion of boy friends. In session 9, after one member brought up the subject of fellatio and "69," there followed a discussion about marriage, intercourse during menses, fertile periods and contraception. The next session they examined the therapist's wedding and engagement rings. When the therapist made her weekly dinner visit to the cottage, questions were asked of her about her husband. The following session, love story magazines were brought into the meeting, and pinching of breasts took place between two or three of the girls.

At session 14 they talked of wearing bras and their disapproval of girls who stuffed their bras. They recalled difficulty with growing up and transition to puberty. Jokes were made of their struggles with parents for permission to wear bras and shave legs. They talked about "going steady." They felt that childbirth was "horrible" and that "the woman gets torn and cut." There was curiosity about the therapist's wedding night. They asked, "What was it like to undress in front of your husband and have intercourse? Would husbands know they were virgins? Would premarital experience be better? Was sex desirable with love or without love?"

Later discussion shifted to less charged concern about weight loss, personal appearance, cottage rules, school, dates and boy friends. They disapproved of girls who "sit with their legs too far apart," "let boys feel them up," or have bad reputations. During these meetings the therapist stressed the value of discussion, self-control and the facing of these difficult subjects.

Adolescent Boys

The group consisted of five boys (13 to 14¼ years of age) meeting in 38 sessions. After this number of sessions, several left the group, and ultimately five more boys (aged 14 to 17) were added. Of the ten, eight had divorced parents. The original five members had no siblings. Their fathers had been absent many years, except in one instance in which the father had died when the boy was 11. After an average of one year of individual casework therapy with each, the therapist felt he had come to a stalemate with these original five boys and, therefore, formed this group.

The original five-member group began by expressing anxiety about adults in terms of fear, mistrust, disappointment, hate and anger. They feared feelings toward their mothers and resented the control the mothers exerted over them. At first, the boys felt that they were in an all-male gathering to tell dirty jokes, fantasy sexual orgies and focus on sex. They were curious to see what reactions they could obtain from the therapist by displaying this material. There were many discussions of homosexuality (more than in other groups going on). Possibly longings for the absent father, previously latent, were more strongly mobilized in the all-male setting. They considered masturbation, which went on in the cottage, or those who masturbated as "queer," but they felt unable to stop it in themselves.

They thought they had to get rough, tough and strong and that they had to prove manhood by sexual intercourse with immoral girls or prostitutes, after which they would settle down and marry a nice woman whom they loved. Intercourse was seen as a way of showing anger and as distasteful, because it always seemed to result in producing "a bloody mess of gore." More tender sexual attitudes made them feel homosexual, sissy or feminine.

In early sessions they expressed fear of homosexual attack. They saw themselves as powerless, helpless children and mother as seductive and frightening. If intercourse were expected of them (presumably with mother?), they would rather be children. They wondered: "What was father like? Why did he leave them? Is sex for fun or anger?" They felt that the therapist must be having sex with their mothers and that mother was a "whore, no good, and probably being raped." At the same time, they thanked the therapist for not rejecting them as their fathers had done. They did not want to be like father, so mother was the only one left to identify with. In addition, they had fears of being men, since they might then seduce women (presumably mother). This led to a regression to oral needs and expressions of reluctance to grow up.

At session 46 there were many personal questions directed to the therapist, because of his engagement and impending marriage. The group members desired to be men, but violence was associated with the sexual act. They linked security with acquiring money but also talked of love and marriage, growing up, graduation, pregnancy, and their earlier life. Subsequently, they discussed babies, birth, seeking an identity and men hurting women. There began to be more identification with the therapist, but they still expressed some fears of getting close and the apprehension that adults were punitive, abusive and undependable. (Undoubtedly, the therapist's marriage aroused fears that he would leave, as other therapists before him had in similar circumstances.)

In early sessions, when anxiety about sexual material precipitated hyperactivity and noise-making, the therapist terminated the session, promising, however, that the discussion could continue in a later session when they were more ready. In previous individual appointments with the same boys, sexual topics had rarely been openly talked about at any length. Strong, unconscious incestual anxieties, especially in the original five members, apparently decreased during the period of group sessions.

DISCUSSION

The general value of group experience for children and adolescents has been widely described in publications elsewhere. By highlighting the special place of discussion of sexual material, we do not wish to unduly emphasize this material, since it is but one part of the varied flow of group discussion. In addition, the conclusions suggested in this presentation cannot be indiscriminately applied to all institutions. The children involved here were primarily neurotic and not strongly delinquent, so that problems with legal authority and internal controls did not occupy a prominent place. However, owing to the nature of institutions and the problems of group living, especially where two to three adults regulate 16 children in a cottage, discussion of sexual material often becomes forbidden and finds only clandestine or defiant expression. At times it seems as if discussion of these issues as a vital part of sexual maturation receives no official recognition or place in the program of many residential centers for children, as pointed out by McNeil and Morse (1964). This is unfortunate, especially because in many residential centers (or institutions) children of disparate levels of experience are mixed together, with the result that sexual behavior and talk are often presented prematurely to many, especially the younger children and early adolescents. Consequent anxiety can cause avoidance of realistic consideration of sexual behavior or a defensive regression and fixation, culminating in inappropriate antisocial or overinhibited behavior.

Placement, of course, also prevents children from using parents as ego ideals, since the parent is labeled "bad" by the fact of the placement. In addition, the parents probably had already withdrawn to angry, frustrated, impotent positions prior to placement. New adult figures for identification are provided in the institutional staff, but it may be some time before these become emotionally significant, if ever. Therefore, the children are thrown onto their own inadequate inner resources, which are weakened by anxiety involving intense, unsublimated and poorly controlled sexual impulses and fantasies.

It is significant that during the several months (occasionally years) of individual casework preceding the group experience here described, little or none of the kind of frank sexual material described appeared. This is a common occurrence in individual therapy with children. There can frequently be mutual anxiety over sexual topics in the one-to-one situation between adult and child. The group situation has the characteristic that, if such anxiety (or, conversely, overinterest) exists in the therapist or members, there will usually be reactions to counteract this. These may be spontaneous, peer-supported pressure for expression, or, conversely, indication of anxiety by hyperactivity and/or absence from the sessions.

The marriage of one of the therapists facilitated an appreciation of the realities of heterosexual relationships. Parenthetically, it is possible to speculate this may have unconsciously influenced the group discussion content and emphasis. However, similar material did appear in the one group in which the therapist was already married, and in another group not reported here.

As might be expected, the initial strong, sexually colored dependence on the therapist aroused fear and mistrust, intragroup hostility and defensive horseplay. The adolescents reacted to the dependence implications in sexual terms, especially the boys, who protested against homosexual implications and projected accusations onto each other and the male therapist. As the sexual threat diminished, sexual topics decreased and the members moved on to identification with the therapist's other adult functions. Sexual energy was liberated to explore heterosexual and other interests in terms of their own identity, furthering their ego development (Fried, 1956).

The adolescent boys had to free themselves from the guilt of unconscious incestual involvement with their mothers, especially after the poor models provided by frequently inadequate or absent fathers. Only then were they able to proceed to see themselves as independent males and to distinguish nonsexual from the sexual expectations of a mature masculine role. The girls were also still involved with unresolved hostile dependent feelings toward their mothers, which interfered with seeing themselves comfortably or happily as mature females.

Contrary to apprehensions frequently expressed about children in a residential setting being allowed to discuss sexual topics, there was no increase in sexual incidents attributable to the group sessions. Some staff members were concerned especially about the discussion of homosexual feelings, but it was felt that the group experience, by reducing anxiety and guilt, probably lessened pressure for inappropriate action. Presentation of this material to the nonprofessional caretaking personnel seemed to promote acceptance and understanding of this previously avoided area.

Through the group experience the children furthered resolution of Oedipal impasses and consolidated more securely their sexual identifications. Guilt, shame, and anxiety were decreased. They were able to progress from preoccupation with aggressive, embarrassed, repetitive use of slang terms to more serious consideration of individual, appropriate standards for adulthood, especially as related to marriage, love and conception. This type of group experience, perhaps alone among the child's many group experiences, provides a forum for discussion of vitally important sexual questions and anxieties with an adult, aided by the security of peer support and peer reinforcement.

It was felt by all those involved in the project that the availability of a consultant was important to its success. Anxieties arose in the group therapists prior to beginning their first groups, and especially during the course of the group experience when the group members were chaotic, rebellious or absented themselves from sessions. The group setting in which consultation was carried on permitted each therapist to receive support from his colleagues, as well as from the consultant. Possibly the consultant's support allowed the therapists to accept and deal more easily with the sexual material presented in the groups than would otherwise have been possible.

This study does not mean to imply that group therapy is the only modality which can facilitate psychosexual development. Casework therapy, family therapy and individual psychotherapy certainly can and do serve the same end. The administrative attitude in the institution itself is also of importance. A repressive attitude can inhibit the freedom and vitiate any gains made in a program such as we have described.

SUMMARY

Material from two groups is presented to illustrate the sequence and significance of adolescent consideration of sexual material in group therapy in a residential setting. Discussion of sexual attitudes arose sooner and more fully in the groups than in previous individual casework sessions. Incestual and homosexual fears were prominent, reflecting unresolved Oedipal conflicts.

It is proposed that group therapy with this age group facilitates psychosexual development, especially in the context of residential treatment. Repressive attitudes of caretaking personnel are circumvented or ameliorated. Sexual incidents outside the groups did not increase. Caseworkers experienced greater comfort and skill in the group setting in dealing with sexual topics. The group members gained a communicative experience with peers and an adult authority, otherwise not available. The group process facilitated progression from the common sexual vernacular to a more adult vocabulary. Lessened anxiety allowed the acquisition of realistic sexual knowledge and attitudes, especially the association of love with sexuality and consideration of the future sexual role.

REFERENCES

ACKERMAN, N. W. (1955). Group Psychotherapy with a Mixed Group of Adolescents. *Int. J. Group Psychother.*, 5:249-260.

BERKOVITZ, I. H., CHIKAHISA, P., LEE, M. L. and MURASAKI, E. M. (1966). Psychosexual Development of Latency-age Children and Adolescents in Group Therapy in a Residential Setting. *Int. J. Group Psychother.*, 16:344-356.

CORROTHERS, M. L. (1963). Sexual Themes in an Adolescent Girls' Group. *Int. J. Group Psychother.*, 13:43-51.

EPSTEIN, N. (1960). Recent Observations on Group Psychotherapy with Adolescent Delinquent Boys in Residential Treatment. *Int. J. Group Psychother.*, 10:180-194.

—— and SLAVSON, S. R. (1962). "Breakthrough" in Group Treatment of Hardened Delinquent Adolescent Boys. *Int. J. Group Psychother.* 12:199-210.

FRIED, E. (1956). Ego Emancipation of Adolescents Through Group Psychotherapy. *Int. J. Group Psychother.*, 6:358-373.

GUNDRY, R. K. (1956). Group Therapy with Delinquent Adolescent Girls. *J. Am. Med. Women's Assn.*, 11:274-279.

MCNEIL, E. B., and MORSE, W. C. (1964). The Institutional Management of Sex in Emotionally Disturbed Children. *Am. J. Orthopsych.*, 34:115-124.

SCHULMAN, I. (1957). Modification in Group Psychotherapy with Antisocial Adolescents. *Int. J. Group Psychother.*, 7:310-317.

—— (1959). Transference, Resistance and Communication Problems in Adolescent Psychotherapy Groups. *Int. J. Group Psychother.*, 9:496-503.

SLAVSON, S. R. (1962). Patterns of Acting Out of a Transference Neurosis by an Adolescent Boy. *Int. J. Group Psychother.*, 12:211-224.

SPOTNITZ, H. (1947). Observations on Emotional Currents in Interview Group Therapy with Adolescent Girls. *J. Nerv and Ment. Dis.*, 106:565-582.

CHAPTER 20

The Peer Group as a Treatment Tool in a Probation Department Girls' Residential Treatment Center

Karl E. Pottharst, Ph.D., and
Marianne Gabriel, M.S.W.

SETTING

THE LAS PALMAS SCHOOL FOR GIRLS serves 100 delinquent adolescent girls, 13 to 18 years of age. On 10 acres of land, there are 10 cottages, each housing 10 girls. A high degree of physical security makes possible the acceptance of girls who are impulsive and unable to exercise consistent control of behavior.

Las Palmas employs a half-time medical director and is classified as an outpatient psychiatric clinic. Fifteen M. S. W. social workers are employed full time (six work in aftercare). Each girl has an M. S. W. caseworker assigned to her. The caseworker is responsible for case management in general, individual casework sessions weekly (or more often), family treatment, group therapy and decisions regarding special discipline, length of stay or furlough privileges. Clinical psychologists and psychiatrists are involved in individual treatment, group therapy and consultation to the residential staff, for about 80 hours per week. Girls not accepted are those with serious physical handicaps, IQ's below 85, psychosis, addiction or overt homosexuality. Most girls accepted have been involved in any one or a number of the following types of behavior: drug abuse, runaway, sex delinquency, truancy, incorrigibility, shoplifting, car theft, etc.

After 1965, the group therapy took place in groups of 10 girls, conducted by a psychiatrist or psychologist, and a social worker, with cottage staff serving as cotherapists. Approximately 85 percent of the families of the girls in residence are seen in family therapy at least every other week. Some are seen weekly. Parent groups meet weekly. In addition to the cottage group therapy meetings, there is a cottage living group meeting, presided over by an elected cottage president. The nine cottage presidents meet weekly as a president's council.

GROUP EXPERIENCE

In 1965, departing from custom of the previous four years, the authors conducted an open-ended group therapy activity in one of the 10 living units. Previously, on-going therapy groups at the school had consisted of six to eight girls selected for group therapy by clinical staff, and meetings were held in the therapist's office or a special conference room. The living unit group was composed of the 10 girls who lived together in the cottage unit, together with unit counselors from the afternoon staff, and cotherapists. This group met every day in the girls' own living room, in contrast to the previous groups, which met once or twice weekly away from the living unit. The purpose of this change was to maximize the girls' involvement in the group and to reinforce the message that the responsibility for self-examination and change is that of the individual girl or group, assisted by staff. Previously, the intimation had been that staff expected self-examination and effort to change but that the peer group would resist.

Several changes resulted. These will be grouped under two headings: (1) changes in interaction between girls, and between girls and staff; and (2) changes in the role and orientation of therapists and other staff.

(1) One change in the level and quality of peer group interaction and adolescent-staff interaction was a *shift from fixity to mobility of role* in confronting interactions. The girl bearing the brunt of confrontations was no longer the same one, session after session. Even powerful or influential girls were confronted, whether they moved into the role or it was thrust upon them. The less uncomfortable position of confronter was occupied by different girls, at variable times and with more frequency. The role of "auxiliary" or "junior therapists," which was prominent in the former group, largely disappeared.

The *variety of issues* to be challenged was also broadened. Instead of one or two girls repeatedly getting "brought down" for sloppy personal hygiene, for withdrawing or whining, almost all girls were faced with a wide range of behavior, including poor work habits, trying to "buy friend-ship," acting "better" than everyone else, lying, "acting crazy," expecting someone else to do one's work, acting "retarded," helpless or phony.

(2) *There was a gradual movement from scapegoating* and retaliatory confrontation *to nonretaliatory and nonpunitive confrontation.* In earlier groups, encounters with weaker peers had often been explosive in nature and frequently served as the channel for displacement of savage hostilities generated elsewhere. "Bad" or weak self-images were projected onto others. In the revised group, confrontation, while still emotionally intense and at times hostile, had a steady, direct, "let-the-chips-fall-where-they-may" quality. Girls did not have to be angry to contrapose; it was done less and less in contexts of retaliation or scapegoating, and more and more in con-texts of "leveling" or "putting it on the table."

Girls relentlessly pressed the one being confronted to the point of emo-tional crisis, undaunted by long, sullen silences or by explosive denials. When the girl being challenged finally dissolved into sobs or choked out some angry, tearful admissions about herself, the confronters suddenly shifted, becoming empathic and supportive. They conveyed that they were able to see her deficiencies or mistakes so plainly only because they recog-nized such characteristics in themselves after having them pointed out dozens of times. They also came up with clinically astute reasons for the girl's un-acceptable actions, in terms of her conflicting roles in her family. Con-frontations were often pressed forward past the point of emotional climax, tears, angry denials or confusion, until the girl made a desperate kind of open commitment to the group that she was going to try to do something about herself or about her problems. In effect, her potential for change became apparent.

Previous concealment of rules infractions in the group sessions gave way to fairly *open disclosure* of these violations, even though this meant going against the peer group code of "not finking." Girls and staff alike felt more freedom in bringing up incidents or in announcing intention to discuss certain matters, so that coaxing, teasing and cajoling a girl into talking at such moments almost entirely disappeared. Neither did they scold or threaten. A direct, no-nonsense approach prevailed. Girls expressed this approach in such statements as, "You might as well get it out. There's no place to hide in this group. Get it out on the table. There aren't any secrets here. The girls that live with you know about it, because it comes out in how you are and how you act. So you might as well talk about it." Occa-sions when a resistive girl was able to prevail against this expectation were rare.

Behavior in the group session *became more mature and integrated,* with less clowning around, better concentration and fewer side conversations. Girls checked each other's excesses and provided corrective reactions to hilarity, silliness, profanity, exaggeration, giggling, etc. Therapists found they were not cast in the role of policemen or disapproving parents as often as before. This change was pleasant and refreshing and freed staff for other things.

Girls respected the right of others to "the floor" and insisted on this right for themselves. A girl who had been interrupted several times would say, "Now, look, goddamit, I have the floor, so will you shut up so I can finish?" Others would say, "Let her finish!"

In our view, this unmistakable movement toward more mature, business-like behavior in group sessions was an outgrowth of the fact that sessions took place not in an official group therapy office, but in the girls' own living unit. Another contributing factor was that all the girls in the living unit comprised the therapy group, instead of the group's being made up of girls selected from different units by therapists and other clinical staff. The therapy group now was the girls' own group, meeting in their own living room. While the precepts for "group therapy" behavior were sometimes subtly, sometimes bluntly, reintroduced and repeated by the therapists, these standards increasingly became the rules of the girls themselves. They, as often as the officially designated therapists, were heard reiterating the rules to each other. The group thus became the girls' *own* group, in which they developed a deep and personal investment.

This last fact is vividly illustrated by the change in the girls' attitude toward the rule of confidentiality. In the former therapist-selected group, confidentiality was chiefly controlled by the therapists, but there were many exceptions. The girls did not trust this system, because they knew things disclosed in group were often repeated to other girls and staff outside the group. In the living unit therapy group the rule of confidentiality coincided with the peer group code of "not taking things outside the cottage." Violation of this maxim seemed to bring about the most jolting and scathing of disapproval from cottage peers. Although staff did not feel as strongly about it as the girls, they did respect the code in their unofficial, casual communications with staff members of other living units. We were aware of a "WE" feeling and the close loyalty that goes with it.

Another *major shift showed up in girls' relationships to staff during the group meetings.* Formerly, girls' communications to staff, particularly to probation officer or cottage counselor staff, consisted predominantly of complaints and demands. Therapist staff customarily countered with interpretations or confrontations of the implied manipulations or "resistances." Girls expressed loud frustration in response to this maneuver and rarely searched for inner feelings to determine the reasons for their complaints.

In the new peer group, complaints, demands, requests, etc., were labeled the "gimmies." The "gimmies" were limited to a definite period of time, perhaps 10 minutes, during the group meeting. They were dealt with on a "reality basis," in positive or negative terms or in terms of the limitations of time available to fulfill such requests. The annoyance of the staff persons in reaction to excessive demands, praise for acceptance of necessary delay or realistic refusal were openly discussed. Girls who were more actively looking into themselves showed impatience with such interactions and joined staff in wanting to get on with the serious business of "group."

In our former groups, staff cotherapists initiated most of the moves to open up serious, significant communication. In the revised group, the girls usually began such efforts, whether with each other or with a staff member. They selflessly brought up the uncomfortable topics, provided openings for anxiety-laden disclosures and waited, encouraged or prodded until the other girl made the disclosure. Staff felt more freedom than before to bring up things about girls' behavior or to suggest that a girl bring out in the group a matter she had disclosed privately.

When a girl had something she wanted to discuss alone with her probation officer or therapist, she was urged to bring it to the group. In a natural way, without coercion or threats, the staff expected that girls would reveal everything to the group of peers and staff; the girls expected this, as well. In this way staff avoided "privileged communications" and separate rules for each girl.

Coalitions and cliques within the peer group now became less common, since there was more openness to the scrutiny and discussion of the larger group, including staff. "In" groups and cliques previously had been a frequent subject of conversation among the girls. Those whose physical size and "strong" manner had dominated others were more often confronted than before. Clinging, appeasing, favor-seeking girls who formed friendships with stronger or better-liked girls were not allowed to hide behind their "poor little girl" facades. Favor-seeking, favor-doing affiliations with staff members were promptly brought to the attention of the entire group.

As a result of this, the kinds of relationships and the unconscious role assignments were more subject to change. Interaction between girls, and between girls and staff, was noticeably more *"game-free,"* that is, free of stereotyped, repetitious, ulterior interaction sequences, frustrating to one person but excitingly pleasurable to the other.

Manipulative games that formerly made up a major part of group interaction were greatly reduced. New or inexperienced girls, who initiated the games of "There's nothing to talk about," or "This place is driving me crazy," or "Try and stop me," were interrupted, ignored or confronted. Injustice collecting ("It isn't fair . . .") was met with the query, "Did you ever stop to think that *you* might have something to do with it?" If someone tried to play the "Therapy Game," ("They say 'express your feelings,' but if you do you get in trouble"), another participant quickly responded, "But what about *how* you were expressing your feelings?" If a new girl announced she was "just putting in time here" (being "busted"), she would be told she could waste her time here if she wishes, but others do not think she is very smart to do so and they do not particularly like her for it.

In group, *girls took responsibility for their own actions* and expected the same accountability from others, whether the act was conscious or unconscious. The authority of the group's realistic perceptions and reactions, in appraisal of a girl's unconscious behavior, prevailed over the individual's right to deny responsibility for her actions on the grounds that she was not aware of what she was doing. The girls seem to go on two premises: "If most of us see you doing something or acting a certain way that is not in your interest or our interest, then we know you are doing it, and we expect you, sooner or later, to be able to control and change it." Secondly, "We will not expect you to change something in yourself that we would not be expected to change in ourselves if you pointed it out to us." Here the group extended a firm, two-way expectation that assisted individual girls to resolve psychosocial crises of autonomy versus shame and of initiative (or responsibility) versus guilt. Cotherapists reinforced this expectation of responsible behavior. Insightful girls were not allowed to use understanding of others' actions toward them currently or in the past as an alibi for getting into trouble.

The peer group focused primarily on making a girl aware of the way she affected other girls and staff, and on the necessity for changing some of her actions. Therapists' focus was on opening up and facilitating communication and on facilitating necessary change. Their point of concentration was *not* primarily on understanding a girl's deviant behavior with the expectation that change would grow out of that deeper understanding. This represented a major shift in therapists' orientation.

Changes in role and orientation of therapists and other staff in the living unit group accompanied the change in adolescent-staff subculture. Formerly, therapists tended to treat every girl in the group "as an individual," with "her own problems." The tendency was to address girls individually in the group, seeking to draw a girl out, in confronting, interpreting her behavior, giving support, etc.

In the living unit group, therapists made comments to one girl that also applied to another, and this was pointed out to both of them; or leaders would ask one girl who was confronting another if what she said did not apply also to herself. If one girl announced good grades, the therapists would show broad interest in other girls' school progress. These leaders directed themselves as much to nonparticipants as to more active members, Distribution of attention and interest, on the part of staff, therapists and group, became more equitable than previously, with the result that girls who would have otherwise "faded into the woodwork" became more involved.

Therapists actively reinforced the social reality that the performance of a girl is tied to that of her peers. Although it was acknowledged that no one can *make* a girl change, it was also recognized that no girl could improve or even understand herself in a solo effort. We were not implying that "other girls can do it all for her," instead of *her* doing it. Rather, we were trying to convey that she had to accept their help and caring, in order to be able to do it for herself. Also, she had to provide help and caring to others to be able to obtain and make use of the help and caring she needed from them.

Some girls were not willing or able to accept staff help *directly* in making *any* changes in themselves. Others could not accept staff help *directly* in making certain *particular* changes. Our belief is that both of these subgroups of girls may be far more ready to accept the help of *each other* directly if the milieu were to emphasize cooperation and open communication, rather than manipulation, conflict, mutual hostility, underachievement, wasted abilities and deceptive double messages. Therefore, in our interventions and suggestions for resolving conflicts and differences, we tried to embody the principle that girls are responsible to each other for their actions, not just answerable to staff.

Human characteristics of staff showed readily in these professional persons. They let it be known that they have limits beyond which they cannot take abuse, limits to their accomplishments, and that they have their natural reactions to insults, excessive complaints, criticism or flattery. They were also more open in expressing feelings of satisfaction with improvements the girls made. We tried to give recognition for changes which pleased us as adults, as well as for actions likely to be recognized and valued by others, including girls' peers.

Staff became far less anxious about not being able to control girls' behavior in the group meetings and found less need to control the group. On several occasions in the former groups, staff members, to avoid scuffles, placed themselves physically between angry, threatening, shouting girls. Once a staff person forcibly held a girl who was about to let her antagonism for another girl spill over into action. In the new groups we simply reminded group members that we were not responsible for their behavior and that their participation in the session was based on their ability to get out their angry feelings in *words, not in blows*. They are expected to remain in control of themselves, no matter what angry feelings they are having.

On occasion, therapists would decide that girls were not making effective use of the time to justify continuation of that particular group meeting and, after announcing this conclusion, simply left the group. Counselor staff then sent girls back to other activity scheduled for that time. The necessity for this was not frequent.

Some staff had apprehension that a girl on the receiving end of massive confrontations might become "traumatized," emotionally hurt or "go all to pieces." This did not prove justified. Such anxieties were replaced by staff efforts to help the girl whose behavior was being examined, to see that the others really were trying to get through to her and, if they were not successful, other, more effective ways, were suggested.

It is apparent that the increased intensity of the five-times-per-week living unit group overcame much of the hostile alienation which had brought these girls to Las Palmas. Our experience confirmed that the peer group, when effectively mobilized, can be a powerful treatment tool.

POSTLUDE

Group Therapy within the Wider Residential Context

Donald B. Rinsley, M.D.

ANY COMMENTARY on the foregoing papers should consider certain general characteristics of the group process, the relationship of that process to the wider aspects of the residential milieu in which it operates, and the symptomatic and dynamic attributes of the adolescents participant in it. First, such a commentary must consider the regressive "pull" which group participation exerts upon the individual group member, with the emergence of introjective and projective identifications, paranoid and depressive anxiety, and manic-denial and related archaic defenses, first described by Freud (3) and later elaborated by Bion and others (1, 2, 7).

Second, as a result of the regressive, identificatory features of group participation, the individual, with his idiosyncratic problems, needs and qualities, may slide into relative anonymity as part of the larger collective; thus, in some instances, one suspects that the therapist's preoccupation with group work of some sort reflects his own discomfort with and need to retreat from the demands of the individual psychotherapeutic process, a misplaced counter-transferential effort at de-intensification which he soon discovers is rapidly shredded when he presumes to conduct a group of wily, labile adolescents.

Third, many publications on group therapy convey the discomforting impression that the groups they describe, usually superficially or phenomenologically, have somehow aggregated by virtue of some general or common feature or problem, such as "delinquency," parental dispossession, and the like, with little if any reference to the past or future of their individual members, or to those of the collective or group itself. Indeed, such writings often appear to have been composed by sociologists with some awareness of psychodynamics rather than by process-trained clinicians.

Fourth, aside from occasional or general references to the milieu or setting within which the group process is stated to occur, many such publications proceed profoundly to ignore the critical mutual relationships of the "group" and the wider residential nexus within which it operates, thereby to ignore the numerous clinical-administrative dichotomies and ensuing multiple-binding communications to which they are subject, a matter with which Blaustein and Wolff, and Pottharst and Gabriel quite rightly concern themselves (v. sup.).

A fifth consideration of great importance concerns the form, depth and chronicity of the psychopathology for which the adolescent is admitted into residential treatment. There is growing awareness amongst clinicians that the adolescent who by whatever route eventuates in the hospital suffers from serious, disabling psychopathology, and not from psychoneurosis, supposed phase-specific "adjustment reactions," or self-limited "turmoil states," terms which often convey euphemistic underdiagnosis of the adolescent's clinical syndrome (8, 9, 12-14, 16, 17). In line with this view, careful study of the adolescent inpatient's family invariably demonstrates matching or analogous psychopathology in the parents and other key family members, which has led over time to serious depersonification of the patient, who has grown up amidst role, age and generational blurring and confusion, diffuse and shifting lines of family authority, and double- and multiple-binding patterns of intrafamilial communication (10, 11, 13-17, 20). Such adolescents are found to have experienced early and severe deprivations and object losses such as to precipitate them into unremitting efforts at protracted pathological mourning with regressive reliance upon splitting defenses (10, 11, 13, 14). Their willynilly inclusion in therapeutic "groups" may otherwise potentiate these archaic defenses, and may lead to therapeutic disaster or, at best, to an "as-if," dissimulative use of the group and the wider residential milieu without significant inner personality change.

A sixth consideration has to do with the timing of the prescription for the adolescent inpatient's inclusion in a therapeutic group, which is closely linked to whether the adolescent is yet immersed in the "resistance phase" of his treatment, or has passed beyond it, made therapeutic identifications with the ward or cottage staff members, hence has begun to perceive the residential setting as potentially helpful to him (12-14, 18, 19). In numerous cases, initiation of formal group psychotherapy while the adolescent continues actively or covertly to resist the therapeutic milieu as a whole simply intensifies the resistances, spreads them out, as it were, and abets the adolescent's use of splitting defenses, now carried over, in addition, to the "group." By the same token, attentively conducted and properly structured groups which meet directly in the patients' living areas serve to minimize the clinical-administrative splits which adolescents so readily exploit from fear of self-revelation, hence may actually supply motivation for treatment.

A seventh matter concerns the use of group psychotherapy in the residential setting in conjunction with ongoing individual psychotherapy. Despite his artful and often stentorian resistances against "closeness," the adolescent inpatient, like his otherwise healthy brother in the community, struggles mightily with the problems and attainment of intimacy. As he works on object-removal and proceeds to devalue parents and their transference equivalents from anxiety over the prospect of regressive re-fusion with them, he nonetheless assiduously pursues closeness as prefatory to the capacity for later, mature object relations. In part for these reasons, group treatment without concomitant or parallel individual treatment proves inadequate for the adolescent inpatient, both as an opportunity for working through problems with object-removal and as a means of exploring and resolving highly delicate, personal issues which are exceedingly difficult if not impossible to express within the peer group. This does not mean that individual treatment should or must be a highly formalized 1:1 process with the adolescent and the therapist closeted away from the youngster's living area; often, in-depth analytical treatment in a 1:1 relationship is better carried out directly in the patient's living area, in a designated area or alcove away but not apart from the mainstream of the ward or cottage goings-on. Ideally, under such circumstances, the patient's therapist also serves as his "ward administrator" or residential psychiatrist, as a guard against the clinical-administrative splits already mentioned (4-6).

A final general consideration concerns a variety of cliches concerning psychiatric treatment of the adolescent, which require the most careful scrutiny. These include:

1. "Adolescents cannot be analyzed."
2. "Intensive (expressive) individual treatment of the adolescent is simply too intense for, and will likely overwhelm him."

3. "Adolescents require a physically active residential program because they have so much energy."
4. "Adolescents need opportunities to express their feelings."
5. "Adolescents dislike talking (i.e., are non-verbal), hence their treatment should heavily stress keeping active and busy, working with their hands, etc."
6. "Adolescents need 'growth experience,' should be guided toward increasingly mature and responsible behavior, and do particularly well in group settings because of their 'natural tendency' to form peer groups."

So far as the first of these generalizations is concerned, and depending upon how one uses the term, analyzed, experience shows that even severely ill adolescents are capable of full engagement in an expressive, analytical process *provided that the therapist, together with the wider aspects of the residential milieu, supplies consistent controls and sets predictable limits for acting out* (4,5). Under such circumstances, the adolescent often demonstrates an arresting skill at observing the "basic rule" of free association for extended periods of time within the therapeutic sessions, as well as the ability to make good use of the therapist's interpretations of transference material. The second, related cliche concerning the adolescent's inability to "withstand" intensive, 1:1 treatment more reflects failure of limit-setting and the therapist's technical inexpertness within the therapeutic sessions than any "inability" on the adolescent's part; these problems frequently express the therapist's regressive, identificatory countertransference toward the adolescent, which in effect "levels" the therapist and abets the adolescent's need to devalue him to the point of therapeutic uselessness.

The third cliche, regarding the adolescent's need for "action," needs critical scrutiny. Often, full-scale "activity" programs, devoid of in-depth process, reflect staff need to deflect and ward off the adolescent by "keeping him going." The key issue here is the staff's uncritical acquiescence in the resistance aspects of the adolescent's apparent inability or unwillingness to communicate verbally, which only further convinces the teen-ager that they are fearful of, hence at root uninterested in him.

The next cliche, regarding the adolescent's need to "express feelings," is reminiscent of the early abreactive-cathartic view of treatment, with its magic-gestural expectation of cure by discharge of affect. The key questions here are: What feelings? How expressed? To whom? Where? When? Within what limits? For the constricted, inhibited, even cataleptic adolescent, "expression" of terrifying, potentially overwhelming aggressive and libidinal affects courts therapeutic disaster; in the case of the labile, roisterous, hyperactive adolescent, careful and modulated control of direct affect-discharge is what is urgently needed; for both, affect needs to be linked with ideation, to promote secondary-process communication to permit understanding of the underlying conflicts basic to the adolescent's particular symptomatic style of intra- and inter-personal relations. The following exchange between a psychiatric resident (PR) and a 15-year-old female inpatient (Pt) is illustrative:

> PR: "You seem to be all bottled-up."
> Pt: "Yea!"
> PR: "Why don't you let some of your feelings out?"
> Pt: "Yeah . . . well if I did I might hit you!"
> PR: "Why would you want to do that?"
> Pt: "I didn't say I *wanted* to do it. . . . I said I *might* do it . . . you're just like my father and I hate him!"
> (At this point, the resident feels he has been "had" and cannot think of anything to say; after about a minute, he finds an excuse to depart.)

The resident's opening statement betrays his irritation toward this under-communicative girl, who responds to it with a monosyllable; the resident's second statement smacks of a "Johnson-Szurek" stimulus to the girl to act out for him, which she perceives, with a warning to him to "back off." By this time, the resident's irritation has reached the point at which he is almost directly projecting his wish to strike the girl into her; she reminds him of his scotoma by abjuring the wish to strike him, then smites him with a direct transference statement which stops him in his tracks. Even after so many gaffes, the resident could well have picked up on the girl's transference statement by inquiring after her feelings concerning and past relations with her father, and might have learned that the father had physically brutalized and sexually abused her, and that she feared the resident (as, in her case, all men) might do the same. A clue to the resident's erotic preoccupation with the girl, and his less-than-conscious fantasies to interact sexually with her is evident in the remark concerning her appearance of being "bottled-up." Supervisory analysis of this opening statement revealed the resident's underlying wish to "open up" (i.e., have sexual relations with) the girl, as well as his deeper need to obtain nourishment from her (bottle=breast).

The view that adolescents are non-verbal (i.e., that they dislike talking, hence are less than desirable candidates for psychotherapy or psychoanalysis), except in cases of demonstrable organic impairment of the central or peripheral articulatory mechanisms, is entirely without basis in fact. Of course, the adolescent inpatient is often less than optimally motivated toward meaningful verbal communication with adult authority figures until he has developed a measure of trust in them; rather, he will often resort to subtle, complex, circuitous verbal and non-verbal metaphors (including "body language" and frank acting out) to convey his anxieties, needs and fantasies, all of which demand careful scrutiny and sensitive understanding in order to translate them into secondary process communication (6). Unless this last, essential aspect of treatment is sedulously applied within the residential setting, therapy quickly founders; it is no wonder that hospitalized adolescents mount repeated assaults upon, run away from, or sink into depressive apathy within inpatient settings in which no one bothers to understand what they are doing, particularly when what they are doing at any given time comprises a prescribed part of their treatment!

The final cliche is, of course, a compound generality, the components of which are often associated together in the views and approaches of therapeutic staff. The phrase, "growth experience," is so vague as to suggest its frequent use as a euphemistic cover for diagnostic and therapeutic ignorance. That adolescent inpatients should be guided toward "mature, responsible behavior," without disciplined attention to the etiology of their symptoms, neatly places the developmental cart before the horse by presuming that the sick adolescent can proceed toward adulthood without first having learned to be a healthy child, a developmental failure ubiquitous amongst adolescents ill enough to require hospital care. The final component of the generalization glosses over the glaringly evident fact that sick adolescents are incapable of generating healthy peer groups; such groups as they are wont to form within the residential setting generally assume the nature of "resistance cliques," the existence of which must be terminated or precluded if treatment is to continue (12-14, 16, 18).

The foregoing remarks may now serve as a launch structure, so to speak, for what follows as a brief discussion of the interesting and informative papers devoted to adolescent groups within hospital and residential settings.

Blaustein and Wolff's paper describes the variety of problems associated with the well-known clinical-administrative dichotomy, and their devoted efforts to resolve them against what one might call great odds. These odds include a mixture of adolescent and adult patients and both sexes on the same ward, attending staff who are not full-time personnel, and full-time staff members not much older than the adolescent inpatients with whom they are expected to work! Optimally, the adolescent inpatient needs older, psychologically healthy staff figures with whom he will hopefully identify himself, not psychologically or chronologically adolescent staff members easily trapped in regressive counter-transference with them, nor sick adults who quickly come to personify the adolescent's own disturbed parents. In addition, part-time or attending staff readily fall prey to the adolescent's redoubtable tendency to split, divide and manipulate staff members, particularly those not in daily, sustained contact with, hence aware of, what he is feeling, thinking and doing. The presence of adolescents of both sexes on one ward very often produces a hothouse atmosphere which absorbs staff energies in actions aimed at "cooling it down," with counter-transference difficulties of the most egregious sort often escaping notice by displacement into apparently unrelated matters. In such a setting, the "adolescent group" thus comes to serve as a limited, small-scale substitute for the all-adolescent ward, with its staff and facilities devoted to the unique developmental and therapeutic needs of this age group. It is to the authors' credit that more than a modicum of success was achieved, although one should venture to suggest at the expense of a more intensive, reconstructive therapeutic experience for the adolescents.

Grold's paper describes a very different setting from Blaustein and Wolff's, but again we are told that attending psychiatrists are part of the residential effort and that adolescents receive hospital treatment alongside chronological adults. Notable in Grold's presentation is his staff's awareness of the need for structure- and limit-setting for the adolescents, including mandatory attendance at Youth Group meetings, appropriate sanctions for rule-breaking, and study hours. It is clear that in the Westwood setting, staff employed adult patients as adjuncts to their own therapeutic efforts with the adolescents, but no mention is made of how adolescent transference to sick adults and the latters' overdetermined responses thereto were dealt with, aside from statements concerning identification, transient relationships, and adult patients' "confrontation" of the adolescents. Under such circumstances, little more than symptomatic sealing-over may or should be expected.

The Constas-Berkovitz paper begins with a preliminary statement that absence of adult patients from the residential setting ". . . may have encouraged concentration of anger at the caretaking adults, since displacement was less possible." This is doubtless true, and entirely proper, as it is in the highest sense untherapeutic for co-hospitalized sick adolescents and sick adults to employ or permit the latter to drain away raw aggressive and libidinal needs of the former, major problems with which the adult patients entered the hospital in the first place! The U.C.L.A. Adolescent Inpatient Ward appears far better suited to definitive treatment of the adolescent, with an all-adolescent population, attention to limit-setting, and separate sleeping quarters for the boys and the girls. Yet, at least within the therapeutic groups, adequate limit-setting appears to have been difficult for the therapists. The authors are quite right that the "bugging" served as a test of the therapist's strength, maturity and dependability, qualities which adolescents urgently need in the adults who look after them. But again, one reads of a "general atmosphere of permissiveness" within the groups, with patients permitted to read books, lie about on the floor, and avert the therapist's presence; one described episode concerns flagrant erotic posturing by a female patient which demanded, but apparently failed to receive, quick and firm interdiction. By and large, the operating structure of any group or individual process, including the controls and limits within which it is expected to carry on, should not differ drastically from those applicable within the context of the wider residential milieu; when it does, it tends toward greater permissiveness, which the involved adolescent may interpret as a vehicle for acting out and splitting; for example, if smoking is not allowed on the ward, it should not be allowed in the therapeutic group, with but rare exception.

The Barter-Buonanno paper sensitively and well describes the variety of counter-transferential "binds" and traps in which the inexperienced clinician may become enmeshed as he works with adolescents, group or otherwise. Of particular importance is the cited example of limited but successful use of counter-transference analysis within the supervisory process, the necessity for which was long ago pointed out by Hendrickson and his colleagues (4-6). Indeed, so intense and painful are these countertransferential problems with adolescents as of necessity to render supervision into what amounts to a profound, if time-limited, therapeutic experience for the trainee. It is for this reason that all general psychiatric residents and fellows in child psychiatry should have a period of training on an all-adolescent ward, an experience which some will attempt to avoid from fear of really looking at themselves.

The Berkovitz-Chikahisa-Lee paper treats the reader to rather more insight into adolescent psychodynamics than the prior articles, and reveals the authors' sound grasp of them as they emerge within a group therapeutic setting. The modus operandi of the groups conveys a close approach to the ideal flexibility of role needed by the clinician who works with adolescents, in accordance with the latters' identificatory and transferential needs and within the context of the therapist's own sound identity and authority. Adolescents are well aware that sexual talk and behavior readily "bug" caretaking adults, who often respond with over-repressiveness or, worse, overpermissiveness. The writers' ability to utilize sexual material in a growth-promoting fashion, coupling it with the deeper aspects of intimacy and love, attests to their own maturity as well as to the adequacy of their consultants, and serves to exemplify the honesty of their wider group therapeutic efforts.

In the final paper, Pottharst and Gabriel treat the reader to yet another example of sensitive group work with adolescents in residence, in this case on an intensive, five-times-weekly level. Once again, the authors demonstrate their awareness of the deleterious aspects of clinical-administrative splits, noting the overall improvement when the group was made a direct part of the overall milieu, rather than sequestered from the latter. With this frequency of meeting, one expects that the group will veer toward transference-analytical work, provided that the therapist is prepared for it, and indeed such did in fact proceed to occur, with the patients offering some astute interpretations under the therapist's watchful eye. The paper is a model of how to conduct what emerges as analytic group therapy of adolescents, and deserves careful study.

The various papers here presented attest to the importance of group treatment of adolescents in residential care, as well as to the gratifying vigor with which it is carried on in many therapeutic settings. It is well to remember that, no matter the setting, a child's direct transferential needs require that good treatment contain the same fundamental ingredients as good parenting—insight, sensitivity, empathy, proper controls and limits, and a maturity which catalyzes healthy identification with the child. Therewith the healthy child is beckoned to grow, the sick child to grow well.

REFERENCES

1. BION, W. R. (1955). Group Dynamics: A Review. *In*: Klein, M., Heimann, P., and Money-Kyrle, R. E. (Eds.), *New Directions in Psycho-Analysis*. London: Hogarth Press.
2. BION, W. R. (1961). *Experiences in Groups*. New York: Basic Books.
3. FREUD, S. (1921; 1955). Group Psychology and the Analysis of the Ego. *Standard Edition*, 18:69. London: Hogarth Press.
4. HENDRICKSON, W. J., and HOLMES, D. J. (1959). Control of Behavior as a Crucial Factor in Intensive Psychiatric Treatment in An All Adolescent Ward. *Amer. J. Psychiat.*, 115:11.

5. HENDRICKSON, W. J., HOLMES, D. J., and WAGGONER, R. W. (1959). Psychotherapy of the Hospitalized Adolescent. *Amer. J. Psychiat.*, 116:6.
6. HOLMES, D. J. (1964). *The Adolescent in Psychotherapy.* Boston: Little, Brown.
7. JAQUES, E. (1955). Social Systems as Defense against Persecutory and Depressive Anxiety: A Contribution to the Psycho-Analytical Study of Social Processes. *In*: Klein, M., Heimann, P., and Money-Kyrle, R. E. (Eds.), *Op. Cit.*
8. MASTERSON, J. F. (1967). The Symptomatic Adolescent Five Years Later: He Didn't Grow Out of It. *Amer. J. Psychiat.*, 123:1338.
9. MASTERSON, J. F. (1967). *The Psychiatric Dilemma of Adolescence.* Boston: Little, Brown.
10. MASTERSON, J. F. (1971). Treatment of the Adolescent with Borderline Syndrome: A Problem in Separation-Individuation. *Bull. Menninger Clin.*, 35:5.
11. MASTERSON, J. F., *The Tie That Binds: Treatment of the Borderline Adolescent.* Boston: Little, Brown. To be published.
12. RINSLEY, D. B. (1965). Intensive Psychiatric Hospital Treatment of Adolescents: An Object-Relations View. *Psychiat. Quart.*, 39:405.
13. RINSLEY, D. B. (1968). Theory and Practice of Intensive Residential Treatment of Adolescents—The Fifth Annual Edward A. Strecker Memorial Lecture. *Psychiat. Quart.*, 42:611. *Also*: Institute of the Pennsylvania Hospital Monograph No. V, Roche Laboratories.
14. RINSLEY, D. B. (1971). *Idem* (Revised). *Ann. Amer. Soc. Adol. Psychiat.*, Vol. I. New York: Basic Books.
15. RINSLEY, D. B. (1971). The Adolescent Inpatient: Patterns of Depersonalization. *Psychiat. Quart.*, Vol. 45, 1. In press.
16. RINSLEY, D. B., Residential Treatment of the Adolescent. *In*: Arieti, S. (Ed.), *American Handbook of Psychiatry, Second Edition.* New York: Basic Books.
17. RINSLEY, D. B., Special Education for Adolescents in Residential Psychiatric Treatment: A Contribution to the Theory and Technique of Residential School. *Ann. Amer. Soc. Adol. Psychiat.* To be published.
18. RINSLEY, D. B., and INGE, G. P., III (1961). Psychiatric Hospital Treatment of Adolescents: Verbal and Nonverbal Resistance to Treatment. *Bull. Menninger Clin.*, 25:249.
19. RINSLEY, D. B., and HALL, D. D. (1962). Psychiatric Hospital Treatment of Adolescents: Parental Resistances as Expressed in Casework Metaphor. *Arch. Gen. Psychiat.*, 7:286.
20. ZENTNER, E. B., and APONTE, H. J. (1970). The Amorphous Family Nexus. *Psychiat. Quart.*, 44:91.

Epilogue

NO DOUBT FEW HAVE been able to read the preceding 22 points of view at one sitting. Some chapters will need revisiting to appreciate the complex interplay of human factors which occurred.

It may have been disconcerting at times to witness the variety of experiences described, some at times even opposed or disagreeing. It is obviously hard to say that there is *one* right or wrong way to relate to teen-agers in small groups.

A crucial factor certainly seems to be an attitude, which is right or wrong. This attitude I would think must include an honest interest, without exploitation of the young persons. However, how does one know when one has arrived at such an attitude? Reading, courses, supervision, and probably most important, self-understanding, whether inborn or arrived at in treatment, all help.

We hope that these 22 chapters have given some appreciation of the dynamic quality and excitement which can accompany the enhanced growth for teen-agers and therapists alike in the small group scene.

> *Good fortune to all in all future work with teen-agers. The future of our world depends on it.*
>
> I. H. B.

Index

Absences from sessions, 15, 69
Ackerman, N. W., 81, 93, 158, 161, 172, 185, 190, 218, 224
Acting out behavior, 40-41
Adolescence
  crisis of, 159-160
  periods of, 9
  special dynamics of, 71-72
  turmoil of, components of, 4-5
Adolescents
  family group therapy and, 153-161, 162-172
  suicidal attempts by, 160
  young, group therapy and, 37-48
Advice, therapists handling of requests for, 76
Age spread, in peer group, 9, 41, 63, 72
Albin, David, 197 fn.
Alienation, peer group and, 3-4, 40
Alliance with therapist, resistance to forming, 37-38
Anderson, Robert, on importance of actively involved therapist, 31-36
Anger
  as response to peer group alienation, 4

suicide and, 104-107
Anthony, E. James, 95, 102, 103
Antisocial individuals, inclusion in group, 11
Aponte, H. J., 242
Authority, problems with, as pitfall of adolescent treatment, 74, 127

Barter, James T., 203, 240
  on countertransference, 204-213
Behavior, acting out, 40-41
Berger, Milton, 121
Berkowitz, Irving H., 108 fn., 122-125, 196, 203, 239, 240
  on "bugging" of the therapist on an adolescent ward, 197-202
  on growth of groups, 6-27
  on sexual attitudes in the residential setting, 216-224
  on younger adolescents in group psychotherapy, 37-48
Berne, Eric, 121
Bion, W. R., 233, 241
Black groups, 126-148
Blaustein, Florence, 234, 238
  on an adolescent group on a psychiatric unit, 181-190

245

Blos, P., 154, 161
Body language, 73
Boszormenyi-Nagy, I., 158, 161
Boys, passive, activating a group of, 121, 122-125
Brackelmanns, Walter W., on younger adolescents in group, 37-48
Brissenden, A., 183, 190
Brown, Saul L., on family group therapy for adolescents, 153-161
Bry, T., 204, 213
Buonanno, Aurelio, 203, 240
    on countertransference, 204-213

Change, developmental, resistance to, 158-159
Chikahisa, Paul, 240
    on sexual attitudes in the residential setting, 216-224
Clinical management, developmental perspective and, 156-158
Clinical reality, 156, 160
Coffey, Hubert, 134 fn.
Cohen, M. B., 212
Cohn, R. C., 212
College group, Oedipal revolt in a, 95-103
Collier, Jenny, 160, 161
Communication, precision of, 73
Confidentiality, groups and, 24, 25, 47, 74-75, 95, 97, 131
Constas, Robert, 196, 203, 239
    on "bugging" of the therapist on an adolescent ward, 197-202
Contraindications to group psychotherapy, 38, 63
Corrothers, M. L., 217, 223
Cotherapists, male and female, 10, 124
Countertransference, 77, 159, 204-213
Counts, R., 159, 161
Crisis-oriented group treatment, 150, 151, 152
Crutcher, Roberta, 121

Davidson, Edwin M., on an Oedipal revolt in a college group, 95-103
Delinquents, inclusion in group, 11
Dependency problems, groups and, 75
Depression, as response to peer group alienation, 4
Developmental change, resistance to, 158-159

Diagnosis, and selection of group members, 49-62
Dreams, telling of, 22-23, 73
Drop-in groups, 108-121, 149-152
Drugs
    active techniques with depressed users of, 108-121
    use by group members, therapist's handling of, 19-20, 42
Duration of group, 15

Ego ideal, 2
Eissler, K. R., 51 fn.
Enns, Harold B., on activating a group of passive boys, 122-125
Epstein, N., 217, 224
Erikson, E. H., 93
    "role diffusion" concept of, 72

Family therapy
    adolescents and, 153-161, 162-172
    focus in, 39-40
Feedback, 190
Fees, 53-54, 82
Felsenfeld, N., 6, 7, 16, 20, 28, 116, 121
Films, use of, 122-123, 125
Fleck, S., 156, 161
Flescher, J., 212
Flexibility, need for, 74
Fliess, R., 212
Follow-up, 189, 190
Forbes, Lorna M., on incest, anger and suicide, 104-107
Fragmented stage of younger adolescent group therapy, 43-44
Framo, J. L., 158, 161
Free association, use of technique of, 73
Freud, Anna, 101, 102, 103, 154, 161
Freud, S., 95, 103, 174, 212, 233
Fried, E., 222, 224
Fromm-Reichmann, F., 213

Gabriel, Marianne, 234, 241
    on peer group in a probation department girls' residential treatment center, 225-232
Geller, Max, on selection of group members, 49-62
Generation gap, 162-163, 197
Ginott, H. G., 28

Glover, E., 213
Goodman, M., 204, 211, 213
Grinker, R. R., 159, 161
Grold, L. James, 239
  on value of a "youth group" to hospitalized adolescents, 192-195
Grotjahn, M., 204, 213
  on transference dynamics, 173-178
Group therapy, adolescent
  active techniques with depressed drug users, 108-121
  activities other than discussion, 25
  as auxiliary therapy to individual and/or family therapy, 38
  auxiliary therapy and, 24-25, 39
  black teen-agers and, 126-148
  "bugging" of therapists, 197-202
  contraindications to, 38, 63
  countertransference and, 77, 159, 204-213
  dangers in, 4
  generic elements characteristic of, 20-21
  hospitalized adolescents and, 181-202
  in a probation department girls' treatment center, 225-232
  maturation of sexual attitudes through, 216-224
  need for flexibility in, 74
  older teen-agers and, psychoanalytic approach to, 63-79
  passive boys and, 122-125
  reasons favoring, 2
  reasons teen-agers attend sessions, 7
  resistance to, 59-62, 116-119, 185-188
  self-selected peer groups and, 80-93
  special problems of, 74-77
  stages of, 43-46
  techniques of treatment pertinent to, 72-74
  when indicated, 5
  within the wider residential context, 233-242
  young teen-agers and, 37-48
Groups
  acting out behavior and, 40-41
  age spread in, 9, 41, 63, 72
  alienation and, 3-4, 40

black, 126-148
"bugging" of therapists by, 197-202
college, Oedipal revolt in, 95-103
composition of, 9-12, 33
confidentiality and, 24-25, 47, 74-75, 95, 97, 131
countertransference and, 77, 159, 204-213
criteria for admission to, 72
dependency problems and, 75
drop-in, 108-121, 149-152
duration of, 15
establishing conditions within, purposes for, 6-7
formation of, 1-2
functions of, 2-3
growth of, 6-27
hospitalized adolescent, 181-202
importance of therapist, 31-36
influence on individual, 2
intake, 11
intellectualization and, 76
interaction within, 13, 39, 122
issues discussed by, 49-50
issues that arise early in, 12-15
limit setting and, 42-43, 48
maturation of sexual attitudes through, 216-224
members
  activity between, outside the group, 23-24, 42, 50
  monopolizing, 21, 117
  new, introducing, 12, 49, 67, 124
  nonparticipating, 21
  number of, 7-8, 65, 96
  preparing for group involvement, 12
  problems of, 10-11
  selection of, 7-12, 33, 49-62
  sexual activity between, 75
  sex of, 9-10, 65, 75, 96, 124-125
  termination by, 41, 45-46, 75-76
network therapy and, 80-93
of passive boys, 122-125
outpatient, 27
probation department girls' treatment center, 225-232
process of, 20-25, 82, 97, 164-168
rules and, 13-14, 42, 49-50
self-selected, psychotherapy in, 80-93

sessions, length and frequency of, 8, 26, 32-33, 41, 49, 63, 68-69, 96, 108, 122, 164, 198
  setting of, 7, 8
  differences relating to, 25-27
  sibling rivalry within, 76
  spirit of, 65-66
  structure of, 6, 7-20, 131, 198-199, 201
  task oriented, 25
  transference dynamics and, 173-178
  walk-in, 11-12
Gundry, R. K., 217, 224

Hadden, S. B., 204, 213
Hall, D. D., 242
Hendrickson, W. J., 240, 241, 242
Hesiod, on generation gap, 162
Holmes, D. J., 211, 213, 241, 242
Home therapy, 81
"Hot seat" technique, 23

Impulse control, setting and, 26
Incest, suicide and, 104-107
Individual, influence of peer group on, 2
Inge, G. P., III, 242
Inhelder, B., 90, 93
Intellectualization, groups and, 76
Intensive Family Therapy (Boszormenyi-Nagy and Framo), 158
Interaction, within groups, 13, 39
Intervention by therapist, 17-20
Intimacy, frequency and duration of sessions and, 32-33
Introspective capacity, setting and, 26
Involvement, therapists and, 31-36

Jaques, E., 242
Johnson, James A., Jr., 121
Josselyn, Irene M., 154, 161
  on adolescent group therapy, 1-5

Kanter, Stanley, S., 102, 103
Kaplan, D. M., 81, 93
Keniston, K., 154, 161
Kestenberg, Judith, 154, 161
Kline, Frank, 178
Kraft, I. A., 183, 190, 205-213
Kushner-Goodman, Sylvia, on a drop-in group for teenagers in a poverty area, 149-152

Langsley, D. G., 81, 93
Language, kind of, used in intervention by therapist, 17
Latency period, 2
Lattimore, R., 172
Lee, Mary Lill, 240
  on sexual attitudes in the residential setting, 216-224
Lidz, T., 157, 161
Lieberman, M. A., 172
Limit setting groups and, 42-43, 48
Loeser, L. H., 204, 213

MacGregor, R., 159, 161
MacLennan, B. W., 6, 7, 16, 20, 28, 116, 121
Management, clinical, developmental perspective and, 156-158
Marijuana, use by group members during sessions, 14
Marks, M., 213
Marmor, Judd, 181 fn.
Masterson, J. F., 242
McNeil, E. B., 221, 224
Mead, M., 172
Mediation by therapist, 162-172
Medication, therapists handling of requests for, 76
Meeker, M., 149, 152
Meeting room
  cleaning up of, 14
  nature of, 8
Members, see Groups, members
Menninger, K. A., 213
Miller, Arthur, 153
Moral judgment, therapists handling of requests for, 76
Morrison, G. C., 160, 161
Morse, W. C., 221, 224
Mt. Sinai Hospital (Los Angeles), 180, 181-190, 191
Mullan, H., 204, 213
Multiple Impact Therapy (MacGregor), 159
Murasaki, Ellen Mauntz, 216 fn., 224

Narcissism, group therapy and, 38
Network therapy, 80-93
Neuropsychiatric Institute (UCLA), 197-202
New York State Psychiatric Institute, 205-212

Newman, Larry, 197 fn.
Non-empathy, group therapy and, 38

Oedipal revolt in a college group, 95-103
Orr, D. W., 213
O'Shea, Charles, on group therapy with black teen-agers, 134-148

Parad, H. J., 150, 152
Parent-adolescent relationship, elements in, 153
Parents, relationships with, 46-48, 74-75
Patterns in Human Interaction (Lennard and Bernstein), 154
Pattison, E., 183, 190
Peacher, Terry, 108 fn.
Perls, Frederick S., 121
Phelan, John R. M., on a psychoanalytic approach to group therapy with older teen-agers, 63-79
Phenomenology, 154
Physically handicapped, inclusion in group, 11, 38-39
Piaget, J., 90, 93
Pottharst, Karl E., on peer group in a probation department girls' residential treatment center, 225-232
Pre-working stage of younger adolescent group therapy, 44
Psychoanalytic approach to group therapy with older teen-agers, 63-79
Psychotherapy, generic elements characteristic of, 20-21
Psychotics, inclusion in group, 11, 38
Pumpian-Mindlin, C., 161

Reach, A., 213
Reality, clinical, 156, 160
Reality clarification, 17
Recordings, use of, 122-123, 125
Referrals, 35, 52, 57
Refreshments, sessions and, 14, 185, 217
Reiser, Martin, on a drop-in group for teenagers in a poverty area, 149-152

Resistance
  to developmental change, 158-159
  to group therapy, 59-62, 116-119, 185-188
Richmond, A. H., 87, 93
Rinsley, Donald B., on group therapy within the wider residential context, 233-242
Ritchie, Agnes, 161
Rockberger, H., 213
Role diffusion, concept of, 72
Rosenbaum, Max, 121
Rubenfeld, S., 190
Rules, groups and, 13-14, 42, 49-50

Scapegoating, 81, 97, 199, 227
Schecter, S., 87, 93
Scheidlinger, S., 20, 28
Schulman, I., 185, 190, 218, 224
Schuster, F. P., 161
Selection of group members, 7-12, 33, 49-62
Self-image, 2, 131, 151, 227
Self-revelation by therapist, 18
Serrano, A. C., 161
Sessions
  absences from, 15, 69
  frequency of, 8, 26, 32-33, 41, 49, 63, 96, 108, 164, 198
  group process in, 20-25, 82, 97, 164-168
  individual supplementing group, 14-15
  length of, 8, 26, 32-33, 41, 49, 63, 68-69, 96, 108, 122, 164, 198
  movement in, 22
  refreshments and, 14, 185, 217
  rules and, 13-14, 42, 49-50
  smoking during, 14
  visitors to, 24
Sexual attitudes, promoting maturation of, in residential setting, 216-224
Shellow, R. S., 185, 190
Short term problem-centered approach, 149
Sibling rivalry, groups and, 76
Silver, Dianne S., on techniques with depressed drug users, 108-121
Slagle, Priscilla A., on techniques with depressed drug users, 108-121

Slavson, S. R., 121, 213, 217, 224
Smoking, group sessions and, 14
Speck, R. V., 80, 81, 94
Spirit, group, 65-66
Spotnitz, H., 218, 224
Stebbins, Dana B., on needs of a group of black teen-agers, 126-133
Stelazine, 54
Strean, H. S., 89, 94
Sugar, Max, on psychotherapy self-selected peer groups, 80-94
Suicide
  anger and, 104-107
  attempts by adolescents, 160
  incest and, 104-107

Task-oriented groups, 25
Termination by group members, 41, 45-46, 75-76
Termination stage of younger adolescent group therapy, 45-46
Therapists
  actively involved, 31-36
  activities of, 15-25
  admission of feelings by, 18-19
  apprehension in, 12
  "bugging" of, on an adolescent ward, 197-202
  countertransference and, 77, 159, 204-213
  dilemmas faced by, 19-20
  functions of, 16
  handling of requests for advice, medication and moral judgment, 76
  importance of personality and style of, 7, 8-9, 31-36
  intervention by, 17-20
  involvement by, 31-36
  legal and moral responsibilities of, 19
  mediation within a group of multiple families, 162-172
  relationships with parents, 4-48, 74-75
  resistance to forming an alliance with, 37-38

roles played by, 16
self-revelation by, 18
sex of, in relation to sex of group, 10
use of first names of, 13-14
younger adolescent groups and, 37-48
Therapy
  auxiliary, 24-25, 39
  family
    adolescents and, 153-161, 162-172
    focus in, 39-40
  home, 81
  network, 80-93
  See also Group therapy, adolescent
Transference, dynamics of, 173-178
Treatment, techniques of, pertinent to adolescent groups, 72-74
Trust, establishment of, 128, 139
Turkel, Stuart, 181 fn.

Valium, 45
Visitors at sessions, 24
Vogel, Lillian B., on mediation within a group of multiple families, 162-172

Waggoner, R. W., 242
Waldman, M., 152
Walk-in groups, 11-12
Ward, J. G., 190
Westman, J. C., 184, 185, 190
Westwood Hospital (Los Angeles), 191, 192-195, 196
Whitaker, D. S., 172
Williams, Frank S., 122 fn., 124 fn.
Wohl, T., 183, 190
Wolff, Helen B., 234, 238
  on an adolescent group on a psychiatric unit, 181-190
Working stage of younger adolescent group therapy, 44-45

Yalom, Irvin, 121, 172

Zentner, E. B., 242
Zuk, G. H., 172